Find Your Balance in These Crazy Political and Social Times

Do the times feel crazy to you? Leave it to Laurel Hughes to come up with fresh high-level understanding of what is happening in America now—an unfortunate malady she calls "cogjam." Laurel's substantial experience with the psychological aftermath of disasters such as the Twin Towers, Katrina and many others gives her unique perspective. She intelligently and coherently diagnoses the widespread symptoms of the American populace's disrupted lives, which strike her as eerily similar to those experienced by people mending from the fallout of major disaster. But unlike traditional disaster, which ends then opens pathways for healing, the roller coaster of raucous noise inflicted by our political and social climate continually throws monkey wrenches into everybody's thinking—and common sense goes out the window.

Beyond identifying the nature of the situation, Laurel provides a clear and useful guide to why this is happening. She delivers a brief but powerful masterclass in cognitive jamming, blending latest brain science and social research with lessons learned during her experience helping disaster survivors.

The bonus is what we are all looking for, the answer to "so what, what do I do?" I had been keeping above the fray as best I could, yet was still feeling a bit crazy at times. Laurel's practical ideas for further adjusting my mindset and achieving balance were a gift—one that I have shared with my friends and colleagues. I highly recommend reading Laurel's book. We all benefit from a little less crazy in our lives. We can also do our parts to heal divisiveness and reinstate the reason and science necessary for the crucial conversations our country must undertake. This book will help you get rid of some of the crazy, and find healthier balance.

> – *Jeannie Coyle Penny, Former SVP HR of American Express, speaker and executive coach to CEOS and C-Suite executives, and author of* Make Talent Your Business.

***

Laurel is committed to the psychological (and related physical and spiritual) well-being of those affected by disaster, social unrest, and the recent resurgence of hate, divisiveness, and global unhappiness. Her book is a coherent, cogent presentation of how we can grow, use negative experience to become more resilient, and ultimately get "unstuck." More than this, The Cogjam Effect offers specific solutions for today's external stresses. Finding our individual paths out of "cogjam" will help us deal with the dismay, fear, anger, and hopelessness that at times displaces the peace, happiness, and fulfillment we seek.

> – *Judy Nicholson, LCSW, Disaster Mental Health C'*

"We are immersed today in a relentless surrounding sound of real and purported existential threats—to our earth, nation, culture, and identity. Dr. Laurel Hughes' The Cogjam Effect illuminates a way to move beyond our current sociopolitical cognitive logjam (cogjam)—"the most powerful driving force behind today's bewildering meltdown." Drawing on her expertise in scientific method and the fields of psychology and disaster mental health, Dr. Hughes explains how our innate, physiological stress response for survival is now making things worse. Using simple and everyday life scenarios, Dr. Hughes teaches us how our feelings, thoughts and actions have unfolded during this challenging time and shows us a way forward. Whether you are politically left, center, right or disengaged from politics altogether, The Cogjam Effect is an important and fast-paced read on how to reclaim a more deliberate, meaningful and hopeful world."

– Rob Yin, LCSW, Senior Social Worker, University of New Mexico Student Health and Counseling; Adjunct Professor, New Mexico Highlands School of Social Work

***

"On a regular basis I observe and experience the cogjam effect. My wife and I have discussed the concepts presented in the book with family members, friends and neighbors. Many attest to their validity and look forward to putting the suggestions into practice. Discussions have also focused on suggestions on how to move forward the book's concepts. Among them: book festivals, presentations at public interest forums, topic-oriented book clubs, newspaper and magazine synopses, textbooks for education courses, newspaper letters to the editor, topic-specific panels at conferences, professional journals, bookstore sections catering to specific reader interests—i.e., current events, political science, psychology, and self-help.

This book clearly offers a blueprint for healing and a path forward, and a practical approach that will prove valuable to those seeking to cope with cogjam, both of which point to likely success. It certainly has for me. I look forward to its publication."

– Bob Porter, LCSW, Disaster Mental Health Manager

***

"Laurel E. Hughes, Psy.D. integrates her disaster mental health expertise and practical life experiences as she sheds light on circumstances in today's world that have most of us perplexed. Her approach to laying a foundation of understanding stress and disaster recovery outlines potential paths for moving forward: behavioral, emotional, interpersonal, and communitywide. She skillfully weaves her scientific background with compassionate insights into common and not-so-common human conditions. Her writing style captures the reader's attention, holds it, and communicates content succinctly with a sprinkling of humor. She makes the reader think, and encourages us in our individual journeys of discovery.

Balance, proficiency, kindness, uplifting energy—all attributes of Laurel Hughes that are evident in *The Cogjam Effect...and the Path to Healing Divisive Community and Fractured Science.*"

--Rebecca LaFollette Taylor: Oregon State Regent 2018-2020, Daughters of the American Revolution

THE COGJAM EFFECT

and the Path to Healing Divisive
Community and Fractured Science

LAUREL HUGHES

Published by KHARIS PUBLISHING, imprint of KHARIS MEDIA LLC.

Copyright © 2019 Laurel Hughes

ISBN-13: 978-1-946277-35-0
ISBN-10:1- 1-946277-35-5

All KHARIS PUBLISHING products are available at special quantity discounts for bulk purchase for sales promotions, premiums, fund-raising, and educational needs. For details, contact:

Kharis Media LLC
Tel: 1-479-599-8657
support@kharispublishing.com
www.kharispublishing.com

Dedicated to disaster relief responders, everywhere

CONTENTS

PREFACE

Life is good. This notion sometimes gets lost in the daily trials and tribulations that tear us into so many directions. However, within each of us lies the power to restore wholeness, peace, tranquility, and life satisfaction, even in these days of what I call cogjam.

My desire is that *The Cogjam Effect* helps all readers gain a better understanding of where this grand drama takes them personally, and what they might do about it. Rather than letting divisiveness and chaos take the reins, we can transform cogjam into growth opportunities—for ourselves, others, and society in general.

Like everyone else, I stand on the shoulders of those who have gone before me. Wisdom shared in this book dates from five thousand years ago to current state-of-the-art brain science. I take opportunity to applaud the National Institute for the Clinical Application of Behavior Medicine. Its excellent "Next Level Practitioner" series and its vast assembly of brain science experts have been keeping me on my toes over the last few years.

Several individuals encouraged and supported me in this effort, without whom it would not have become the book it is today: Rick Hanson Ph. D., Rob Yin LCSW, Jeannie Coyle Penney, David Penney, Bill Hughes, Bob Porter LCSW, Becky Taylor, and Judy Nicolson LCSW. Thank you for your caring contributions. And, many thanks to the motley collection of writers groups I've been involved with over the last few years. I would not be the writer I am today without you guys.

Please note: all professional encounters mentioned have been fictionalized

CHAPTER 1
......
Storms Over the Horizon

A **DISASTER MENTAL HEALTH** career changes how you look at people, though probably not in the way that first comes to mind. Myths abound regarding notions of how disaster affects us, which could explain why lead news stories have yet to notice how we teeter on the edge of a nationwide mental health disaster.

But the confusion is understandable. The field of disaster mental health is so new that even many health professionals are not aware of what it aims to remedy. Look at how the big screen sets up disaster scenarios: hordes of extras portraying victims running around and screaming, making poor choices, and likely to be devoured by the monster of the week. Media coverage of real disasters isn't much better, highlighting the flashiest scenes of chaos, destruction, carnage, and misery.

But it sells, and for good reason. In spite of how ghoulish it makes us look, we're wired for it. This macabre trait has kept us alive for thousands of years. It's certainly annoying when traffic slows for everyone to scrutinize some driver's unfortunate fender bender. But in other circumstances, the overwhelming urge to zero in on mishap saves our skins, or someone else's.

Even as smoke billowed from the ill-fated Twin Towers, the typical reaction was not to run in panicky circles. Those who encounter threat as severe as the events of September 11th most often become focused—assessing the danger, then tuning in to whatever course of action offers the best protection for themselves and those they care about. Or in some cases, people run toward disaster and provide aid to those at risk. Panic only stirs when people come to believe they've run out of options.

Even social conventions and taboos may be temporarily sidelined if they hinder this effort. People become more abrupt and insistent, even forceful, as they do what it takes to win out over peril. Likewise, strangers who ordinarily steer clear of each other may work hand in hand—pulling survivors from earthquake wreckage, helping sandbag rising shorelines, guiding others away from approaching wildfires, or even joining an eighty person chain of beachgoers to rescue a family caught in a riptide. The importance of preserving life rises above all else.

Is anything about this beginning to sound familiar? If not, hang in there. It will soon become up close and personal.

My observations of survival in the world of disaster response are consistent with what science says about stress and the human body. Extreme arousal chemically encourages us to tune out everything other than what, right at that moment, will save the day. Things like engaging in social niceties or thoroughly analyzing a situation take time—not the wisest choices, when speed is of the essence. Sometimes we can only survive by letting lightening-speed gut reactions lead.

Another myth is the belief that after experiencing disaster, emotional damage is inevitable. This idea probably grew legs because of better mainstream awareness of posttraumatic stress disorder, or PTSD. Fortunately the idea that disaster always leaves behind long-term emotional debris has lost some of its traction. Sometimes, yes. Always, no.

Resilience, or resiliency, has gained greater understanding. We know that we're designed to rise up and overcome adversity, not be overwhelmed by it. If it were the other way around, our species wouldn't have lasted this long.

Also slower to catch on is the concept that not all of what disaster does to us is bad. In addition to posttraumatic stress, disaster brings posttraumatic growth. Seeing people apply altruism, compassion, and previously unknown strengths during dire threat and recovery was one of the reasons I volunteered for so many disaster assignments. Both the people involved and the work itself were inspiring.

Of course, some survivors do succumb emotionally—especially those experiencing additional ongoing life challenges: limited resources, medical issues, family crises, and others. But even this does not necessarily mean a mental health diagnosis looms in their futures. Most recover from their symptoms using the same resilience practices they've relied on their entire lives. Often, they pick up a new trick or two for down the road.

So far, this sounds pretty good. Here we are, bolstered by innate programming for handling stress and arousal that natural selection has been keenly tuning for millennia. By now it must serve our needs like a well-oiled machine. Right? And this capability is always adaptive, ever on the lookout for survival's best interests.

Guess again.

One day I was walking through a parking lot and didn't notice the pothole in my path. As luck would have it, I stepped right into it—my legs collapsing. Down I went, gaining a sprained ankle and scraped knee to show for the adventure. However my upper body was fine, even though it too had smacked against the asphalt.

I can thank my stress wiring for this piece of good fortune. Within milliseconds after my misstep an adrenaline rush revived learning from my karate days, when I was well practiced at falling and not getting hurt. In less time than it takes to think "don't forget to roll," my cheek was already resting against sun-warmed gravel. Unscathed, at that. Conscious thought had taken a backseat so older hardwired learning could grab the steering wheel.

Now, fast-forward a couple of weeks. I was home, my ankle on the mend. I was heading toward the back of the house to help corner the cat for a trip to the vet. My husband suddenly called out "here she comes!" The frantic cat scrambled around the corner and I leaped into action, managing to grab her just as she shot by.

However, as I did so, I didn't take into account my ankle, which was still far from a hundred percent. Hardwiring prompted me to use it in an ill-advised manner. I ended up on the floor again (though in fairness to my fight or flight, I did once again roll as I fell). Fortunately, I didn't re-injure the sprain. Well, much anyway. It hurt a little more for a day or two.

But the stress response isn't organized around stopping to consult recent memory. It acts on what it's got, at the speed required for the most compelling course of action.

This story isn't unique. Most people easily recall incidents when knee-jerk reactions got them into trouble. We've all been there, which brings us to the present, where knee-jerk reactions are running rampant.

Everybody is so on edge over socio-political strife that most everything we hold dear is slowly eroding. Expressing our anguish and enduring the reactions of others to stress has driven us into communitywide counterproductivity. Many common social decencies seem to have lost their hold. Frequent assaults to science and common sense leave us feeling as if thinking and reasoning have made a run for it, or even blasted off for Planet X.

It's still the good old reliable stress response on the job. It's only trying to step in and save the day, doing what it always does when arousal overwhelms. But somehow it has lost its way.

The result of fight or flight's boundless zeal is that we no longer experience mere stress. It is turning into, or has already become, trauma—a common outcome after excessive adversity of any sort. What is especially fascinating about our current predicament is how we've found a way to do it in unison, such that it self-perpetuates. Somehow we've interwoven our fight or flight instincts and reactions into one big, hyper-juiced, free-for-all.

As well intentioned as the human stress response may be, I have come to believe that its misguided overreactivity is the most powerful driving force behind today's bewildering socio-political meltdown.

THE COGJAM EFFECT

It has been several years since I last boarded a jet headed for a disaster zone. I had assumed that phase of my life securely shelved, and that I was free to chase after more frivolous pursuits. Having mere social events bring a mental health disaster to me, instead of me going to the disaster, wasn't on my radar. But that's exactly what happened.

There's nothing flippant about this suggestion. Over the last year or so, I've observed behaviors, emotions, thoughts, and other reactions that are hauntingly similar to those I saw while helping people work through disaster trauma. The difference, however, is that today's home front behaviors don't seem aimed at neutralizing a true threat. At least, not the type of threat the stress response is designed to neutralize. Instead, citizens and public figures alike are reacting to "threats" in ways that only further gum up the works. In its innocence, fight or flight is putting us at increasingly greater risk, rather than protecting us.

I call the stress response innocent because such a primitive part of the brain drives it, structures largely identical from primates to chickens to alligators. During arousal, this primitive brain filters or blocks input from the more advanced cerebral cortex, and pushes back against anything that might become a distraction. This way, fight or flight more easily focuses efforts and forges onward. Time seemingly stands still while logic, scientific learning, and common sense become less accessible—perhaps temporarily put on hold altogether—so the primitive brain can do its job.

Once the threat is over, stress dissipates and people let down their guard. More sophisticated reasoning comes back online. Those who took it out on each other recognize and accept that stress was to blame for any hostility or abruptness. They forgive and reconnect and things go back to normal.

I remember the recovery cycle well. All disaster survivors work at getting their lives back to normal, each in their own way and at their own pace, bless their resilient souls. But sometimes, immediate demands such as figuring out where to get food, finding shelter, and satisfying other post-disaster needs require a little prodding or assistance.

That's where my colleagues and I stepped in. Being able to walk alongside survivors as they advance from "deer in the headlights" to refocused and high functioning was a fantastic perk. Especially since we knew they could do it. More often than not, they did not disappoint us.

But...what happens if the threat isn't completely over? Or, if we suspect that an additional threat dangles nearby, waiting to drop on us? The primitive brain will not back down if it still perceives storms on the horizon.

And then, what if the when or where of an expected assault can't be predicted, and there's no control or course of action to avoid it? These two factors make the perfect storm for ratcheting up the stress level of any situation: 1) inability to predict when the threat will hit; and 2) having no way to exercise control over it.

Today's politically charged social climate is a vignette of these stress boosters. Diabolical geniuses couldn't have set it up it any better. We're constantly bombarded by assaultive or confusing rhetoric, and we have no idea when the next set of fireworks is going off. Or, which form they will take this time; or who or where they might hit. About the only way we could take complete control over exposure to such input would be to go live by ourselves in caves. The one thing we can truly be sure of is that it will happen again.

Many cope by doing life in a constant state of alert. This strategy offers at least some sense of safety and protection. But such a choice also means gut instinct will be doing business as usual. Fear reactions easily egg on ill-advised flare-ups, which in turn ignite others' fuses. More fireworks explode and everyone's fight or flight reengages. Rational thought decreases, reactions increase. People get traumatized and feel less able to cope. More flare-ups follow. And the dance goes on, music courtesy of the human stress response.

Our higher reasoning is better than this. It could defuse the whole thing if we let it. But with the never-ending stream of incoming assaults, better judgment doesn't have much chance to get completely back online. It often ends up missing in action, held captive by the stress chemistry that keeps clogging up relevant neural pathways.

For the sake of shorthand, I came up with a name for this viciously circling cognitive logjam: the cogjam effect. That's where we are now—more or less stuck, drifting in a politically perpetrated cogjam.

How cogjam plays out these days doesn't really need an introduction. We're already more familiar with it than we'd like to be. We run across some form of it almost daily. Civil conversation can suddenly become a perverse ping-pong match, as nagging fears and anger compel companions to bring up, and try to somehow work through, that which distresses them. We are saddened to see family relationships and lifelong friendships head for a fiery demise. And let's not even get started on the hostility and nonsensical thinking stirred up by social media posts. Thanks to the wonders of modern technology, all we have to do is pick up a device to find ourselves accosted by yet another assault to sensibilities.

Unfortunately, some of us are coping by becoming numb to it, as if resigned to the abuse. Many have learned to avoid talking about the situation altogether, let alone address the emotional impact of what's been going on. However, from a mental health perspective, sweeping it all under the rug is deadly. Only with systematic examination can we come to realize what is happening to us, how it affects feelings and behavior, what we can do about it, and how we might keep it from happening again in some future era.

BUT WAIT, THERE'S MORE . . .

The turmoil doesn't end with the stress caused by the vicious circle. Consequences of today's cogjam introduce additional stresses that further fan the blaze.

Uncertainty. Murky dichotomies, like fake news versus reality, and blurred lines between evidence-based facts, opinion, and "alternative facts" create confusion. Confusion always pumps up stress, and the nonstop streams of inflammatory and contradictory messages feed it well. Keeping ourselves safe and secure requires knowing what's going on around us. Ignorance cripples ability to detect incoming threats. In addition, extensive confusion and polarization among those who lead creates worries over whether they are truly able to deal with an outside threat, or handle other natural or man-made catastrophes. We feel unsafe. The primitive brain can't ignore this.

Growing self-doubt. We were born programmed to reason scientifically. We've been using scientific reasoning to make sense of the world from the day we first realized that shaking the yellow rattle makes a neat noise, or that raising a fuss brings Mommy running. From that point forward, we've built onto and fine-tuned those earliest inklings of cause and effect, developing perceptions of reality that support successful lives. Therefore, the hostile and irrational commentary is not only stressful in and of itself. The rhetoric also takes aim at our very foundations. It undermines the basic game plan we use for determining the firmness of the ground beneath us. From a mental health perspective, losing faith in whether we've got all our ducks in a row—regardless of whether such thoughts are conscious or subconscious—is one of the most destructive outcomes of cogjam.

Challenged social lives. Essential to overcoming stress and trauma is social support. Talking about concerns or simply joining with friends, family, co-workers, and others is one of the greatest balms we've got for recovering from any adversity. We are wired that way. But then, we're also wired with the stress response, which judges staying alive to be more important than public relations. Alienating personal support networks due to impulsive outrage and defensiveness annihilates a primary resource for recovery, not to mention introduces new stress over toasted relationships. In addition to creating and perpetuating cogjam, the ongoing political pot stirring robs us of what we desperately need to heal the emotional carnage left in its wake.

Increase in hate crimes and other violence. Some people are especially vulnerable during times of stress. Their reactions take things too far, perhaps even physically acting out on their fears and frustrations. To them, it feels like fighting back or protecting themselves from harm. But that's not what it really is. It's desperation, or feeling too inadequate to address the situation in a more productive manner. Hate crimes and other interpersonal violence do nothing to help the real problem. However, they do create a need for the rest of us to keep checking over our shoulders for random attacks.

Guilt and shame. We don't like who we appear to be turning into. On some level most people feel bad after treating others poorly, no matter what the circumstances. Given the many negative feelings and behaviors that come with cogjam, excessive self-criticism may rear its ugly head. Not only because of what we've thought, said, or done, but also because of this weird inner struggle to pull off something so simple as being reasonable. Some feel out of control altogether. Without understanding what's really going on, we worry that something is seriously wrong with us. And for the record: no. Any new symptoms you see in yourself over current affairs do not necessarily mean a looming mental health diagnosis. Chances are, it's only cogjam at work.

Absence of leadership or clear direction for getting out of this mess. Cogjam didn't happen overnight. Today's polarization built up its first head of steam among politicians. Conservatives and liberals alike have had decades of practice with taking pointless swipes at each other, opposing each other for obstructionism's sake, vilifying those with opinions other than their own, and generally whipping up the masses into an indignant frenzy. Which, of course, encourages and perpetuates outbreaks of fight or flight among the citizenry. The DC Beltway contingency fell victim to cogjam long before the rest of us, driven by its own brand of irreconcilable fears. Expecting them to take control or show us the way out is not realistic.

The bizarreness of it all. You can't make this stuff up. If somebody pitched a novel containing such outrageous features, the author would have gotten nowhere. Editors reject stories if they're too unbelievable for the reader to feel comfortable stepping into them. Yet, here we are. Not understanding the how's and why's of this modern day *Game of Thrones*, plus having no idea how to overcome it, is as stressful as anything else listed above—especially when our top-drawer reasoning keeps getting stuck.

Without decisive effort to still the perpetual whirlwind, cogjam is positioned to disrupt both scientific reasoning and fundamentals of socialization indefinitely. The implications are disturbing, at the least. Entire lifetimes of making sense of the world may no longer feel aboveboard, or as if crumbling to the ground, as attacks to sensibilities go on and on. Instinctual and early-hardwired childlike reactions will keep trying to rescue us, faithfully stepping in to fill the void—which, of course, are fraught with processing errors. We've certainly seen no shortage of those lately. Simply wondering how people believe some of the things that come out of their mouths, especially when we know them to be more on the ball than their commentary suggests, further feeds confusion and stress. We may feel as if cogjam has our collective sense of community circling the drain.

Without calmer heads to prevail, cogjam will remain unchallenged, and the driving force of fight or flight will continue to trump all.

SEEKING ANSWERS

I wouldn't be writing this book if I didn't see a way out. That would be too depressing.

There are indeed solutions. I've watched too many disaster survivors bludgeon their way forward to doubt it. We can do it for this disaster as well. I can feel it, practically taste it. I've already seen heartwarming cases of recovery—hardy souls finding their own unique formulas for coming to their senses, shaking off cogjam's effects and healing both sensibilities and relationships. I suspect most everyone has seen bits and pieces of this around them, but haven't recognized it for what it is: resilience, entering right on cue.

For here is where the answer lies:

- Regaining our lost inner footing, so that we heal both fractured science and disrupted community

- Reestablishing who we really are, the unique individuals we've been since day one, as well as the ways in which we are all truly one
- Getting back to original game plans for drawing logical conclusions, and determining fact from fiction
- Refortifying our deserved self-confidence

The world needs to make sense again. Rather than letting cogjam control us, we need to take the reins. We need to turn cogjam into a growth opportunity.

The path I propose requires stepping back for a stroll down memory lane, even though we are unlikely to remember its earliest alleyways. Examples from my own past experiences help illustrate that much of what I am about to share did not get its start with higher education. The building blocks and lessons in everyday living stepped into their rightful place long before then.

Observing, assessing, and drawing conclusions during our first explorations of the world took us many places. The genes we carry and input we gathered along the way worked hand in hand. They not only shaped general thought processes, but also the unique ways we perceive ourselves, how we interact with others, and our overall worldview.

We can bring this original learning back online again. If we fully reengage our existing strengths, they can be drafted to battle cogjam. Once on the scene, chances are they will spontaneously volunteer for it.

The first half of this book builds basic understanding. What goes on inside us and among us, that so readily promotes the cogjam effect? What strengths and vulnerabilities do we all have, and how do we identify the roles they play in our individual cogjammed states? More detailed information is shared about stress's effect on the body, especially during disastrous circumstances. Classic reasoning errors that lead to faulty conclusions are dissected and explored.

Disaster recovery is explained, including the role of individual differences. Some people have traits that put them at an advantage for healthy recovery. Others are especially prone to cogjam, through little fault of their own. They may spend their entire lives in it. Such individuals have an especially tough road ahead when it comes to finding their way out. But they are also the ones who require the most understanding and compassion, regardless of whether there's any chance they'll ever see the light.

Compassion is key. Compassion heals, for giver and receiver alike. It is one of the first corners of our souls to reignite if we are to find our way out of darkness.

The second half of the book outlines many potential paths for moving forward: behavioral, emotional, interpersonal, and communitywide. The act of bringing the hidden out into the open is in itself healing. For once the dynamics of an oppressive entity are laid bare for all to see, it loses much of its power.

It can no longer sneak in the back door to influence thoughts and behaviors because it is automatically unmasked. If we see it, and recognize it, we can do something about it. Confusion clears when underlying patterns become visible.

Perpetrating confusion is actually a strategy batterers employ to control their victims—one minute lashing out, and the next minute acting loving and caring; or claiming to be happy about something, then at other times outraged over it, all the while pointing fingers at the victim as somehow responsible, messed up, or "wrong." Many intelligent and well-adjusted individuals have been taken down by batterer-induced confusion. The bewilderment produced by cogjam can do likewise. But just as recovering battering survivors can identify and rise above the confusion, we too can overcome the impact of cogjam abuse.

For the record, I have no particular iron in this political fire, no partisan ax to grind. I have identified myself as an Independent ever since the day I registered to vote. And even though what we're facing today is largely a politically caused disaster, I try as I can to steer clear of reinforcing the posturing and polarization. It's not easy.

Nor do I purposely point fingers at any particular party or individual. Without a doubt, some examples will remind you of reasoning blunders or behaviors you've heard or read about. But it can't be helped. A wide range of illogic is gumming up the works. We need to lift the hood and start taking things apart if we're to figure out how we're going to get out of here. Dissecting thought processes lessens the temptation to give in to errors, as well as makes us less vulnerable to getting drawn in by those of others.

THE PATH FORWARD

Just as the specific impact of cogjam varies from person to person, so will the solutions. There isn't any one right answer. Each of us can examine how and to what extent cogjam has taken us hostage, and do our darnedest to wriggle from its grasp.

Angry protest-type behavior does help let off a little steam. And it's certainly better than having someone climb on the roof of the IGA with an AK-47. But distressed crying up at the sky brings no remedy for healing the emotional impact of today's political strife. It only pumps up more fight or flight reactions among those having alternate views. Lashing out at those around us is not a sign of strength, productivity, or even effective self-defense. It is only vulnerability and fear making themselves known, goaded on by misguided arousal.

It's time we take control. Even if a spaceship swooped down tonight and swept the unsavory elements cinched within the DC Beltway from the face of the planet, the die has already been cast. Trauma is here, and it's having its say. Communitywide mental health vulnerabilities have settled in.

If we're among the lucky ones who've already realized how we shoot ourselves in the foot with cogjammed thoughts and behaviors, there is still a need to seek answers for moving beyond them, both within ourselves and in our interactions with others. And, even if we've already successfully tamed our own disturbing thoughts and interpersonal behaviors, we need to understand where they came from in the first place, so we do not again stumble so easily.

Cogjam must be addressed directly, as only we, as individuals, can address it. That is the aim of this book: to offer a path that leads toward an end to the bleeding, healing the damage, and doing whatever possible to bring this vicious cycle to its knees. No matter how trite the term, we are indeed resilient.

What led you to pick up this book? What nuggets did you hope to find? I suggest you've chosen the right book if you seek to:

- Be part of the solution, rather than part of the problem
- Take control over what currently spirals out of control
- Discover strengths you never knew you had
- Experience greater inner peace
- Clear up confusion, and regain self-confidence and sense of certainty
- Heal and strengthen relationships with those you hold dear
- Better fend off the slings and arrows of ongoing dysfunctional politics
- Help choose and plant seeds for the next era—which can only sprout from the muck left behind by cogjam

We can get unstuck. This, too, will pass. And just as we had the power to create an adverse society, we are also able to capitalize on the posttraumatic growth that will follow. The healing of fractured science and disrupted community will rise from the blood, sweat, and tears of many individual battles—just as recovery unfolds following any disaster. And on this occasion, in addition to laying hands of healing on a community swirling in the wake of disaster, I explore my own learning and healing, as I too seek my path out of cogjam.

Pages to follow describe how to recognize our own cogjam status, decide what we want for ourselves, and what we might do about it. We cannot take control of others' choices or behaviors, but, we certainly have control over our own and what we do to either end or perpetuate mass mental health disaster. There is indeed hope.

Let the journey begin.

CHAPTER 2

· · · · · ·

Enemies Within

THE COMMON VIEW of today's strained society is of two extreme positions duking it out, with both trying to claw their way to the top of the food chain. This certainly paints the most tangible picture of what we see and hear. And it's definitely the arena stirring up the most cogjam misery.

However, I beg to differ in regard to what it is we're really looking at. I suggest that this conflict we've entered into reflects something much deeper and more profound, an allegory of epic proportions. What we experience today is only a bump in a story that has been unfolding for many thousands of years.

Our current cogjam saga is merely one more skirmish breaking out in an ancient inner battle, one that fired its first rounds when the cerebral cortex became big enough to throw its weight around. Finding ourselves in this spot was inevitable—at least, so say the musings of this Monday morning quarterback.

Both sides are formidable. When it comes to self-protection, the gut brain really knows its stuff. Its "star-power" benefits species of lesser and greater developmental advancement alike. Biologically speaking, it is finely tuned and high functioning. Without it, earthly fauna wouldn't have proliferated with such diversity and resilience.

On the other hand, this larger cerebral cortex of ours is a relatively new kid on the block. Nonetheless, its ability to think its way out of tight spots also helps us flourish—especially in times of self-defense, when physical adeptness alone won't do the trick. Without it, our species probably would have gone the way of the dinosaur.

Meanwhile, world order did not sit around and go stale. Societies advanced in complexity. Social standards and practices snowballed, eventually becoming etched into patterns and principles of how groups satisfy their members' needs. For our particular species, getting along with the other guy became as great an asset to day-to-day survival as being bigger, stronger, or quick enough to punch out the other guy first.

The human race hasn't outgrown the need for a stress response, and never will. A certain amount of arousal is critical for both motivation and general effectiveness. But the importance we place on some of that early wiring is beginning to become obsolete. The guy in a spear fight with a neighboring tribe needs a completely different set of survival strategies than a business owner battling a magnate threatening a hostile takeover. Surviving in a complex social world requires more thinking.

All would be well if the two brain functions knew how to play together nicely. But that's what's only beginning to get sorted out in the grand story of the evolving brain. More typically, no matter how gently or firmly the gut brain tries to block cognition, the logical brain becomes all the more insistent. It fully believes it is the better lobe for the job. As a result, the limited flexibility of the stress response can become self-defeating.

Thus the real conflict is not one of opposing social attitudes, differing philosophies and worldviews, or cartoonishly polarized political parties. It is the ultimate battle between fear and logic, two evolving brain functions going head-to-head. What spins around us today is merely the joint echoed cry of each individual's inner struggle between logic and gut.

We live at an evolutionary crossroads. Something—or perhaps many things—will need to give before the human race either successfully adapts, or watches the inner battle implode.

WHO IS FEAR?

Consider a lizard. Not a big scary type, but one of those cute little green fellows that like to hide under rocks or in drainpipes. He harmlessly goes about his day basking in the sun, seeking yummy grubs, finding cozy shelter, and making a few baby lizards along the way. He also remembers to be cautious, ever wary of his surroundings and moving quickly from one place of refuge to the next.

Suddenly, there's a large movement. It looks like something is heading his way.

"What's that?" It's too soon to tell. "But what if it's a predator, a roaming herd, an approaching car, or ..." *Horror of horrors.* "A seven year old with a terrarium?"

He scurries off as fast as his little legs will carry him.

But alas, so many species are bigger, faster, and stronger than our lizard. He ultimately finds himself cornered. As soon as opportunity arises, he faces his unidentified foe, and chomps at it with all his might.

He never meant anyone any harm. All he ever wanted was to mind his own business. But, staying alive comes first. Most of us are likely to cheer on our little friend, hoping he escapes to sun himself on a rock another day.

What feelings did you notice as you read this story? Did you join those of us who cheered him on, hoping he would fight off his foe and return to his relatively carefree, lizard lifestyle?

That's compassion bubbling to the surface, a trait so enmeshed in the human condition that it can even get percolating over a fictional lizard. Understanding who fear is, and what we have to offer it, presents our first opportunity to enlist compassion as an ally for healing. For each of us has that little reptile within us, in the form of the gut brain: minding its own business unless a threat looks poised to annihilate its very existence. The gut brain feels every bit as vulnerable, and is just as easily frightened, as that little lizard.

Gut instinct is not the enemy—though at times it seems like it is, given how the most severely cogjammed among us so readily let their gut control their commentary. Likewise, feeling threatened creates more of our own discomfort than the intellectual exercises we take part in over confusing social quandaries.

But gut instinct is really only that little lizard trying to save his hide, a corner of our beings that deserves compassion as much as any other. And to employ compassion for anybody, or in any context, we must also be able to use it to comfort our own vulnerabilities.

The path to healing divided community and fractured science begins with giving that poor little guy a break. He needs to feel safe. He wants to be listened to. He needs to sense enough support to be able to step down. He needs to rest.

The logical brain can be of assistance here, beyond its ability to actively choose the way of compassion. It has both the flexibility and resourcefulness to work either with or around the gut brain's rigid insistence. It's not so different from how we would interact with an innocent toddler who constantly squalls or gets underfoot. The logical brain needs to step up and be the adult of the situation. And to do so—not to mention negotiate a viable truce—it needs to know exactly what it's dealing with, both physically and functionally.

A MIND-BODY SUPERHIGHWAY

An exquisite network of neurons fast tracks the gut brain's survival tactics.[1] The polyvagal system is a complex neural web. The vagus nerve stretches from tailbone to brainstem, with tentacles reaching out to connect with most every organ in the body. The vast majority of these nerves are sensory, taking in cues that hint of lurking threat.

However, the polyvagal system works both bottom-up and top-down. In other words, in addition to bringing important information to the brain, it also has neural pathways that promote physical defensive reactions. And especially crucial to our quest to arrange a truce, the top-down wiring transports guidance from thinking and willful centers of the brain.

When the gut brain punches the panic button, events unfold at lightening speed.[2] Adrenalin is released, which in turn pumps up cortisol production. These two work together, both creating an energy boost and supporting muscular activity needed for fight or flight.

Cortisol's contribution goes on in the background. It increases blood pressure and blood sugar, transforming whatever is available into quick sources of energy. The body becomes less sensitive to pain, so any injury sustained in battle is less likely to slow efficiency. Cortisol also temporarily puts the immune system on hold. The immediate priority is fueling response to crisis.

Adrenalin's job is frontline, getting the body going. Heart and respiration rate go up. Certain blood vessels dilate—energizing and nourishing muscles, while vessels in body parts that don't play major fight or flight roles constrict. Voice rises in volume and pitch. Anger may spike, a motivational energizer. Peripheral vision lessens and tunnel vision takes over, which limits distraction from the enemy or escape route. Digestion slows down or stops altogether, so it won't tie up energy better used elsewhere.

After the threat passes, the system backs down. Body chemistry returns to baseline.

But in the socially oriented world of cogjam, the threat never gets off our backs—no matter that these skirmishes rarely involve immediate threat to life or limb. Depending on the stress of the day, they're more likely to be threats to belief systems, egos, relationships, or freedoms. Or, they imply the possibility of future actions or outcomes that would keep us from getting whatever is either needed or dearly desired.

But gut-brain wiring can't make such distinctions. It doesn't see the difference between existential threat and physical threat, or understand the ele-

1   Porges, S. W. (2011). *The polyvagal theory: Neurophysiological foundations of emotions, attachment, communication, and self-regulation.* New York: Norton.

2   Gardner, D. (2009). *The science of fear: How the culture of fear manipulates your brain.* New York: Penguin Group.

ment of time. In fact, sense of time often disappears altogether during extreme arousal. All the gut brain knows is "threat" and "right now." And it has only one way to handle that: sound the alarm. The panic button gets punched and full-fledged infusions of adrenalin and cortisol follow. Over, and over, and over.

Given the above, we might guess that those who are most juiced up are also the ones most likely to jump into the thick of political battles. Not long ago, a group of researchers tested such a hypothesis.[3] They measured cortisol levels, checked out the individuals' political activity, and then compared the two.

They found that those with higher baseline cortisol levels were actually *less* likely to become politically involved than those with lower baselines. We can throw together a little street logic to explain it: politics are stressful, and if you're already stressed out to the max, why go out looking for more?

But these individuals were less likely to even vote, as compared to those with lower cortisol baselines. They didn't take advantage of the one thing they were truly empowered to do, as far as getting in their two cents' worth. It didn't matter that there was no need to tell anyone how they voted, or even whether they voted. It was as if they had simply given up, the opposite of what cortisol and adrenalin are supposed to get rolling.

It doesn't add up. If they're that extremely and regularly stressed, why aren't they the ones most likely to strike out against a problematic status quo?

FIGHT, FLIGHT, OR . . .WHAT?

Answering this question requires taking a closer look at typical stress reactions. The term "fight or flight" has been used to describe the stress response since the 1930's. Fighting back or fleeing are the most obvious solutions during threat to life or limb. But circumstances of dire threat vary. Sometimes neither fight nor flight is well suited for ensuring safety and security.

Recently, additional behaviors have been identified as natural stress reactions. Apparently these too proved sufficiently useful to be passed along in the grand scheme of survival: freezing, calling out, and feigned death.

Freezing. For months, various news media broadcasted clips of the explosions at the Boston Marathon mass casualty disaster. You may recall that immediately after the first explosion, many spectators neither ran off nor appeared to look for someone or something to fight. Instead, they quieted and remained still. Their attention centered on figuring out what the heck was going on. Then a second bomb clarified the situation and people went into action.

In addition to encouraging intense focus when a threat is still murky, freezing can be a way of becoming invisible. One morning, my good-sized Labrador

---

3   French, J. A., Smith, K. B., Guck, A., Alford, J. R., & Hibbing, J.R. (2011). Paper presented at the Annual Meeting of the International Society for Political Psychology, Istanbul, 2011.

and I were taking our usual stroll through the neighborhood. Out the corner of my eye I picked up on something unusual. Glancing across the street, I spotted one those urban coyotes I'd heard so much about. The animal was standing stock still, partially hidden by shrubbery. Her head was fully visible, and her eyes were clearly zeroed in on us.

Fortunately, my dog did not notice her presence. We passed by without incident—unless you count my own jumbled urgings of fight or flight. But the lesson: even with her obvious presence, freezing in place saved the coyote from an altercation with a larger animal.

Calling out. Yelling, screaming, or otherwise calling out sometimes comes with that lightning strike of adrenalin. Doing so can be lifesaving if it alerts others to mortal threat that can't be overcome individually, or lets others know of danger ahead. Those loud noises might also scare off more timid perpetrators of assault.

Feigning death. Sometimes when a creature is cornered or captured, it acts as if it's dead. It becomes limp and unable to be roused, though usually still conscious. It may suddenly "come to life" and escape if the predator drops its guard. On the face of it, feigning death may seem more like a good way to end up mortally wounded. Or eaten. But predators sometimes lose interest if their prey stops fighting back. Some predators also prefer to eat only new kills, rather than animals that are already dead, a habit that protects them from illness due to spoilage.

Getting back to the original question: what caused those overstressed would-be voters to shut down? Yes, it could be some form of freezing—waiting to see how things pan out before daring the risk of engagement. Figuratively feigning death and hoping nobody goes around kicking the bushes might also be a way to feel safe—coping by trying not to be noticed.

But another piece to the puzzle is the more likely culprit. And it's one that frequently fits the jigsaw gestalt of disaster.

LIFE IN THE UNIMAGINABLE

What makes cogjam a mental health "disaster?" For that matter, why is anything defined as a disaster? We hear those ruled by black or white thinking use extreme terms like "disaster" and "horrible" to describe anything they find at all unfavorable, as well as use words like "fantastic" or "incredible" to refer to whatever they have aligned themselves with. In fact, using limited speech and extreme terms during conversation has been tied to stress-related "gene signatures"—inner markers of habitually heightened stress and/or other emotions.[4]

4   Mehl, M. R., Raison, C. L., Pace, TWWW, Arevalo, JMG, & Cole, S.W. (2017). Natural language indicators of differential gene regulation in the human immune system. *Proceedings of the National Academy of Sciences*, 114, 12554-12559.

We might expect this, since the gut brain loves extremes. Extremes simplify decision-making.

But for the purpose of our topic, the definition of disaster relied upon is the one established by emergency management and other groups who step in when communities are in distress.

Disaster is an adverse incident that significantly disrupts community functioning. It results in material, human, infrastructural, environmental, and/or other losses that go beyond the community's ability to cope by usual means. Addressing vital needs and getting day-to-day functioning back to normal typically requires assistance outside of usual community resources and practices. [5]

Disastrous incidents can be naturally caused—such as hurricanes, floods, pandemics, wildfires, earthquakes, and tornadoes; or manmade—such as bombings, explosions, releases of hazardous materials, and arson. Note that manmade does not necessarily mean intentional. War, mass shootings, and the like, yes. But much of manmade disaster is purely accidental, unfortunate by-products of our human fallibility.

That's what cogjam is about: a man-made disaster, but for the most part unintentional. Yes, there could be abusive sociopaths out there who purposely try to perpetuate it. It would certainly be a good way to keep others traumatized and more easily manipulated. But the majority of cogjam more likely stems from our communitywide struggle to cope with the multiple conflicting perspectives generated by so many advanced brains.

Specific fears reported have changed more toward immediate concern over basic personal wellbeing. Frequency of fears stemming from socio-politically related consequences has also risen above that of more traditionally noted ones. For example, in both 2016 and 2017, an annual survey found that corrupt government officials were the top fear. However in 2017, the percentage of those who reported having this fear rose from 61% to 75%. Most of the other top ten fears changed in actual type. Losing a loved one, terrorism, and economic instability moved down in the rankings, replaced by such fears as not being able to get health care, not having clean water to drink, and getting into a nuclear war.[6]

Such fears are more visceral and absolute, based on circumstances that are dangerously closer to threatening basic day-to-day living or even possible death. It's certainly excuse enough for the gut brain to claw its way into the front seat and grab the steering wheel. Perhaps this change in reported fears shows us that the gut brain has jumped in already.

---

5   FEMA (2017). *National Disaster Recovery Framework.* Retrieved from www.fema.gov/national-disaster-recovery-frame-work.
6   Wilkenson College of Arts, Humanities and Social Sciences (2017). *America's Top Fears 2017: Chapman University Survey of American Fears,* October 11, 2017.

Cogjam therefore fits within the definition of disaster because:

- It has released a landslide of mental health impact on our communities.
- The resulting stress or trauma has excessively challenged most individuals' abilities to either cope well or overcome it.
- It disrupts and at times overwhelms community functioning.
- Exceptional effort is needed to overcome its breadth of impact, beyond usual means of coping and mental health resources available.

The gut brain can't ignore the uncertainty, frustration, and fears generated by the broad fusion of conflict that cogjam brings. But the gut brain is the wrong tool for surviving it. Therefore we suffer similarly to those living through other disasters—not because of lost homes, lifestyles, loved ones, physical health, or neighborhoods, but as a result of the nationwide drop in sense of wellbeing, both jointly and individually.

SEEKING TO COPE

Everyday living has its own run-of-the-mill rough patches. For these, our coping typically turns to personal resilience, our social support network, or seeking the advice of professionals. These recovery resources apply equally to dealing with mental health consequences of any life disaster, no matter how major or minuscule.

But with cogjam, all three of these recovery resources are in some way challenged:

- There's no readied playbook for overcoming cogjam. It's too new and bizarre. This slows or impairs figuring out how to apply our usual coping and resilience.
- Social support networks are upended by the interpersonal turmoil. We are no longer so certain who our friends are, perhaps even unsure of how to approach them for support during this drama. Conflicting views leave many relationships strained, among friends and family alike.
- Mental health professionals are in relatively limited supply, even more so regarding those who work specifically with trauma. There are plenty of ways to go about mass psycho-education. But the specialty field has yet to nail down cogjam as a malady, let alone establish how best to guide others out of it. Without that kind of internal agreement, how to go about treating it is not clear-cut.

Regardless, establishing cogjam to be a nationwide mental health disaster does little in itself for getting a national recovery plan on its way. Even if mental health professionals had an agreed-upon protocol, our nation does not identify anybody as responsible for heading it up. The *National Response Frame-*

work mentions mental health as a corollary concern during criminally caused incidents, natural disasters, public health emergencies, and the like. But there is no official plan for when we're faced with widespread mental health carnage standing on its own.

So in the interests of moving forward, we best not count on some white knight agency or organization suddenly galloping in to save us any time soon. We need to take charge ourselves, perhaps as it should be. And we will need to get creative.

Our first step: recognizing usual symptoms of disaster.

DISASTER IMPACT

Symptoms that turn up following disaster stem from the same chemistry that causes the human stress response. Fight or flight works great while in the throes of surviving—running from the wildfire or tornado, or pitching in to help rescue someone trapped in aftermath debris. But the human stress response wasn't designed to address the ongoing stress that comes with long-term disaster circumstances. Our bodies can't be flooded with cortisol indefinitely without consequences. When hanging around for extended periods, it has been linked with problems related to:

- Immune system effectiveness
- Muscle tissue and bone density
- Obesity and gastric functioning
- Thinking skills
- Increases in subjective feelings of tension and stress
- Lower self-esteem
- Long-term changes in neural patterns, such as those associated with PTSD

Back when I was doing fieldwork, I had a standard speech I usually delivered about ten days into a disaster operation. It emphasized the importance of workers making themselves take breaks, as well as days off when possible. Otherwise accidents, injuries, and illnesses would take their tolls. These maladies pretty much always launched a spike in frequency a couple weeks into a major disaster operation, regardless. Nonetheless, I like to think that my dutiful warning encouraged at least some people to take better care of themselves.

Cortisol can be blamed for increased incidence of illness during extended stress, given how it affects the immune system. The greater number of accidents and injuries, however, is better accounted for by adrenalin—not due to excess, but because its level eventually nosedives. Our adrenal glands can't produce the bucket loads of adrenalin required to satisfy a continually punched panic button forever.

Remember that we need to maintain a certain baseline of arousal just to go about our daily lives. If the tank gets too close to empty, our engines begin to sputter. Mental errors go up, and behavioral effectiveness goes down. We make mistakes that get us injured. And without adrenalin to motivate us, we sag.

These added vulnerabilities interfere with taking the bull by the horns and guiding it out of cogjam. Even without new cogjammed behaviors cheering on dysfunction, struggling stress chemistry has siphoned away the motivational energy needed for solution seeking.

This is probably the best explanation for why individuals with the higher cortisol baselines did not bother to vote. They had run too low on adrenalin— their bodies could take no more.

Evidence of lower adrenalin also shows with cogjam. Given how long we've been dealing with it, you may already have noticed the following in yourself or among loved ones:

- Becoming resigned to our predicament
- Moving into denial that the problem exists, or that it's of any importance
- Social withdrawal
- Basic lack of energy

Avoidance-type behaviors can be part of the coping solution for some of the uncontrollable negativity floating around. But they do not help us find solutions. They do not help us figure out why cogjam entered the scene in the first place, so that we might avoid it down the road. If overused for coping, avoidance behaviors leave us stuck or adrift.

Moving forward requires more. And avoiding it in the future requires clear understanding, planning, and intention to take a different path.

COMMON DISASTER SYMPTOMS

There are other ways arousal chemistry meltdown shows itself. Just as individuals have their own unique ways of coping, they also have their own ways of going downhill when they reach their limits. However a person usually breaks down is what likely will be left swirling in the wake of flailing fight or flight.

Of course, new reactions turn up as well. As future chapters will illustrate, that can actually be a good thing.

Identifying and understanding our personal battles with cogjam requires a brief review of the physical, emotional, cognitive, behavioral, interpersonal, and spiritual consequences that may turn up in the mix. The symptoms listed below are those most commonly seen in the aftermath of disaster. They are by no means the only possible symptoms.

Likewise, they are not unique to disaster. Other life experiences, illnesses, genetic issues, and the like are also associated with developing such symptoms. And yes, the vastness of this motley crew is reminiscent of a Chinese menu. Still, it provides a good starting point for nailing down that which ails us.

- Physical: Fatigue, nausea and other gastrointestinal problems, dizziness, headaches, muscle tremors, sweating, chest pain, difficulty breathing, feeling weak or hollow, sensitivity to noise, elevated blood pressure
- Emotional: Shocked or dazed, fearfulness, anxiety, anger, irritability, loneliness, sadness, guilt, impatience, numbness, guilt, shame, losing enjoyment of usual pastimes
- Cognitive: Decreased ability to make decisions or solve problems, difficulty concentrating or remembering things, confusion, calculation difficulties, short attention span, constant mental replays that try to get the past event to turn out differently, recurring dreams or nightmares, and inability to get thoughts of the disaster to stop
- Behavioral: Sleep difficulties, changes in appetite, increased startle reflex, tearfulness, crying for no apparent reason, avoiding activities that serve as a reminder, staying excessively busy as a distraction, increased alcohol and drug use
- Interpersonal: Isolating self from others, frequent conflict, angry or other such behavior alienating others, overprotectiveness towards family or friends
- Spiritual: Questioning personal religious beliefs, blaming God for what happened, displaced anger toward authority figures

As the complexity of these lists imply, my suspicion of cogjam having become a national disaster was not because any one symptom or syndrome shouted at me "this is disaster caused." What gave it away was the collective trauma. It was the distraction, guardedness, pervasive sadness, easily triggered anger, sense of confusion, regularly derailed logic, and occasional sense of hopelessness. It was seeing relationships among lifelong buddies reduced to dust, as well as marriages and other family relationships becoming strained. It was the decrease in effective emotional and interpersonal functioning of the community as a whole, no matter which community I observed. To my horror, most everyone seemed to be making preferred selections from that Chinese menu.

POSTTRAUMATIC GROWTH

Fortunately, posttraumatic growth is as likely to be a consequence of severe adversity as is suffering (and after slogging through that last section, we could all use the good news). In addition to unpleasantness, good comes from disaster.[7]

We grow. It's growth that only takes place when adversity is disorienting enough to pull the resilience rug out from under us. It forces us to step back and reexamine both ourselves, and what we take for granted. In self-defense, we build greater resilience. Such rewards are up for grabs anytime we face significantly overwhelming challenges.

The most commonly reported outcome of posttraumatic growth is discovery of a new appreciation for life. At least, those who experience posttraumatic growth typically agree it's part of what they gain. But there are other reported benefits as well:

- Greater sense of personal strength and empowerment
- Greater intimacy in relationships
- A new sense of priorities, or what really matters
- Finding more meaning in life itself
- Elevated spiritual development
- Seeing new paths and possibilities for the future

What spectacular color this adds to cogjam's depressing murkiness. Imagine the potential: cogjam may well advance us in ways that otherwise never would have been possible, both as individuals and as a community. There truly is a light at the end of the tunnel.

7   Joseph, S. (2013). *What doesn't kill us: The new psychology of posttraumatic growth.* New York: Perseus Books Group.

CHAPTER 3
......
Oil for the Wheelhouse

N O MATTER WHAT the version of assault, the stress response is about survival. The chemical blocking and narrowed focus that follow are one cause of the disrupted thinking that plagues us when we're all worked up. However, cogjam introduces an additional element to the formula, thanks to this larger cerebral cortex of ours.

We enter into a state of what we could call cognitive distress. Cognitive distress slips onto the scene because of repeated assaults to the intellect. Supposed realities might be drawn out of thin air and insisted upon. A source might say one thing one day, then something else the next. An individual's actions might be the exact opposite of what he or she had just made a big deal of valuing. Others' flow of logic simply doesn't seem to add up. We see people behave in ways that few would have ever predicted.

Things don't make sense anymore.

Feeling like your rational self is under fire ignites a deeper fear. It singes the very roots of self-confidence, and self-doubt sprouts in its place. Except when we experience cognitive distress, the actual source of the anxiety is not so easily pinned down as with a more easily identified threat. Not being able to figure out where uncomfortable feelings come from stirs up an even greater sense of vulnerability and self-doubt.

The trauma of intellectual assault is most looked at in studies of battering relationships, such as when one partner attempts to control the other by undermining the other's intelligence, or keeping him or her in a state of fear or confusion. Outside of such relationships—what has come to be called "gaslighting"—the topic has attracted relatively little attention.[8] Fortunately, the past several decades of cognitive research have built an arsenal of well-developed weapons that are more than qualified to fight intellectual trauma. We will put them to good use as we go along. First, however, we need to re-steady ourselves on the trail of common sense.

What exactly is common sense? What constitutes valid logic? This chapter revisits what we all used to know about establishing fact from fiction, before so much of it scurried down a rat hole.

REVIVING SCIENCE

While the primitive brain bends toward the whims of instinct, what goes on in the logical brain is similar—if not identical—to concepts and reasoning built into formal science. Our brains have always used science-like practices to make sense of observations, absorb new ideas, and build a knowledge base for a successful life.

Snippets of folk wisdom hang around over many generations because such observations and conclusions agreeably meld with how our brains operate. In fact, I take the liberty of scattering a number of old sayings throughout this and other chapters. They help illustrate how ingrained the main ideas of scientific reasoning are within our collective wisdom.

The biggest difference between common sense and scientific method is that scientific method is more organized and thorough than casual observations and interpretations alone. Therefore, it serves well as a platform to which to secure our cognitive anchors.

But if scientific method is truly so tied to the mind's natural ebb and flow, how did science get battered into such a fractured state? How could people become so much more susceptible to making snap judgments or accepting what others say without thinking it through?

Fight or flight is not the only perpetrator of rushed conclusion drawing. The speed of Western society itself has evolved, especially technologically. The internet environment promotes and supports faster-paced lives. We want to know what we want to know, right when we want it. Googling obliges such whims, providing us with instant results on any topic. Often we don't bother to check original sources. If Siri or Alexa says it, we figure that's good enough. We

8   Welch, B. (2008). *State of confusion: Political manipulation and the assault on the American mind.* New York: St. Martin's Press.

accept it and move on. Cogjam only ramps up the magnetism of that instant gratification.

Some of the antics filtering down from the political arena show similar shortsightedness. In their frenzy, members of all parties are at times guilty of treating reality as if it's something to proclaim, rather than deduce. Unless, of course, it involves an opposing side's proclamation. Then shortcomings in reasoning are pointed out as obvious. And often, they are.

This political hamster wheel might be amusing if it weren't so tragic. Not just because cogjammed thinking limits how well government officials can achieve their goals, but also because these practices are so freely modeled, reinforced, and spread around in the mainstream. Consciously or subconsciously, we're biased to follow the paths indicated by our leaders.

But the impact of such role modeling is clear—and widespread. All it takes is a look at social media to see how playing fast and loose with facts and inferences has caught on as a national pastime. We didn't act this crazy before now.

That's because we are better than this. Healing fractured reasoning requires reestablishing the intelligent give and take we were born to put to use, as did the ancestors who gifted us with old wives tales and urban legends.

A THUMBNAIL SKETCH OF SCIENCE

Back at the university, experimental design and statistical analysis earned a reputation for being as dull as ditchwater. Or when finals week rolled around, was labeled something significantly more execrable.

This chapter is not a formal review of scientific method. It does not serve as preparation for performing formal research. Rather, it aims to show the relationship between science and the garden-variety common sense used every day by everybody, regardless of educational level.

If the pieces don't immediately come together for you, don't worry about it. The bullet points at the end of the more complex explanations highlight the main points. And the most important concepts will be revisited as they apply later.

DEFINITION

When I was in the fourth grade, we learned that "science is the study of the world around us." This definition stuck with me because my understanding of science has never wavered far from it. Three social science degrees and decades of continuing education later, and nothing has crossed my path to violate this simplest of definitions.

Until now. Or rather, I see a whole lot of evidence that many people either didn't learn that early lesson, or are ignoring it. Nudges from the gut brain are frighteningly adept at getting us to accept "facts" prematurely. To better understand such reasoning blunders to be blunders, we first must nail down exactly what evidence-based thinking is.

What really is this thing we call science? Some respond by saying it's biology, physics, psychology, and the like. While those topics are typically listed under science or social science categories in college course catalogs, that's not what science is. Those listings are actually *fields* of scientific study. In other words, they are specific topics that use scientific practices and procedures to gather information and draw conclusions.

Others sometimes answer this question by saying it's what scientists do—a circular explanation, of course. Such a definition easily comes to mind because we so commonly turn to scientific experts to explain unfamiliar or complex topics. Scientists are our go-to guys and gals. We expect them to be able to most accurately represent their particular knowledge base.

Therefore we learn to be selective about whom to consult when in need of advice, no matter what the issue. We are more likely to believe we have a tooth cavity if the dentist tells us than if an accountant diagnoses it. Dentists go to school for a long time to learn how to do what they do. So do CPAs—and we'd be more likely to consult them than our dentist if we had problems with tax returns. Such individuals have graduate degrees, or other advanced training and experience in their fields. They know what they're talking about. Right?

Well, yes, up to a certain point. Those who go in for required training and credentials in a particular field generally come out agreeing on the basics. It's hard not to, and still be awarded a degree or certification.

However, the wonder and beauty of scientific inquiry is that "reality" has never been etched in granite—at least, not in a manner the human brain can comprehend. Ongoing investigation continues in every field imaginable. We constantly dig up new factoids. These must be logically wedged in with other accepted facts to be of any use to us.

At first, expert opinions on how to incorporate such new discoveries differ, perhaps widely. Over time more study and lots of discussion take place. Eventually, a general consensus is established, and the new information becomes part of the revised agreed-upon knowledge base. These constantly shifting sands are one of the reasons why scientists' opinions are so valuable. They are the ones most likely to be aware of the current lay of the land in their particular field.

The intellectual negotiations of scientists mirror how we put together consensual reality for anything. If everybody agrees that an object before them is a table, then reality is that it is a table. In some past culture, everyone might agree that this same object is a sacrificial platform. That would be their reality. Absolute reality, if there is such a thing, doesn't make much difference. Functioning well in our world relies, in part, on meshing with the consensual beliefs of those we live among.

Regardless of majority agreements, every field has its controversial topics. And as might be expected, there are controversial practitioners to go with them. With people being people, there will always be some who significantly stray from the status quo. They include the visionary geniuses, but at the other end of the spectrum are the half-baked crackpots. Those at both ends, as well as everyone in between, still know their way around their field better than those of us standing on the sidelines. But without a way of applying further scrutiny, how do we tell which is which? Is it wise to blindly trust credentials at the end of a name?

While credentials provide initial guidance for whom to consult, having an idea of where the credentialed individual's information is coming from is also important. Experts should be able to describe the type of data, the logic of their conclusions, and how or why it applies to the question asked. They should also be aware of any major differing opinions. Having this level of exchange lets Jane and Joe Public sort out facts and opinions for themselves.

Second opinions from additional experts can be beneficial, too. But again, experts are only as competent as the data they work from. If they truly know their stuff, they can explain why they think what they think. No concept is so complex that it can't be broken down into parts to be further digested by the average consumer.

In short, science is about *how* we observe, assess, and draw conclusions, regardless of the topic under study or who is studying it. How scientific method systematically goes about it is at times boringly pedantic, as you may well conclude as you follow along in this chapter.

Hang in there. The extra care pays off in the end. The systematic practices of science provide the most accurate picture possible because they account for as many potential variables as an experimental design allows. Ability to arrange for such control in casual personal observations is rare.

In other words, scientific method lets us be more certain of what the outcome of an investigation truly represents, which conclusions are most appropriate, and how to best use the information in the real world.[9] Experimental design and number crunching data works the same no matter which field we investigate. Math is math.

---

9   For a more in-depth review of scientific method, try Corbin, J. & Strauss, A. (2015). *Basics of qualitative research: Technique and procedures for developing grounded theory*, 4th ed. Los Angeles, CA: Sage.

Sometimes people talk about science as if it's an entity unto itself, that "science says this." In everyday language, this statement is shorthand for saying "scientific inquiry has found this." Some take the former literally. That's a mistake. And a problem.

Science is only a tool. It does not "say" or believe anything. That would be like saying a compass, yardstick, or abacus holds beliefs of one sort or another. They are only measuring tools, supplying us with concrete pieces of information. Likewise, scientific method is one more relatively objective strategy for assessing observations. The individual assessor is the one who makes inferences, draws conclusions, and adjusts beliefs, based on what the tool shows and how it meshes with what the person already knows.

Of course, there are also non-scientific tools that help make sense of our experiences. Intuition is one. Spiritually based enlightenment is another. What we take in by these means isn't any less real.

But success at anything means using the right tool for the right job. Existential questions are difficult, at times impossible, to answer through scientific method. They're too subjective, among other things. Likewise, if we want to know how much two plus two is, we don't meditate or pray about it. We simply do the math our brains are designed to calculate.

In summary:

- Science is a tool, not a person or field of study.
- Scientific inquiry is merely a more structured and detailed version of common sense.
- Scientific experts and their opinions—not to mention our own—are only as good as the data from which they draw their conclusions.

THE FLOW OF SCIENCE

Scientific inquiry takes place in four stages:

1. Establishing the hypothesis we wish to investigate. What are we trying to prove?
2. Gathering appropriate data, and deciding how to go about observing and measuring it.
3. Fitting findings into the greater knowledge base. What logical deductions we can make with the new information?
4. How new understanding might apply to a specific situation or individual.

That last step is the most important, yet comes closer to being an art form. It's one of the reasons people are said to "practice" certain fields—as is the case for law, or medicine—rather than always being able to provide the absolute right answer. They come up with the best answer they can, based on their familiarity with the knowledge base and the relevant details of the specific person or situation before them.

This can be said of science in general. The principles of scientific method help us find the best possible answer, or the most probable answer, for whatever we face—on a smaller scale, but still better than what we can come up with by relying on single observations or reports of others. Through careful evaluation, scientific method can control for many of the missteps that cogjammed reasoning so easily creates.

THE CURIOUS CASE OF TED AND THE THIRTY PUSH-UPS

Let's say your coworker, Ted, is long tormented by boring morning meetings he must attend. It takes everything he's got to force his eyes to stay open. But when he returns to his desk after today's meeting, instead of looking glum and frustrated, he's walking on air.

When you ask what's gotten him so ethereal, he says he's found a solution for getting through those meetings. His miracle cure: performing thirty push-ups before entering the boardroom. While a bit taxing, he says that ever since he started doing it, he's been more fully participating. He hasn't missed an important piece of information all week, and is convinced that the push-ups increased his ability to focus. He insists that you would also benefit from his morning regimen. All day long he spreads his evangelical message throughout the office.

What do you think? Are Ted's conclusions about push-ups and improved attention span scientifically sound? For the record, research does suggest a relationship between exercise and ability to focus. But for our purposes, that's not the point. What we're evaluating is the probability of whether it was true for Ted in this particular instance, and whether what he did might benefit others in the office as well.

You may already have a question or two about Ted's conclusions, or have that vague feeling that something isn't up to snuff. This is natural. When we hear about these types of instant cures or conclusions, common sense questions inevitably cross our minds.

Experimental designs are set up to address those common sense questions. Specific features of the designs arrange so that alternate explanations for data coming out the way it did are less likely to apply. Following are several natural questions we might ask about Ted's results, and what scientific method might do to improve clarity of cause and effect.

Could Ted's attention span have been better that week, regardless? This is a question about whatever else went on with Ted that could have affected his attention span. For example, maybe the week before he'd been going to bed at a reasonable hour instead of staying up late with the Xbox. Perhaps he ate a real breakfast that morning, instead of picking up a quick latte during his mid-morning break. The previous week the boss might have read him the riot act for daydreaming during meetings, which inspired him to try harder. Maybe his being oblivious to something everybody else heard at the meeting resulted in an embarrassing faux pas; he didn't want to go through that again. And on, and on.

We can write off these alternate explanations if we base conclusions on more than the experiences of single-participant Ted. After all, "one swallow doesn't make a spring" (one of those old adages I promised). So let's say we recruit a hundred of his fellow workers, and have them all do thirty push-ups before morning meetings. It's highly unlikely that all of the workers would have the same ongoing life history as Ted. Therefore, improvements due to differences in recent history would average out in the end.

Common sense works the same way. In our day-to-day lives we usually base ongoing beliefs on more than one piece of evidence. For example, we expect the sun to come up in the morning because we've watched it happen so many times. After experiencing a total eclipse, we don't figure the sun is about to be blotted out forever. We recognize it as an anomaly, given our previous experiences. Likewise, a historian who finds only one reference to a specific accounting of a past event is less likely to believe it over multiple references presenting a credible conflicting story. Common sense applies to all fields, not just science.

In addition to Ted's individual differences, we might wonder about natural growth and adjustment processes. Suppose his boss's boring drone takes a while for anybody to get used to. Perhaps Ted just happened to reach the apex of his learning curve the week he did the push-ups. If this were so, his ability to focus would have improved without them.

This brings us to the realm of the wily control group. Control groups are the spoilers of unwanted subterfuge. They get this name because they "control" for the possibility that the result would have happened anyway, with or without the treatment under study.

We can create a control group for our experiment by dividing participants into two groups, the experimental group doing push-ups and the control group doing business as usual. Since the random natural growth factor applies to everybody, improvement by those in the experimental group that is better than those in the control group is less likely to be due to natural growth.

Is this truly something that would benefit anyone, or are the push-ups only a good answer for Ted? "That's comparing apples and oranges" is the folksy version of this potential issue. It refers to those occasions when what's good for one isn't always good for another.

Suppose Ted has an attention deficit condition of some sort, one that is especially sensitive to exercise or lack thereof. If this were the case, Ted's conclusion about push-ups improving focusing skills might be true for him. But it wouldn't mean much for everybody else. Unless, of course, others in his office suffer from the same problem.

Suppose there's an unfortunate neurological condition affecting many of the locals because of past contaminants in the water system. It so happens that doing push-ups helps with the symptoms of this particular ailment. What if everybody who'd been affected by the contaminants ended up in the push-ups group, with no affected individuals in the other? An improvement might be seen among those doing the push-ups. But, the results still wouldn't necessarily apply to those without the neurological condition.

This is why scientists use random assignment to group membership. The idea is to make sure that every participant recruited for the study has an equal chance of being in the experimental group or the control group. Random assignment uses drawing names from a hat, choosing every other name on a list, or any other strategy that avoids biasing which group a participant ends up in. For our study, random selection gives us a pretty good chance of making sure that focus-challenged participants are evenly represented in both groups.

In the real world, we don't have the luxury of such maneuvering. But we still use the basic idea. If a friend recommends a practice or product that works well for him, we commonly hash out second, third, or even fourth opinions with others while we consider it. It's not because we don't trust the friend. It's because experience has taught us that a happy and healthy life is more likely to be achieved when we're thoughtful, rather than impulsive about what we do or believe.

What makes Ted so sure his attention span improved? In other words, Ted may have seen an improvement in attention span only because "we find what we're looking for." This has to do with the objectivity or subjectivity of observations.

We are all hopelessly subjective when it comes to assessing ourselves, or things that matter to us. We experience our inner existence in ways that can be assessed by no other. These feelings are pervasive, and they color our observations—thus the saying about seeing the world through rose-colored glasses. We can try to be more objective. But completely weeding out subjectivity regarding ourselves is extremely difficult, if not impossible.

Objectivity is about establishing what is agreed upon—consensual reality, if you will—or at least getting as close to agreement as possible. It's kind of like how sports shows have one narrator who reports the play-by-play, and another who is a commentator. Play-by-play is simply recounting actions as they take place, what everybody sees happening. Commentators, on the other hand, throw in their two cents' worth about what's being observed: speculating why a particular player did something, whether he thinks the referee got the call right, or anything else that represents interpretation or opinion rather than clear and obvious facts.

For our study, we could probably get everybody to agree on something as obvious as Ted's eye color. That's relatively easy. Assessing improvement in focusing, however, is a more complex proposition. Without building some form of objectivity into our data, the results will be difficult to fit in with the rest of reality.

Test scores are concrete, and equally observable by all. Suppose we create brief multiple-choice quizzes that cover the content of each meeting's agenda. We give them to participants of both groups after their morning meeting, and see how much they recall. Their scores let us compare the two groups of participants with more objective data than simply eyeballing how on-task they look, and giving subjective opinions.

In daily life, we consider objectivity and subjectivity all the time, though we may not be aware of it. How often do we say something like "that's just Fred" after he lets loose an oddball comment? Life experience shows us that everybody has his or her biases. Because of them, we sometimes take their opinions with a grain of salt. Some individuals' biases get so far outside the norm that we brush off what they say altogether.

By the same token, we're more inclined to believe those who tend to be objective. Perhaps we trust their opinion because they ground what they say with evidence from good sources, are consistent in their message, leave emotion out of it, tend to look at both sides of an issue, or are in other ways thorough in how they go about presenting information. Even if we don't know why, or don't even recognize that we're doing it, on some level we all take note of which people are more—or less—reliable.

Did the push-ups only work for Ted because he believed they would? I wish the placebo effect didn't get such a bad rap. When you think about it, it's a downright miracle that our bodies can heal or otherwise get us to perform better if we simply believe what we're doing will make a difference. Why haven't we zeroed in more on this, and found a way to benefit from it? Instead, the placebo effect is typically treated as an annoyance to weed out, something that gets in the way of studies about pills, procedures, and the like.

If Ted has found himself a placebo that helps him pay attention, hooray for him. We should all be so fortunate. However, his success doesn't tell us much about global cause and effect between push-ups and attention span. To sort out possible placebo effects, our control group needs to receive a treatment, too. That way we can expect the possibility of placebo-based improvement to be pretty much equal for both groups.

Let's give the placebo group a funny story to read just before the meeting. If everybody improves, but the push-ups group still gets better quiz scores than the funny story group, we can assume there's more going on here than a couple of placebos.

How do we know the differences between the two groups are due to a real difference, rather than an outcome occurring by chance? Suppose your friend is about to flip a coin ten times. He asks for your best guess about how many times it would land heads or tails. You'd probably go for five a piece. After all, it's a fifty-fifty proposition.

Your friend flips the coin. But he gets six heads and four tails. Does this mean there's something wrong with the coin? Of course not. You based your guess on the expected average of many, many coin flips. The next series might just as likely be the opposite, four heads and six tails. Both fall within the realm of expectable outcomes.

But what if the coin came up heads ten times? Would you then say there's something fishy going on, or would you accept that it happened by chance?

There's a similar difficulty with our attention span study. Chance alone suggests that our experimental group and control group will not produce identical scores. Either one, or the other, is highly likely to achieve at least a slightly greater or lesser value. How much higher or lower do they have to be to represent a true difference, rather than only an accident?

Inferential statistics show the probability of an outcome representing a real difference, rather than something happening by chance. A full discussion of inferential statistics is well beyond the scope of this book, not to mention most people's levels of interest and patience. Let's leave it with this understanding: certain types of data use certain experimental designs, and specific statistical analyses and calculus-derived tables are used to tell us whether differences between groups are significant.

Statistical significance: this brings us to that saying about there not being any one right answer. Even when using fancy statistics, we don't get an absolute yes or no with experiments like whether push-ups help attention span. Depending on the level of certainty we're aiming for, statistics generally indicate whether it's a ten percent, five percent, one percent or even lower probability that the quiz scores came out they way they did by accident.

Regardless of which of these levels of probability we decide to go with, the controls built into this system give Ted a higher level of certainty than he had with his original experiment. And the answers found and conclusions drawn are dramatically better supported than what comes from taking a guess and hoping it's right.

So even when we get as picky-picky as we did with Ted's hypothesis, applying the prescribed number crunching only shows how *probable* it is that better quiz scores indicate a true difference between the groups. There are always exceptions to the rules, and unknown factors often play roles. Unforeseen possibilities are endless. All scientific method can give us is the most probable answer, based on the available data.

We can't leave the discussion of statistics without mentioning "fishing error." Fishing error is when we get results that are statistically significant, but they are actually one of those one/five/ten chances in a hundred of coming up by accident. This is why scientists perform the same study multiple times before getting overly excited about their results, a practice known as replication. Chances of getting the same fishing error multiple times are miniscule.

So even though we can't be a hundred percent sure about accepted facts, there's no reason not to get as close as we can. The human race has been getting along relatively well with such a mindset for some time. All cultures put together a consensual reality that most can live with, even in today's complex world. And when making predictions and life plans, we're certainly better off hedging our bets in ways that respect probabilities like a fifty-fifty coin toss outcome, rather than hoping for that chance of getting all heads or all tails. Yes, anything is possible, philosophically speaking. But improving chances for a happier and more productive life means aiming toward the probable. Common sense, right?

In summary:

- Scientific experiments are set up to weed out possible alternative explanations for what we're trying to figure out.
- Scientific method increases objectivity, and reduces the influence of subjective opinion.
- We can only demonstrate high or low probability levels of something being correct, rather than one right answer.
- Scientific method draws conclusions from multiple sources, and replicates new findings to lessen the chance of coming up with a particular outcome by accident.
- The gut brain, unfortunately, is significantly less concerned about common sense. In fact, it doesn't think at all about probability or statistics. It is designed to recognize a threat and then react, an all or nothing proposition. Whether the perceived threat is inevitable or highly unlikely is not part of the equation.

This is one of those junctures where logic can step in and give a stressed brain a little guidance. Yes, being struck by lightening is a possibility. But we don't spend our lives hiding from or worrying about such a low-probability event.

DRAWING INFERENCES

Life experience makes us increasingly wiser, or increasingly more foolish—perhaps even when based on the same collection of life experiences. The make-or-break of it is how we process whatever information comes our way. Here's an example.

Back in the sixties, a flurry of research looked at gender differences and nature versus nurture. One particular study tried to show that by nature, the female gender is more dependent on others than the male gender. The researchers drafted a group of infants who were just beginning to move around and pull themselves up. They assumed that at this early age, the influences of nurture wouldn't have had much chance to take hold. They brought them and their mothers into a waiting room with a crib-like pen. They instructed the mothers to set their infants in the pen, and stood back and watched.

As to be expected, most infants were not pleased with being dumped in a strange place. But how they reacted differed some, based on gender. More boys than girls pulled themselves up against the rail, pounded against it, or experimented with other possible means of escape. On the other hand, more of the girls than boys only sat in place and burst into tears. The researchers concluded this was because girls are generally less independent than boys.

Their conclusion stood until another set of researchers reexamined the data. It so happened that the original study had tracked how much time each infant spent in the pen. Not surprisingly, the girls on average were out of those pens faster than were the boys. The research reviewers suggested that the outcome was not a matter of dependence or independence, but rather communication. Babies who wanted out communicated their displeasure by means of the only language skill they had. This revised conclusion is consistent with mainstream developmental findings that, in general, girls avail themselves of language earlier than do boys.[10]

Herein lies a most critical distinction, from the standpoint of sorting out observations.

Note that both conclusions, though very different from one another, came from the exact same set of data. No matter which way the scientists interpreted

---

10   Eriksson, M., Marchik, P. B., Tulviste, T., & Gallego, C. (2012). Differences between girls and boys in emerging language skills: Evidence from 10 language communities. *British Journal of Developmental Psychology, 30*, 326-343.

the results, the amount of time infants spent in the pen was the same. Which infants sat and cried or got up and climbed against the rail was the same.

That's because gathered data itself is objective, as much as it can be. But at the point of drawing conclusions, subjectivity and human fallibility make their grand entrances. We must respect the difference between these two stages of scientific inquiry to avoid tripping into a rat hole. It's a practice we already may be aware of and do regularly, even without having to dissect specific thoughts and behaviors to the *nth* degree.

Here's a more everyday example.

You arrive at a neighborhood barbecue. Chef Lenny acts dejected, saying that one of the other guests, Leo, thinks he is not very good at grilling. You know Leo well, and that it would be highly unlikely for him to openly say such a thing. So you ask him what Leo actually said. It turns out Lenny overheard Leo tell someone his burger was hopelessly undercooked.

However, you know from past outings that Leo likes his meat singed into shoe leather. Therefore his comment was more likely a statement about personal preference, rather than Lenny's grilling skills. You point this out to Lenny. He breathes a sigh of relief.

Two different perspectives, based on the same comment: this is why going back to the objective information is so important. What if you took it all at face value, and came down hard on Lenny for trashing Leo? Or, chastised Leo for suggesting Lenny would say something like that? We avoid major interpersonal fallout by keeping an open mind and not jumping to conclusions. We consider other relevant information before acting when circumstances matter.

Both of the preceding examples demonstrate why it's a bad idea to reject a scientific finding whole-handedly just because something about it doesn't sound right, or opinions conflict. That's throwing out the baby with the bathwater—better known as all-or-nothing thinking, a common conundrum we'll be exploring later in greater depth. If we reject scientific expertise because of interpretational disagreements, we miss out on learning to be had at the point of data collection.

A different set of cautions applies if we go the other direction, and decide there is in fact scientific merit to a new interpretation. In the infant study, the second set of researchers cannot say there's no difference between genders regarding dependency, even if considerable additional data supports the language factor. It could be both inferences are correct—perhaps baby girls are both more dependent than boys, and earlier to use verbal communication. A do-over with appropriate controls is needed to clarify the picture.

This is the usual way of scientific investigation. Failure to demonstrate only means we're still working on the question. Scientific method supports conclusions based only on what it can demonstrate. Otherwise, it sticks to "I don't know." It supports "no" only if it can directly demonstrate it.

Therein lies the rub in the world of cogjam. Fight or flight mentality absolutely detests "I don't know's." When in dire straits we can't protect ourselves very well without having a good idea of what's going on around us. So out of desperation we latch onto whatever conclusions are available, and choose a course of action that leads us to feel, or actually to be, safe.

If we don't distinguish the difference between real and imagined or anticipatory threat, our inner lizards goad us into jousting with windmills. Science gets lost in the shuffle. We position ourselves to get wrapped up in premature conclusions, when there may not have been any need to draw a conclusion in the first place. Rather than protect ourselves or loved ones, we introduce the risk of misguidance, rather than reduce existing risk.

Cogjam strikes again.

In summary:

Effective use of science means respecting the difference between the actual concrete data and the logic used to draw conclusions about the observations.

Scientific findings are about concepts that can be and actually are demonstrated, rather than assuming their opposite must be true if data does not support the original belief.

Immediate fight or flight reactions are not too concerned about either of the above.

SANDRA AND THE SUPPLEMENT

Newly adopted information doesn't get left to stand on its own. We introduce it into the bigger picture. Where does it belong on our cognitive shelves? Even those who know scientific method inside out can get tripped up by this one. That's one of the reasons why anything appearing in reputable scientific journals goes through so much peer review before put in print.

Let's start over with a new example.

Sandra has pesky skin rashes that come and go. She reads in her HMO newsletter that not getting enough vitamin B-6 can cause rashes similar to hers. With a little internet research she finds a CDC report suggesting that in the diets of USA citizens, vitamin B-6 is inadequately represented more than any other nutrient. Thus bolstered by factual information from a reliable source, she decides to increase her vitamin B-6 intake. Over time, she discovers she isn't getting those rashes anywhere near as frequently.

Sandra is on cloud nine. She not only found the cause of her plight, but also succeeded in researching and applying what appears to be a legitimate cure. She comes to you and crows over her success. Then she asks about any rashes you've had lately. When you admit to the occasional scaly patch, she tells you with unquestioning certainty that vitamin B-6 deficiency is the culprit, and that you need to increase your intake.

What do you think? Sandra's information came from valid sources. And it did seem to work for her, assuming it's not a placebo effect.

Unfortunately, this story is an example of the old saying, "a little knowledge can be a dangerous thing." The structure of Sandra's logic used illustrates two problems: single-factor thinking, and premature hypothesis acceptance. Her reasoning strategy goes like this: If you have a vitamin B-6 deficiency, you will get skin rashes. Therefore if you get these skin rashes, you must have a vitamin B-6 deficiency. Right?

Wrong. There are a kazillion other reasons people get scaly patches that have nothing to do with vitamin deficiency. Given that the treatment seemed to work for Sandra, chances are it was a true success for her. But given all the other possibilities, whether it would do any good for your own occasional scaly patches is still unclear.

Realistic application of new pieces of information requires taking into account the other related factors, especially ones that may disconfirm the original assumption. Drawing an absolute conclusion on the basis of a single new piece of information is not only illogical. In some cases it's also an ingredient to the recipe for disaster.

Sandra also dropped the ball when she assumed that putting together accepted facts in a logical manner creates new facts. It doesn't. It creates a new hypothesis that needs to be checked out. Her reasoning took her down a rat hole because she accepted her hypothesis as true without first testing it, or checking for other relevant data.

There are indeed valid inferences to be made from "if A, then B" propositions. For example, "if not B, then not A" can be concluded from an "if A, then B" statement. In the case of the vitamin B-6 story, it looks like this: if the deficiency (A) always results in this type of rash (B), and the rash isn't there (not B), it's safe to say there is no B-6 deficiency (not A).

Thankfully there are less nerdy ways to go about drawing sensible conclusions, which better reflect what we do naturally. In short, respecting the following basic guidelines helps pave the way to more logical conclusions:

- Consider the source.
- Consider more than one piece of information when applying a conclusion beyond its original context.
- Don't forget to look for possible disconfirming data.
- Rather than paranoid rejection or jumping in with both feet when encountering new information, practice healthy skepticism.

It's not like we don't already know how to do this. Logic-based falsehoods end up in our laps more often due to not following through all the way with our best thinking than basic ignorance. Thinking it through takes time and effort, and that "if A, then B" jazz can get complicated—especially so when we're simultaneously floating in cogjam haze.

CHAPTER 4

······

Erring Is Human

THE HUMAN BRAIN—such an incredible organ, and it does so much for us. Rallying under the flag of evidence-based thinking, its many functions faithfully move us forward.

It does it so well. Throughout our lives we're rewarded with an ever-growing arsenal of tactics for promoting intellectual advancement, healthy belief systems, a solid understanding of who we are, and fitting in with fellow human beings. And as is true for most every other critter, we use newly adopted reasoning to polish the evolutionary brilliance of the stress response.

Yet this is the snag, where these two gifts—capacity for scientific thinking and primitive reflexes—tangle at critical moments. Left unchecked, self-protective behaviors typically win out over logical protest. The gut brain is more tightly and efficiently wired than the relatively newer cerebral cortex. Self-protection turns first to those maneuvers that have had time and opportunity to hardwire, regardless of whether its automatic behavioral repertoire is due to reflex, instinct, or early training. When seeking quick answers while stressed, specific features of past learning make certain solutions or explanations seem more reliable than they really are.

Some of the concepts I'm about to share take a while to absorb. We so easily accept many of these common reasoning errors as logical that our wiring must do heavier lifting to get itself on a different track. So as you read this chapter, allow what will sink in to sink in, and don't worry about the rest. Important concepts are revisited repeatedly later, as they apply. With repetition this stretch of the path out of cogjam will become clearer, step by step.

THE MANY PATHS OF RATIONALIZATION

As with fear-based behaviors, interpretations and conclusions drawn when we're all worked up may or may not be our best. When battling through the heat of the moment, temptation to accept a logical hypothesis as reality rather than something to be checked out can be powerful indeed. But putting the cart before the horse in this manner is actually a form of rationalization.

Taking advantage of a second barnyard analogy: "Why did the chicken cross the road?" Comedians have suggested too many alternative answers to list. Many of them even turn out to be legitimate answers. But the only one who knows for sure why the chicken crossed the road is the chicken.

Multiple logical conclusions can be drawn about most anything. But even if all of them are valid possibilities, they can't all be right—especially given how they often conflict with one another. Logical conclusions and factual reality are two different things.

Rationalization is what happens when we adopt a plausible explanation as fact, without giving it further scrutiny. Sometimes we turn out to be right. But more often than not, we're wrong. Acting on assumptions that haven't been checked out can and often does get us into all kinds of trouble.[11]

This is because rationalizing trots along in the opposite direction of scientific thinking. Instead of systematically observing and assessing and then drawing a conclusion, rationalization starts with a conclusion, often promoted by gut-brain influences, then draws on past knowledge and personal biases to build a hypothesis to support it—better known as confirmation bias.

Actually, up until that point all may be well. It's taking that next impulsive step—accepting the newly created hypothesis without first finding a way to check it out—that gets us into hot water.

Rationalizations and their built-in inferential leaps have a way of piling up. They're the building blocks of how we unwittingly build mindsets for housing life experience that make us increasingly more foolish over the years, rather than wiser.

I'm reminded of commentary among politicians over the last decade about the mission to pull together a national health plan. When liberals ran the show, certain stump announcements proclaimed that conservatives didn't care whether citizens had health care, since they refused to support the Affordable

---

11   Cohen, M. (2015) *Critical thinking skills for dummies.* Chichester, W. Sussex: John Wiley & Sons, Ltd.

Care Act. Later I heard the exact same proclamation coming from the conservatives—that since liberals weren't willing to abandon the act and go along with their proposed plan, they didn't care whether citizens had adequate health care.

Yes, making such public announcements is as divisive as all get-out. But more relevant to our current objective, what's wrong with this picture?

This: both collectives start with a conclusion: "they're the bad guys." Therefore anything the bad guy lobbies or votes for is assumed to be a product of this intrinsic "badness." The end result is that neither side gets so far as examining and considering the other's ideas. They don't bother to explore whatever supports the other guys' beliefs, wants, or needs, or even who they really are. Thus they gain nothing that could realistically clarify those assumptions of "badness."

Instead, it only reinforces the rationalization that they're bad guys. The sniping does nothing to get either side closer to their goals, either, even if such antics do satisfy urges of their gut brains. The main accomplishment of this approach is setting opposing gut brains in motion for their next defensive swipe.

Conspiracy theories are also the stuff of rationalizing.[12] Pieces of information get cut and pasted together to support—or at least not contradict—conclusions like:

- The moon landings were all fabricated on film; they're a hoax.
- The Holocaust never happened.
- Elvis is alive and well.

Actual factoids and logic used to support conspiracy theories may be legit. And the conclusions drawn from the limited data may make perfect sense, based on what made it into consideration. Isn't that enough?

No. Not if disconfirming data is never sought, let alone considered. Technically, "theory" is an inaccurate label for conclusions drawn in this manner. The above examples are actually conspiracy hypotheses, ideas that have not yet been adequately checked out or put to the test of scientific thinking. But when the gut brain seeks targets to blame for a murky sense of foreboding, it finds exactly what it's looking for in conspiracy theory thinking.

All the same, in some situations we really do want the fear response to take charge. We don't always have time for the luxury of thinking through this, that, or the other possibility of how best to get out of harm's way. Our only choice may be a quick rationalization: punting with the first viable solution that comes to mind. It's better than nothing.

12   Barkun, M. (2003). *A culture of conspiracy: Apocalyptic visions in contemporary America*. Berkeley: University of California Press.

After things simmer down, however, nothing stops us from reexamining whatever we chose to believe or do in the heat of the moment. In the best of circumstances we perform a critique (or an autopsy, as the case may be) of how choices worked out after the fact. Who hasn't mentally replayed past difficult episodes, or talked them over with friends or a significant other?

After-event review comes second nature. It is an excellent opportunity for considering missed information, as well as thinking up other ways to handle similar situations. Coming to terms with what we did and how it worked out prepares us for the next sticky wicket, steering us away from repeated misjudgments and making the best of glowing successes. It's a critical step to learning from experience, not to mention building resilience.

Then there's this cogjam thing, popping up again like whack-a-mole. If a crisis keeps pulling the blinds over measured thinking, how does that ray of reflection manage to sneak through? Treadmills like our current socio-political strife neither respect nor slow down long enough to do much objective critiquing. Learning itself may become stunted, or take us into dastardly directions—like vilifying or deifying people based on their political positions.

DENIAL—OR, "AIN'T NO PROBLEM HERE"

The zenith of ill-advised logic is actively choosing to ignore the obvious. Scarlett O'Hara of *Gone with the Wind* had her recurring line, "I'll think about that another day." Once stated, as far as she was concerned, the problem of the moment no longer existed.

But it worked for her, so her storyline goes. At times, it works for all of us. Whether we consciously or subconsciously bury awareness of scary realities, doing so is an effective way to emotionally cope with an overwhelming situation. After all, if we decide there's nothing to fear, the primitive brain leaves us alone. Besides, if we sat around and thought about all the scary things that could possibly happen in today's world, we'd probably never leave home.

But extraordinary care needs to be taken when using denial. The category-5 hurricane will still go whichever direction it's headed, even if you convince yourself "it will never land here" and refuse to evacuate. The lioness will not decline to serve you as main course if you choose to ignore a scary pair of eyes glowing in the bushes. Once again, to be effective, denial needs to be the right tool for the right job.

Denial is extensively studied in cases of substance abuse.[13] Addiction is an extremely difficult nut to crack. It can and often does become deadly. It limits or ruins lives of addicts and their loved ones alike. However when feeling

---

13   Goldstein, R. Z., Craig, A. D. Bechara, A., Garavan, H., Childress, A. R., Paulus, M. P., & Volkow, N. D. (2009). The neurocircuitry of impaired insight in drug addiction. *Trends in Cognitive Science,* 13, 372-380.

hopelessly at the mercy of an addictive substance, denying the significance of the illness allows for escape from the terror of many potential bad or scary consequences. Getting from day to day is easier without interference from the primitive brain's kicks in the gut. But denial also backfires for addicts, since it interferes with addressing what needs to change and could be remedied.

For some, denial contributes to cogjam symptoms because they deny whether logic itself is important, saying things like "I trust my gut to lead me." Good, they well should—in certain circumstances. However the remainder of this chapter raises the curtain on many forms of havoc wreaked when the wrong tool is used for the wrong job.

SINGLE FACTOR THINKING

Behaviorally, fight or flight has a single goal: protect the self or loved one. It rolls out a brief episode of tightly narrowed focus. When the lion, wildfire, or flash flood is no longer on our tails, we stop running.

This is where similarity between fear-based gut reactions and thought lives relating to fear head different directions. It's a crossroad where the logical brain meets one of its toughest challenges. While fight or flight behavior usually ends once the threat is gone, if never challenged, immediate conclusions about why it happened and how to avoid it may hang around indefinitely.

Cogjam deals out such knee-jerk conclusions in spades. Burdened with bucket-loads of protective rationalizations, our thought lives are easily led astray. Being trapped in a bubble of single factored thinking—the opposite of scientific reasoning—poisons both depth of understanding and long-term perspective. And thanks to classical conditioning, fear has its way of cementing in the strangest things.

Little wonder we're having so much trouble coming to agreement with others. "My way, or the highway" is one manifestation of single factor thinking. The gut brain finds an answer it believes will take care of a threat. Therefore it will not budge, and clings desperately to whatever it thinks will save the day. Negotiation is out. Extreme behaviors like mindless opposition, throwing a verbal or physical punch, and dropping bombs are in. Whatever it takes.

It's not that we stop trusting logical protest. It's about the gut being the more persuasive of the two. Gut instinct and reflexes are so often right, like when we jump out of the way of an oncoming car or snap our hand back after it brushes against a hot oven rack. Besides, emotional decision-making feels so satisfying in the moment, and is so much easier to do. These perks alone reinforce it into the overall game plan, even when it ends up encouraging faulty logic and problematic behavior.

On top of it all, the logical brain can strengthen gut-brain reactions as it dutifully stores and retrieves memories of those times when fight or flight reactions did indeed save the day. It has little problem teasing out good reasons to cave in favor of gut instinct, when doing so seems to fit the situation. But it can't stay parked in that space indefinitely. Somewhere along the line, logic needs to retake the steering wheel.

Another potential road bump is the murky disconnect between brain and gut. The logical brain doesn't speak the language of feeling. All it hears coming from gut instinct is a cacophony of disturbing rumblings. What the gut senses and cries out about sounds blurred. The logical brain can only note and label the discomfort. If a situation needs immediate interpretation, the best the logical brain can do is think up or look around for a likely explanation of the distress, so something can be done to take care of it: rationalization, in all its biased glory.

BLACK OR WHITE/ALL OR NOTHING THINKING

We take in too much information to be able to store and consult every bit of learning as individual pieces. So we need a good organizational system, and shorthand to get us to the right knowledge base with the least hassle. Ever the good scientist, the brain does this by clustering together input that seems similar or repetitive, and assigning labels or other cues to help find it.

This is how our brains create prototypes. Take the word "flower." Flowers come in many shapes and sizes. But if you ask people what a flower looks like, they usually describe something similar to a daisy. They know full well that not all flowers look like daisies. But a daisy certainly represents the most common and well-recognized shape. And if they drew a very basic sketch of a daisy, everyone who looked at it would likely guess it was intended to be a flower. In this manner prototypes help with both organization and communication.

But they have a downside—like when assumptions treat prototypes as if they are realities, rather than shorthand reference tools. That's where stereotyping comes in. We may assume members of a certain category of society are all the same—often based on uncomplimentary features, thanks to the negativity bias. Racism, ageism, sexism, and other such "isms" are well known for their roots in stereotyping. And as most everyone well knows, stereotyping is a first-rate promoter of divisive community.

Judging any group of people to be all the same is absurd. We already know this, at least on some level. Those having either liberal or conservative political views are fully aware that those in their own party do not agree on everything, and that members differ in numerous other ways as well. But especially in this time of extreme divisiveness, those in opposing parties aren't cut the same slack.

This common reasoning error, also known as overgeneralization, is another example of how the gut can override logic in ways that are destructive, rather than protective. It narrows its single-factor focus onto the threat of an opposing group's agenda, and then interacts with anyone having such views as if that's all there is to them. It may also stop and get in a few swipes, as long as it's slithering through the neighborhood.

Understanding that every member of a group couldn't possibly have the same exact views or personal traits is not rocket science. We also have lifetimes of observing how taking swipes at one another only increases divisiveness, and decreases chances that the other side will listen. Furthermore, we've seen that such acting out usually doesn't get us whatever it is we really want. But such tidbits of emotional intelligence have difficulty finding their place amidst cog-jam fog.

Negotiation and compromise are impossible if the gut nixes checking out ideas and logic—as represented so well by conservative/liberal stalemates and their mutual demoralizing behavior. For example, below is a list of questionable conclusions that illustrate this pattern of illogic, drawn from political issues of late:

- Some Muslims are terrorists; therefore all Muslims should be kept from immigrating.
- Some Mexican illegal immigrants have criminal records; therefore all Mexican immigrants should be treated like criminals.
- Some journalists are unethically biased in how they present their stories; therefore all journalists are unethical, and anything they say is fake news.
- The current health care program has problems; therefore everything in it is flawed and it should be dumped.

And you can probably come up with plenty of other examples, given the surplus piling up over the past few years. When relying on this brand of reasoning, solutions like blocking immigration from predominantly Muslim countries, building a wall on our southern border, discounting anything reported by a journalist as fake news, and throwing out both the good and the bad of the current health care plan all make perfect sense—at least according to the gut brain. But for the logical brain to willingly go along for the ride—*aye, yi, yi yi.*

Incidentally, a bit of a scandal lurks in the shadows of this scenario.[14] Truth be known, the gut is having a desperate love affair with black-or-white/all-or-nothing thinking. They are virtual soul mates. The gut brain gleefully endorses

---

14   Gardner, D. (2009). *The science of fear: How the culture of fear manipulates your brain.* London, England: Penguin Books.

"good versus bad" distinctions. Its sole reason for being is to detect and react, based on whether circumstances are judged safe or dangerous. It needs a very simplified categorization strategy to get this done before the lion catches up. Categorizing people, perspectives, or anything else as all good or all bad makes identifying threat a lot easier. The gut brain thrives on oversimplification.

Prototypical shorthand assessments are just the ticket. It's love at first sight. The logical brain, of course, is perfectly capable of stepping in and introducing common sense into this impetuous affair. But as far as the gut brain is concerned, gray areas only make for muddy waters. Gut reactions function with an on/off switch, not a dimmer switch. Thus it sees the logical brain as an interloper. Getting rational thought into the picture amidst so much passion takes a lot of effort.

Opposing political opinions rarely involve the immediate life-or-death circumstances for which the fight or flight response was intended. We'd never know it though, considering how politicians so often seem to let gut reasoning take the lead.

On the other hand, look at it from their perspective. As far as their careers go, opposing political opinions may well represent life or death. Given the complexity and expense of election campaigns these days, our representatives no longer simply look out for the interests of their constituencies. They are in the unenviable position of also needing to satisfy those who finance their campaigns, which often isn't individual voters. Plus, they need to walk the lines of party planks.

The needs and aims of these three factions may not coincide. The resulting conflicts of interest hack away at politicians' increasingly precarious stumps. It's a no-win situation, and probably terrifying for any elected official who values staying in office. The temptation to give in to gut reasoning must be profound, indeed. And as long as the status quo for election campaign practices continues, it's a safe bet that cogjam will always be riding shotgun.

But then, here are the rest of us. We don't experience similarly dire consequences just because someone expresses an opposing opinion. Yes, if certain policies got put in place they could negatively impact us down the road, perhaps in ways that are very significant. But that's not an emergency situation. There's still time to step in with a measured response for the here and now. Or even choose to do nothing, for the moment. It's not like we're about to die or be maimed. If anything, we trip up more from unthinkingly blurting out thoughts or opinions than because of what the other guy has to say.

Gut shortsightedness also blinds us to important limitations and potential. For political groups, it often plays out like this: you like the good in your party, and therefore defend everything about it as good, even though it has logical limitations. The existence of the bad ceases to matter because there's good involved. On the other hand, you dislike the bad in the opposing party, in spite of its other values that hold merit, and therefore react to everything about the party as if it is bad. The good doesn't matter.

There are actually pros and cons to pretty much any position. But the gut doesn't consider this. It's focused on identifying targets to attack or flee from. So we end up settling for rationalizations, which by design maintain the status quo. Dismissing the other side's claims gets really easy: "They only believe that because they're [insert preferred political party designation here];" or "They're only saying that because they don't want [whatever the home team supports]." It makes no difference if claims made by opponents are evidence based. This stance discourages entry into the intelligent discourse that might lead to finding and trying out solutions.

And when we invest ourselves this strongly into such single-minded goals, we demolish the chance of meeting in the middle ground shared by all: the desire to ensure free, safe, healthy, and happy lives.

FUNDAMENTAL ATTRIBUTION ERROR

On social media and elsewhere, people sometimes spout off slights like "Haters!" or "Dividers!" when referring to those with opposing views. It doesn't seem to matter how much merit or thought the expressed ideas contain, or how carefully and tastefully the ideas are presented. Even vague mentions of a position can bring on an attack. Part of the reason is that good ol' black or white business doing its usual thing.

But there's more to the story. The fancy social science label for this phenomenon is "fundamental attribution error"—blaming adversity on specific individuals, when the problem is really about a situation.[15]

Most knee-jerk reactions that fuel cogjam are based on relatively vague fears. We imagine possible consequences of opposing views, and fear they will negatively affect us or those we care about. Or, we to some degree align our socio-political views with who we are as individuals, such that our very selfhood feels threatened by alternate views. Or, ego involvement interprets them as saying "you're wrong, stupid, etc.," or somehow questioning our values. Our intelligence or reasoning ability may feel attacked, or vulnerable.

Socio-political polarization is an abstraction, a situational rather than concrete threat. No matter how tempting, we can't realistically hang responsibility for our predicament on any specific individuals or groups of people. It took a long time for us to get here, and every side has knowingly or unwittingly had

15   Ross, L. (1977). "The intuitive psychologist and his shortcomings: Distortions in the attribution process". In Berkowitz, L. *Advances in experimental social psychology*, 10. New York: Academic Press. pp. 173–220.

some hand in it. That's why it's so critical that each of us figure out how to take responsibility for our corner of it and do our best to heal.

Devoting time to considering what's right, best overall, truly important, or what might happen in the future was not so relevant to the original human survival plan. Staying alive was in the here and now. There were plenty of immediate needs and concerns to go around, without dredging up mental pictures of what might go wrong down the road. Primary survival goals had to do with gathering food, eating, making babies, ensuring safety and security, and fighting off the bad guys. If none of these goals needed immediate attention, people typically rested. Some primitive societies still function this way.

But here's where we sit now. While socio-political fears generally don't concern dire threat to here and now survival, we still have to reckon with an inner lizard that is trying to fight off or flee from a concrete enemy. Though poorly armed, the gut brain nonetheless refuses to let us down during abstract or future-oriented threat. In its valiant efforts to come to the rescue, it activates step one of the tried and true: identify a predator, enemy fighter, or other hazard about to do harm. Once identified, that's easy to address. You engage in battle, or run for safety. Piece of cake.

Unless you live in modern society. During highly charged political give and take, the gut brain easily identifies a target: whoever states the offending position. Let the finger pointing begin; let solution finding go away, now completely irrelevant. The gut brain wins out over the logical: "The threat is that guy over there, not a situation. What's this 'situation' BS, anyway? What's that ridiculous 'advanced' brain fluttering around about? Let the bad guy have it with both barrels. Problem solved."

Ahem. Well, yes. If the goal is to simply chase off or escape from the "enemy," such behavior serves us well. If the goal is to alienate others or make new enemies, it'll work for that, too. And if the perceived enemy is a hefty portion of society or allies with whom we must work together to have happy peaceful lives, cogjam gets us disaster.

CORRELATION AND CAUSATION

Not long ago, I joined a social media discussion with some others who were hashing through current politics. Topics went heavy into the nonviolent resistance angle, such as protest marches, rallies, and so on. I stated a caution about making sure such activities are actually pathways to solutions in today's here and now, rather than an indiscriminate cry to "resist!"—an approach that might needlessly fuel fight or flight in others, and only further the cogjam stalemate.

A major-league keyboard kerfuffle followed. Others in on the chat were certain that the anger element of past civil rights efforts was the critical aspect. After all, change occurred after a lot of angry protest. Got to do the same now. End of story.

As discussion continued, I mentioned the differing leads of the primitive brain and logical brain. I brought up the value of using measured response and ways in which gut reactions can be shortsighted. I tried to introduce the idea that protest can happen in ways that don't so drastically ramp up divisiveness and acting out.

But I bombed at getting my point across. At first, nobody even hinted of letting go of the belief that acting out primitive angst was the critical part of the solution. The gut brains elbowing their way into discussion so passionately clung to their preferred coping style that distinctions such as what to express versus how to express it could not even be heard. Or, maybe it was only because I was doing a lousy job of writing that day, my own gut brain interfering. *Sigh.*

Regardless, the core issue was this belief that angry protest happened, then change happened; and therefore angry protest caused change. Technically, it was legislative actions championed by various individuals that directly resulted in civil rights changes. Protests do appear to influence future legislative actions, and have played major roles in civil rights efforts in eras when communication options were more limited. Taking to the streets was one of the best options our civil rights predecessors had.

But they didn't fill the marketplace with an angry mob of peasants carrying torches and pitchforks who then stormed the castle of the oppressive ruler. These days taking such an approach would get them far too many unwanted side effects. Instead, they implemented courses of action appropriate for the 1960's. Likewise, we can seek best practices for getting views out in this new millennium, where social media and other lightening-speed repetitive communications unwittingly become weapons of mass destruction rather than platforms for solution finding.

What form might this new, more selective approach take? I can hardly wait to see what we come up with. But to follow through, we first have to find our way out of the existing mire.

Like, the bit of errant logic we're about to pick apart—the structure of the reasoning used within the previous example, rather than the actual issue at stake. Possible misinterpretation of the historical events stems from assuming that if A and B happen together, one causes the other.

It's a common reasoning error. Everybody occasionally falls victim to it. But in reality, there are four possible explanations for why A and B happen at the same time:

- A did indeed cause B.
- B actually caused A.
- A third unknown variable caused both A and B.
- A combination of the above contributed.
- There is no relationship between A and B; their occurring together is an entirely random event.

So the anger acted out really could be part or all of the explanation for progress in civil rights. But it also could be the other way around, that beginnings of changes in civil rights attitudes resulted in people becoming more willing to show they were angry. Or perhaps the culturally shifting tides of what was considered socially acceptable both moved forward civil rights, and had people expressing previously suppressed anger. Or the two weren't connected at all. They simply both happened at the same time.

Scientific method has ways of testing the above hypotheses. But that's not the point. What's relevant to our mission is to understand that premature and sometimes errant assumptions may follow if we accept any of the above hypotheses without checking them out. Though there's more work and discipline involved in this route, forgetting to do so keeps us lost in the weeds.

GUT-FRIENDLY MEMORY TRAITS

Cognitive scientists have been picking apart ins and outs of reasoning bias for the past century. In addition to the attractiveness of certain reasoning errors, they have found that specific features of our memories increase the likelihood that certain elements of an event are more likely to come to mind when we seek solutions or explanations, especially in times of high stress.[16]

Recency. Recent memories reside closer to awareness than old ones. They easily come to mind because they're so available. For example, suppose the evening news reports on an e-coli outbreak in your area. It is traced to a certain brand and type of packaged greens, a product you use regularly. The next morning at the supermarket you see that the guilty greens have been pulled from the shelves.

However you don't feel right about buying safer greens of that brand either, even though you know they have completely different origins. Your logical brain knows better. But your gut brain urges you to change brands altogether. Thanks to the memory of recently viewed images of sick people—as well as a possible assist from classical conditioning—you may very well alter an old habit, even if the real risk has already been taken care of.

16   Gardner, D. (2009). *The science of fear: How the culture of fear manipulates your brain.* London, England: Penguin Books.

Air travel following the events of September 11th is a good example of this happening en masse. Even those who had been comfortable with flying for their entire lives were hesitant to get on a plane again. The industry suffered, in spite of care taken to ramp up security. If anything during the months immediately following the incidents, the airways were safer from terrorist attack than they'd ever been. Nonetheless, the primitive brain regularly overruled the logical. It took about a year before most people moved past it. As memories faded, so did fear of flying, even though risk had not changed much from what it was the year following the incident.

Emotional loading. Memories get highlighted during high arousal. Chemical adjustments help the brain cement in details about whatever proved dangerous. This promotes the next generation of safety cues for handling future situations. We often hang onto vivid long-term memories of highly emotional experiences—such as a scary encounter with a mugger, or where we were and what we were doing when first hearing about the events of September 11th. Likewise, we better remember the content of meetings or speeches if it is presented with a slant toward stirring up emotions.

Politicians take advantage of this as a matter of course, often throwing in the negativity bias for good measure. Negative information stands out more, since the gut brain actively looks for it. Many politicians play up the negative about their opponents and their agenda, perhaps spending more time talking about that than their own plans. At times the negative is exaggerated beyond all reasonable expectation. It fuels strong emotions on both sides.

As we listen to flimsy stump speeches overburdened with emotion, we may smirk over how the speaker is going way too far. But when we get to the voting booths, the emotionally loaded speech will better come to mind than views that had been shared by the calm and collected guy or gal, even if what the latter candidate says is more realistic.

Novelty. The gut brain is always on the alert for the unusual, scanning the environment for mismatch between what is expected and what is actually there. The logical brain throws in an assist by adding memory and analytical intelligence to the scanning process. This is why we've survived without the teeth, claws, speed, or strength of many other species. We literally got by on our wits, noticing and studying novel input. When we got that niggling sense of "what's wrong with this picture," we gave it priority until we could figure out if threat was involved.

Once an oddity is judged harmless, the gut brain accepts it as one more feature of the expected. This is called habituation. It's the same as when we at first notice sounds like rush hour traffic picking up, rain on the roof, or a conversation going on in the background; then eventually tune it out, going about our business as if it weren't there.

We can do this even in the presence of a potential risk that is not relevant at the moment, or low probability. This is a good thing. The world is full of dangers. Constantly reviewing everything that might go wrong would take up the entire day. But until we reach that point of habituation, a novelty resides relatively close to the surface of awareness, making it more available when looking for an explanation or trying to make a decision.

Extremeness. How much more available would we expect a memory to be, then, if all three features applied: recent, emotional, and novel? The events of September 11th, the JFK assassination, the Challenger disaster, and similar incidents both cemented longer-term detailed memory and remained in ongoing awareness for longer periods than did most of our other life exposures. The recent Supreme Court hearings to confirm Justice Kavanaugh and their impact on our nation may well join this collective. There's something about the extreme that seems to take more time for the brain to sort out and set aside.

For example, one of my past disaster assignments was New York City's Twin Towers relief operation. Several weeks after the main event there was a second incident in the area, a major scaffolding collapse. Its thunder blasted out as loud as any lightning strike. It sent up a huge cloud of dust, and injured or killed several construction workers. Many of those nearby first jumped to the conclusion that the explosive bang and plume were evidence of another plane attack, or a bomb going off—traumatizing, indeed.

While interacting with citizens in the thick of it I discovered that the scaffolding collapse, though startling and tragic, was not the traumatic event most often entering conversation. Instead, the new incident brought into awareness lingering issues over the Twin Towers disaster. It became a healing opportunity, a serendipity sprouting from the depths of the primitive brain that now could be sorted out by the logical—a phenomenon we also may be able to take advantage of in the face of lingering cogjam.

Meanwhile, here is a more current example of recency, emotional loading, novelty, and extremeness contributing to a future outcome.

During the last presidential election, participant activity at some conventions left observers aghast: foul language, lewdness, tantrums, trashing behaviors, and other capers more expected of wayward preadolescents than grown men and women. Especially notable was a repeated chant of "Lock her up!" when referring to one particular candidate.

When the time came for voters to make a decision, on the basis of memory features, would this chant reside close to the surface of their awareness? You betcha. It was recent. It was emotionally laden. Exposure to that level of social audacity is novel. The sights and sounds of so many adults behaving the way they did were certainly extreme. It's a home run.

Furthermore, the catastrophizing encouraged over the candidate upped arousal chemistry even higher, further limiting objective thinking. Then there were the memory-cementing bonuses of simplicity and repetition, introducing the same brief chant whenever opportunity arose. Whether this tactic came about by intuition or design, the campaign may have hit a high mark in executing emotional manipulation of a large group.

And that's without yet having considered the ways of herd instinct.

CHAPTER 5

······

Roaming with the Herd

A **FEW DECADES AGO** a charismatic anti-tax ideologue took his dog and pony show across the countryside. He told everyone who would listen that federal income taxes were supposed to be voluntary. He advised citizens that filing tax returns a certain way allowed them to opt out. Thousands joined his whirlwind of evangelical fervor, taking his advice and further spreading the word.

It did not end well for them. The zealot's thesis was based largely on his interpretation of the phrase "voluntary tax system." He used it out of its original context. The phrase in the tax regulations was actually referring to practical aspects of collecting taxes. In other words, citizens were to voluntarily perform the task of establishing how much they made, what they owed, and then get it to the appropriate treasury—certainly an advancement over tax collectors going door to door and demanding whatever they decided citizens should pay.

Claiming that the taxes themselves were voluntary did not keep the zealot's followers from suffering the consequences of their choices. These people were not dummies. They were at least bright enough to hold down jobs that generated enough income to be worth protecting. They should have been able to see the flawed logic. Perhaps many did, on some level.

But it did not prove powerful enough to counteract the impact of herd influence.[17] There is safety in numbers, as the saying goes. However equally true is that going along with the herd can produce the infamous fate of lemmings over the cliff, as in the preceding example.

We do need the herd. In addition to providing safety and support, it is a vital source of information and example. Observed group practices, role models, mentors, coaches and the like are necessary to find our way through society and reach our full potential. No man is an island, as the saying goes.

However in all things moderation and a dose of healthy skepticism is the still the healthiest approach. Anything taken to an extreme becomes absurd or even maladaptive, as much as the gut brain might balk. The bottom line: we need to listen to the herd, but temper input with common sense.

Which most of us do, at least most of the time. We begin tracking the actions of role models as little children, and never stop learning from observed behaviors. What we do with what we learn, however, changes over time. Thanks to brain maturation most of us become more skilled at putting new learning through the sifter of common sense, and adjusting our knowledge base to assimilate it, accommodate it, or toss it into the discard pile.

We also learn to be selective about whom to believe or copy. By the time we're adults we are well aware that copying what certain other people in our lives do or say is not a good idea. Such wisdom aligns with that old admonition to "consider the source" when deciding what to believe.

Even though influences of herd instinct affect us daily, in the back of our minds always lies some level of awareness that others' choices are not always practical, effective, socially adaptive or acceptable, or even safe. We factor this into our choices and beliefs. Some obvious examples:

- A tall man escaping a wildfire by jumping over a wide chasm could mean curtains for a short-legged woman who tried to do the same. For her, survival requires something other than what the guy in front of her did. Instead, perhaps squeezing through a hole under a nearby brick wall, a solution that wouldn't necessarily work out for the large man.

- Adopting a friend's habit of cheating on tax returns because he seems to get away with it does not mean doing so will not create consequences for yourself—or for him either, as far as that goes. If a course of action violates your values or personal ethics, you will suffer consequences of conscience as well.

- Offensive and insulting language seems to be turning up almost everywhere these days. Copying it, however, is guaranteed to alienate most people. It also degrades personal image and decreases the credibility of

17   Junger, S. (2018). *Tribe: On homecoming and belonging.* New York: Hachette Book Group.

those who use it. Social consequences for indiscriminate language use range from losing jobs or friends to inciting fistfights and worse. In recent times, we have watched life-long relationships destroyed by such behaviors. Learning from such outcomes and recognizing their causes can act as a buffer against imitating the ill advised.

IDENTIFICATION WITH THE AGGRESSOR

Why do people stoop to copy offensive behavior, anyway? It's not like we don't know any better. Kindergarten learning aside, over our entire lifetimes we observe the results of it with our own two eyes. We know how it affects us. We know how it affects others. And thanks to another saying, we know that "whoever throws the first blow is the one who lost the fight." But lately we see that kind of trashing going on everywhere, even among those highly placed in government or who follow faiths or other moral codes that frown upon such behavior.

That's because when we're overstressed, joining in with the crowd is an easy solution. It helps us feel less vulnerable, or more empowered to protect ourselves. After all, it's what everybody else is doing, or so we tell ourselves. So we cave. And at least for a while, we feel less stressed. Until, of course, we realize what we've done and live with the consequences. Or perhaps we never acknowledge it, and keep creating more cogjam.

Psychodynamics has a fancy term for this: identification with the aggressor.[18] Most formal discussion of it surrounds the study of abused children who later become bullies or batterers themselves. Even though they have firsthand knowledge of how miserable it is at the receiving end, it doesn't stop them. They learned to survive during emotionally trying times by copying whatever they saw their batterer do to come out on top.

Actually that personal experience of being a victim is what makes bullying behaviors so attractive. Victims who adopt the aggressor's abusive behavior feel stronger, or more in control. It soothes feelings of weakness, inadequacy, or being at the mercy of their own past/present batterer. But as a present-day solution to conflict, it's only a primitive reaction to threat and trauma-based fear, rather than logical strategy for handling adult challenges.

As current affairs go about exposing real or imaginary dirty laundry, we don't have to look far to see that copying bullies is not limited to those surviving a difficult childhood. Many adults show themselves to be similarly vulnerable as they resort to snide remarks, name-calling, tantrums, and other childish behaviors as they grope their way through socio-political turmoil.

18   Howell, E. F. (2014) Ferenczi's concept of identification with the aggressor: Understanding dissociation structure with interacting victim and abuser self-states. *American Journal of Psychoanalysis*, 74, 48-59.

As adults we know better. And thankfully, a number of light bulbs appear to be clicking on. Many people are already backing off of this style of coping, though its preponderance on media broadcasts may not reflect it. Unfortunately, there are other fully-grown men and women who keep right at it full steam ahead, seemingly ignoring the expected natural consequences.

But it fits right in with herd instinct. The idea of going along with the crowd carries that allure of safety, and feels so naturally good when we're overwhelmed.

And there's a good reason why going along with the crowd feels this natural. Certain chemistry actually encourages herd instinct, the same as adrenalin creates fight or flight.

OXYTOCIN

Oxytocin is an ingredient of our neurochemistry that promotes social bonding.[19] It turns up in love relationships, childbirth, breastfeeding, and other social attachments. Interestingly, states of anxious arousal also release oxytocin.

When I first considered this I recalled an acronym we tossed around on the disaster trail during high-stress assignments: DII, short for "disaster induced infidelity." I also recall packed neonatal wards in Portland, Oregon area hospitals about nine months after Mt. St. Helens blew. Then, of course, there's the baby-boomer population that turned up after World War II. Being collectively thrown together for heavy-duty stress appears to strengthen at least one type of social bonding among those who endure it.

But in addition to encouraging attachments to specific individuals, oxytocin promotes bonding within groups. In the world of disaster response, we called the instant joint efforts of workers and community members "disaster bonding." Similar ties develop in other groups that regularly deal with emergency, combat, and other high-stress occupations. The friendships that form in such scenarios may last a lifetime.

Benefits of group bonding explain why oxytocin turns up during high arousal. Living by our individual wits alone is not always enough. In primitive settings, surviving encounters with the stronger and mightier may well require help from others. Group cooperation might be the only way to successfully fight off an attack from a neighboring tribe or larger and stronger predator.

The threats modern society faces may not be quite the same, but we continue to find safety from certain threats by virtue of our numbers. We need look no further than the Las Vegas mass casualty shooting to see how people can be

19   Neumann, I. D. (2008). Brain oxytocin: A key regulator of emotional and social behaviours in both females and males. *Journal of Neuroendocrinology*, 20, 858-865.

naturally compelled to help one another, even when they themselves are still in the midst of mortal danger.

Oxytocin thus enhances ability to succeed as a group. Likewise, it is a modulator of fear and anxiety, lessening intensity of flight or flight emotions to more manageable levels. It also results in feeling more inclined to respond to social stimuli. Such effects certainly explain why ancestors blessed with a healthy supply of oxytocin were more likely to survive and pass on their genes than those who were not. But there's still that downside: oxytocin has us feeling drawn to follow the crowd, even when doing so is irrelevant or contradictory to everyone's best interests.

Fortunately, herd instinct doesn't completely prevent the logical brain from stepping in, any more so than does the stress response. The key point is to realize that this neurochemical hijacking is going on, in addition to what adrenalin does to us during times of fight or flight. Taking into account chemical influences is critical for stepping back and finding the calmer and steadier thinking that keeps us from joining lemmings piled up at the base of the cliff.

GROUPTHINK

Bonding among the overstressed can get really out of hand. Whole groups may adopt ways of looking at and addressing problems that drift way beyond the mainstream. Sometimes the resulting thinking and behaviors defy all logic, at least as observed by those on the outside. It can even take shape as mass denial that a problem exists, such as denying the Holocaust.

But it's a means of coping. The thinking, even if quirky or maladaptive, offers certainty when so much seems unclear. It has the tug of strength in numbers, too. Stress lessens and group members feel more able to cope, as well as more empowered by being part of a joint worldview.

Everybody is vulnerable to the potential of groupthink.[20] Even scientists are at times guilty of accepting conclusions simply because they have been well circulated in their midst, perhaps in situations where stress has little or nothing to do with it.

Take for example the once popular estimation of how much of the human brain we use.[21] Somewhere along the line, the value of ten percent got drawn from a hat. It was passed around as the best estimate from that point forward.

But how could anybody possibly know? PET scans show those parts of the brain that are active at the time of picture taking, and most every area lights up for something. EEG's only show activity in the form of brain waves recorded.

20   Baron, R. S. (2005). "So right it's wrong: groupthink and the ubiquitous nature of polarized group decision making". *Advances in Experimental Social Psychology*, 37: 219–253.
21   Boyd, R. (2008). "Do people only use 10 percent of their brains?" *Scientific American*. Retrieved at https://www.scientificamerican.com/article/do-people-only-use-10-percent-of-their-brains/

X-rays, MRI's and the like reveal portions of the brain that are missing or ab-
normal. But we don't have adequate technology for detecting the total number
of neurons that are either firing or just sitting around at any point in time.

In truth we still know so little about the brain that there's probably plenty going on we have yet to figure out. Given that unused neurons tend to be
pruned out, we're most likely using whatever is still there: the whole brain.
Nevertheless, even though most scientists were familiar with this existing disconfirming data, the ten percent rule had a long and happy run. The more the
true believers circulated this belief among each other, the more convinced they
were that they were right. An urban legend was born.

Another example is the extreme health risk once associated with eating
eggs.[22] An egg-consumption taboo hung around for about forty years. It first
got rolling when scientists discovered the connection between cholesterol and
heart disease. Egg yolks are high in cholesterol. Physicians put two and two
together and decided that people should eat no more than two a week.

But that advice was based entirely on a hypothesis they'd pieced together,
not an outcome study demonstrating that fewer eggs decreased the number of
people developing heart disease. Fortunately, as good scientists they went about
testing the long-term effects of egg consumption. A major longitudinal study—
an ongoing one, that regularly provides many valuable and widely accepted
health findings—revealed that those who ate more eggs did not appear to have
any more problems with heart disease than did those who ate fewer. The surprised researchers wrote up their findings and tried to get them into print.

But it took years for their report to see the light of day. The researchers
could not get a publisher to take them on. The establishment had been passing
around that "no more than two a week" advice for so long that they refused to
believe what the study resoundingly demonstrated, regardless of how many
thousands of individuals had been assessed.

Today there is general acceptance (albeit begrudging, among some) of more
frequent egg consumption. Recent research has also shown that the cholesterol
we consume doesn't do much to cholesterol levels anyway. It only reduces how
much of it the liver needs to produce for the body to get by. Also helping is that
the medical culture is moving away from this business of vilifying certain foods,
and instead advising 1) a balanced diet, and 2) moderation in everything. This
cultural adjustment—or about-face in herd direction, if you will—assisted with
eventual acceptance of a more evidence based egg-consumption standard.

As the above examples illustrate, resistance to disconfirming data is stronger when it's glued in with a jointly accepted view. Over time such perspectives

22   Rong, Y., Chen, L., Zhu, T., Song, Y., Yu, M., Sen, Z., Sands, A., Hu, F. B., & Liu, L. (2013). Egg consumption and risk
of coronary heart disease and stroke: Dose response meta-analysis of prospective cohort studies. *BMJ*. Retrieved at http://
www.bmj.com/content/346/bmj.e8539

can become increasingly more extreme or polarized, especially when disconfirming data is kept out of the picture. The rationalizations become part of the cultural norm. That the beliefs are only collections of inferential leaps never enters consideration.

A while back I was watching a television interview of a prominent politician. A journalist asked him about a recent poll, which appeared to indicate the opposite of what the politician had just suggested. The politician scoffed, stating that the polls were fake news. Several minutes later the journalist asked a question about a different topic. The politician stated his opinion, and pointed out that the polls supported his beliefs. The journalist responded, "so if the polls agree with you, they're true, and if they disagree, they're fake news?"

The politician answered with a non-response. But the look on his face pretty much said it all. In all likelihood this man did see the ridiculousness of what he'd just said. But for the sake of the herd he stuck to his guns—in front of millions of viewers, no less. That's groupthink in action. Logic, values, or even personal self-respect becomes less important than maintaining the group message. Such reasoning practices give cogjam a potent shot in the arm, as well.

Cults have reputations for using groupthink to control their memberships. They entice troubled individuals with unique solutions to living and thinking that will supposedly help them relieve the stress of whatever ails them. Also well known are many disastrous consequences suffered among those who succumb to cults, such as giving away all assets to cult leadership or writing off relationships with former friends and family members. A few of the more infamous cults, such as those of Jonestown or Waco, Texas, turned into tragic mass casualty incidents. These outcomes illustrate the frightening power groupthink can have over group members.

Little wonder, then, that our society is so polarized. Huge numbers of citizens align themselves on one of the many sides of today's political extremes, clinging desperately to one another for safety and comfort, and almost guaranteeing limited exposure to alternative views. The divisiveness we see now might not have become so profound if not for all the inbred rationalizing—liberally sprinkled with joint catastrophizing, and both of these inciting the primitive brain to squelch logic and pump up emotions. It is the way of herd instinct, gone awry.

In summary, the greater and more extensive the fears, the more we polarize into herds. The greater the polarization, the more frightened we become—once again, the vicious circle of cogjam. All the same, it doesn't take away the choice to listen for and march to the beat of our own more levelheaded drummer. It only takes more conscious effort, as well as willingness to soothe and put to bed our inner lizards.

REGRESSION

As explained earlier, we sometimes select problematic reasoning or behaviors simply because they've been hardwired longer. Here's an example I ran into not long ago.

I was standing in a buffet line with a group of well-educated and respected professionals when a political hot potato fell out of the pot. One person with an especially vehement position blamed a certain public figure for an unfortunate status quo. As she reached the end of her rant, her sentence required mention of the politician's name. At first, she only stammered. Finally she blurted out the one name to find its way off the tip of her tongue: " . . . Fatso."

The rest of us were taken aback. Plus, working hard not to show it. An uncomfortable silence followed.

The guilty party began to flush. "Sorry about that. That was really rude."

I, for one, was fascinated. And as is probably true for many who read this, it wasn't the first time I'd been with a gathering of sophisticated individuals and heard comments that were similarly oversimplified, divisive, and counterproductive. But engaging in name-calling that was this childish seemed like a whole new realm.

"You're not the only one who gets that frustrated," I told her. "I've wondered myself about it. Why do we feel so drawn to saying stuff like that? How about you? When was the last time you ever called somebody that name?"

She smiled sheepishly. "Probably grade school. I have no idea why I said it just now."

I believe I do know why. In the midst of her frustration, my colleague's search for an appropriate word had been struggling upstream against a double-whammy. Coming up with a socially acceptable response had been thwarted not only by her strong emotional biases, but also by the bizarreness of the socio-political situation itself. There's also how much exposure she might have had to name-calling in the media, making it feel as if maybe it's now okay.

Socially acceptable ways to respond to profound illogic and inappropriateness in high places do not easily come to mind. The social challenges we routinely face are rarely this extreme. We don't get a whole lot of practice with them. Left at sea, we may grab onto any passing life raft, in spite of its dubious-looking holes.

Furthermore, when exposed to the bizarre, consensual reality feels challenged. People used to accept the value of scientific thinking. Everybody went along with a fairly similar view of what constitutes socially acceptable behavior and common sense. Evidence-based beliefs were once universally respected. Most of us—outside of politics—have not regularly dealt with this alternatively factual universe. In the past when those among us said things that went too far, we jointly recognized the belief or statement as oddball, and found diplomatic ways to move on.

In this era, even the definition of "oddball" is no longer agreed upon. Thinking up something to say in the face of alternative universe facts is an unfamiliar proposition. Both tact and sophistication need to be in it somehow, for any solution to succeed. Yet these require heavy-duty mental gyrations—which, of course, are in relatively short supply during cogjam.

I suspect that my embarrassed colleague had been caught up in just such a cognitive whirlwind. Trapped by her temporary loss for words, a longer-wired response from childhood popped out and filled the hole. Phenomena like this are actually well known, though I have not (yet) seen them notably applied to how we've been acting amidst socio-political strife.

It's commonly called regression. When we're overwhelmed, we sometimes return to a level of functioning that is less mature or advanced than our usual thoughts, emotions, or behaviors.[23] Examples of regression are easiest to notice among traumatized children, given how their behavior changes so much from year to year. During severe stress or following significant trauma, an eight year old might return to bedwetting. A five year old might insist on having a baby bottle or pacifier. A seventeen year old might abandon nightly carousing with his buddies, choosing instead to stay wherever his parents are. These coping choices are usually temporary, abandoned once resilience comes up with more age-appropriate options.

Regression recovery among adults requires either looking for or being open to other options, ones supported by the logical brain's aptitudes and influences. Overcoming cogjam-related regression means pulling ourselves out from under this chemically laced security blanket the gut brain keeps trying to throw over us. And then, actively seeking out inroads to less divisive and destructive solutions.

It's a formidable task. Walking against herd direction presents its own set of risks. But they're better than risking outcomes like the entire herd drinking poisoned Kool-aid or losing their lives in a compound shoot-out.

And the added bonus: it means we get to be ourselves again.

---

23   Jung, C. G. (1993). *The Practice of Psychotherapy*. London.

CHAPTER 6
......
Coping Gifts Differing

S O FAR OUR exploratory trek has mainly visited features we all share: the intricate wiring of fight or flight, corresponding social and emotional programming, and how it typically affects our behavior. Occasionally noted were our differences, such as our diverse styles of behaviorally, cognitively, emotionally, and socially coping with life's trials and tribulations.

Considering individual differences is relevant not only to understanding our own strengths and vulnerabilities, but also to being able to compassionately respond to others as they handle (or perhaps do not handle) their distress. The deck is somewhat stacked in this regard, thanks to issues of both nature and nurture. This chapter looks at pluses and minuses of different cards we may be dealt as we seek to cope with adversity.

RESILIENCE

The inner fortitude human beings can bring forth in hard times is stunning. Psychological resilience truly is a gift, and resides in all of us. It's a coping process we each personally design and apply, a general overall approach for dealing with the bumpier paths of everyday living.

Such strategies and tactics are therefore finely attuned to specific needs and experiences. That's why resilience is so effective. It's always evolving. We continually re-chisel its form based on what works, what doesn't, and other individual learning.

Generally speaking, we aren't consciously aware of the master plan we use unless we've given it a lot of focused scrutiny. Usually we just pull it out and use it as the need arises.

Exploring the concept of coping dates back to the beginnings of psycho-dynamic thinking. Freud is most credited with revealing the importance of defense mechanisms—subconscious coping for when things get tough. My studies and impressions have lead me to believe that three traditional defense mechanisms are the ones most likely to be used among those who better cope during disaster: intellectualization, humor, and—of all things—denial.

In the best of all worlds, we pull out the right one of these for the right job:

- Intellectualization is a useful defense during heated discussion, or any other stressful situation that benefits from heavy input by the logical brain. Temporarily shutting out emotions and focusing on reasoning not only helps avoid distraction. It also helps produce effective solutions.

- Denial resides at the opposite end of intellectual scrutiny: we block out and ignore the problem's very existence. It works out in some of those situations we cannot change, but still must somehow slog through in order to function or save ourselves.

- Humor falls somewhere in between, as far as keeping it real. It can be used to lighten an uneasy situation, broaden perspective, temporarily step away from its significance, or all three. Having a good laugh has the added benefit of stimulating multiple organs in ways that relieve tension and lessen the overall stress response.[24]

Other defense mechanisms are more limited in the benefits they offer:

- Rationalization, often used during less effective reasoning, is one. It's okay if we need a quick answer to latch onto during a crisis. Not so, if it gets in the way of long-term planning or effective decision-making.

- Withdrawal can be adaptive if used as an opportunity to step back and lick wounds. But if it becomes a permanent rest stop, it's a problem.

- Then there's fight or flight's all-time favorite: letting loose and acting out. Great for when you're fighting for your life, but not so great if you pick an argument with your boss, or get yourself arrested for road rage or assault.

24   Mayo Clinic (2016). Stress relief from laughter? It's no joke. Retrieved at https://www.mayoclinic.org/healthy-life-style/stress-management/in-depth/stress-relief/art-20044456.

There are many others. How much of these influences stem from learning or instinct is not particularly important. What matters for stress response purposes is the value they all share: letting us temporarily deal with or create distance from the gut brain's insistent squalls—at least, long enough for coping to take place.

However as previous examples reveal, there's far more to resilience than psychodynamics simmering beneath the surface. And resilience usually doesn't mean escape from uncomfortable emotions that come with crisis, either. In fact, feelings generated by the gut brain provide important information to take under consideration during the deliberation process.

Resilience is about thoughts, behaviors, and emotional reactions that increase likelihood of getting through a fracas relatively unscathed, or at least in as good shape as could be expected. It is often referred to as the ability to "bounce back" from adversity. Those most likely to have well-functioning resilience generally have traits or abilities found with:

- A positive self view, including realistic confidence in strengths and abilities.
- The ability to assess difficulties, problem solve, make viable plans, and follow through.
- Effective communication skills.
- Sufficient self-control to manage impulses and strong emotions.

These aptitudes fall within the domain of the logical brain. They pull together the reasoning, self-discipline, and flexibility necessary to pick up on and adjust to personal, practical, and social realities.

The gut brain doesn't give a hoot about any of these. It cares only about what might or might not fit in with the immediate need to push the panic button. And then, cheering on whatever action gets it closer to feeling safe again. Outside of adopting new cues for threat, future practical or social impact is pretty much a moot point for the gut brain.

In addition, the ability to change and grow in the face of personal failures requires the ability to admit to being wrong, or making a mistake. The gut brain is no fan of these maneuvers. Such admissions acknowledge vulnerability. Vulnerability implies susceptibility to threat.

This is one of the reasons those caught up in cogjam get so defensive. They may argue their polarized points until they sound ridiculous, at times regressing to insults, snide remarks, name-calling, and other childish behaviors. The gut brain won't back down on its own. Defending against vulnerability is all it knows. It pulls out all the stops, and gives it everything it's got. So in spite of contributing useful intuitive feedback, the gut brain can become more a liability than an asset to resilience building.

The logical brain, on the other hand, has the capacity to focus on the positive—how we might grow, rather than what might go wrong. It can focus on finding effective ways to cope, rather than become overwhelmed by fear-based impulses. It has the flexibility needed for considering and trying out new ideas and behaviors. The gut brain is not good at these.

The field of positive psychology studies the many elements of human functioning that make life worth living, as opposed to working from the angle of whatever isn't going right.[25] Hooking our cognitive wagons more securely to the positive than the negative is associated with multiple mental and physical health benefits:

- Longer lives
- Greater resistance to the common cold
- Better cardiovascular health
- Less likelihood of depression
- Lower levels of distress
- Better ability to cope with hardship

Effective resilience therefore not only gets us through crisis. It also guides us toward additional new strengths. In turn, these strengths offer greater resilience for the next adversity—a darn good reciprocal arrangement. Furthermore the end result is exquisitely personalized, befitting the individual who participated in its creation.

In other words, we experience post-traumatic growth.

BUILT-IN VULNERABILITIES

While those with well-functioning resilience are better shielded from adversity's sticks and stones, personal challenges can put people at a disadvantage. Certain conditions spawned by both nature and nurture hinder scientific reasoning and social functioning from the get-go. Those so affected are more susceptible to regression and other instinct-driven missteps. They are especially vulnerable to cogjam and likely to have a harder time digging their way out of it, as examples to follow will illustrate.

A rare silver lining to the events of September 11th and the Middle East war casualties is the flurry of brain science, stress, trauma, and resilience research that quickly followed. We now know so much more about brain functioning. New knowledge is pointing the way to more successful treatment of many conditions, both physical and mental. This goldmine also holds answers that can help overcome the influence of cogjam.

25   Lopez, S. J., Pedrotti, J. T., & Snyder, C. R. (2015). *Positive psychology: The scientific and practical explorations of human strengths*, 3rd ed. Los Angeles: Sage.

THE STORY OF PHINEAS GAGE

Phineas Gage was a nineteenth century railroad worker who regularly handled explosives, the ultimate cause of his undoing.[26] One day while tamping down powder with a rod, a spark ignited. The powder exploded. The rod shot from the hole like a missile, landing some eighty feet away. Unfortunately, the trajectory getting there went right through poor Phineas' skull.

To everyone's amazement, Phineas survived. But his personality and behavior changed. Before the accident, he was described as what today we might call a "man's man"—a strong, steady, hard worker who was well liked by all, always ready to step up when something was needed. After the accident, he was described as unsocialized and impulsive, almost animal-like in his self-absorption. His employers made the observation that he was "no longer Gage." Between his rude and insensitive behavior, impulsive angry outbursts, and difficulty staying on task, they had no choice but to fire him.

Based on these reported observations, we might suspect that Phineas' symptoms were due to losing too much cerebral cortex, and that the primitive brain was all he had left to keep the show going. We might likewise conclude that long-term memories, intelligence, and capacities for logic and self-control had exited his skull along with the lost brain tissue.

This did not turn out to be true. Following a long recovery, he moved on. Years later he was referred to by others as a shrewd businessman, apparently doing quite well for himself. His ability to control impulses and rein in antisocial behavior improved, as often happens when individuals suffering from brain damage reestablish lives within tight concrete systems like running a business.

So the logical brain was apparently still functioning. And despite the severity of his brain injury, Phineas went on with his life rather successfully. Did he just get lucky? What's really going on here?

Actually, he was lucky indeed. The location of the hole in his preserved skull suggests that the rod traveled through an area where the limbic system and cerebral cortex hook up. In other words, the primitive brain and most logical brain structures were still there. But the two were not sharing information as they had before—at least, at first. Thanks to neuroplasticity, his neural pathways appear to have been able to arrange alternative hook-ups, eventually giving hubs of logic and willful behavior more control over his impulses.

Not everyone who suffers brain damage is so fortunate.[27] Though Phineas' social and impulse control problems are common among those with such in-

26 Fleischman, J. (2002). *Phineas Gage: A gruesome but true story about brain science.* Boston: Houghton-Mifflin.
27 Ponsford, J., Draper, K., & Schonberger, M. (2008). Functional outcome 10 years after traumatic brain injury: Its relationship with demographic, injury severity, and cognitive and emotional status. *Journal of the International Neuropsychological Society.* 14, 233–242.

juries, for many their gut brains are forever oversensitive to stress. Acting-out behaviors remain difficult to keep under control.

Dealing with cogjam is especially challenging for such individuals. With their fight or flight response so inclined to punch the panic button, they are less able to rein in angry impulses, and in turn more frequently spur on others' stress reactions. Since milder forms of traumatic brain injury tend not to be obvious, we can't easily identify which angry people are dealing with an underlying physically based challenge.

But we still need to live with them, and to do so adaptively and with compassion. We succeed at this by recognizing and accepting the concept of coping gifts differing.

Not all brain function abnormalities are the result of accidents, strokes, tumors, and other more obvious injuries. Conditions caused by certain genetic programming and environmental influences paint a similar picture.

DEVELOPMENTAL DISABILITIES

Developmental disabilities limit the types of reasoning and behavior we can realistically expect of some. Most of us already take this into account. We often act differently toward those who behave poorly if we know them to be significantly disabled. We cut them greater slack for error, and may explain things differently or more patiently to make sure they understand. If anything, I suspect we err more on the side of not giving disabled individuals enough credit for intelligence, or expecting too little of their abilities.

Cogjam is as much a coping challenge for them as it is for those with brain injuries. Their logical brains have specific weak areas, depending on the disability or condition. Thus their social skills can be challenged from the start. Plus, they must also deal with the challenge of figuring out what to do with cogjam-based monkey wrenches thrown into their social lives.

One set of conditions lends itself especially well to explaining the interplay between disabilities and cogjam. It has received considerable attention over the last few decades.

Diagnosis of autism spectrum disorders is still on an upswing.[28] This is in part due to our having figured out that many previously hard-to-explain conditions are actually something akin to autism or Aspergers syndrome. But another reason is our age of advanced technology. Many of those so affected now fill more visible—and in fact, very productive—roles than had been possible in years past.

---

28   Johnson, C. P., & Myers, S. M. (2007). Identification and evaluation of children with autism spectrum disorders. *Pediatrics*, 120, 1183–215.

So we are more aware of their presence. And, that they appear to be growing in number: in the Silicon Valley during the technology boom, the number of new diagnoses of autism among children in the area surged. At any rate, given its apparent frequency, chances are good that someone in your life has some degree of autism or Aspergers.

Originally, the autism diagnosis was only assigned when the patient's hypersensitivity, odd behaviors, and social impairment were near to catastrophic, such as that stereotypical patient who sits in the corner all day spinning an ashtray, or the central character in the movie *Rainman*. Over time healthcare professionals noticed there were other patients with similar oddities, but not so severely impaired. They also found that autism-like symptoms seemed to run in families, though varying widely in which aspects played out in which family members. Closer study of genetic influences and brain functions soon followed.

While environmental exposures appear to play some role, evidence suggests that autism spectrum conditions are largely genetically caused.[29] So far around 30 genes have been identified as more frequently present among those with autistic traits. Minor differences in certain brain structures have been identified as well, at least for some of these individuals.

How this fits in with cogjam coping is this: the difficulties Phineas Gage experienced are similar to what those with autism spectrum conditions cope with from the day they are born. There's some form of disconnect between the emotional and the logical, such that emotional intelligence doesn't take hold as it otherwise might.

This begs that we return to discussion of the polyvagal system—our sensory wiring for the stress response. When it comes to primitive brain structures, mammals enjoy at least one important advantage over non-mammals. The mammalian survival plan more effectively uses social connections. It capitalizes on them in part by "reading" others and communicating intuitively, both verbally and through body language.

A system of more advanced vagal wiring creates this advantage.[30] In addition to the neural network situated largely within the trunk, mammals have a facially oriented vagal system—thus the term, polyvagal.

The mammalian vagal system both takes in intuitive cues and helps communicate social information to others. Muscles are wired to produce automatic facial expressions, based on what the individual is thinking or feeling. They also facilitate the wiring that so nicely expedites speech. However this facial

29   Freitag, C. M., Staal, W., Kauck, S. M., Duketis, E., & Waltes, R. (2010). Genetics of autistic disorders: Review and clinical implications. *European Child and Adolescent Psychiatry*, 19, 169-178.

30   Porges, S. W. (2011). *The polyvagal theory: Neurophysiological foundations of emotions, attachment, communication, and self-regulation*. New York: Norton.

wiring is both expressive and receptive. In other words, in addition to listening to a conversational partner's oral sharing of thoughts, observation of facial expressions reads and interprets nonverbal communication—based on what is seen, heard, or otherwise absorbed by the observer's mammalian vagal system.

The signs and symptoms of autism or Aspergers are consistent with what might be expected of a poorly functioning mammalian vagal system. Communication skills are often impaired, and speech might sound flat or stilted. Facial expressions may seem wooden much of the time. When those affected do smile or frown it often looks forced—because it is. They learn what faces are supposed to look like at certain times, and try to imitate them. But their facial information often isn't as naturally or spontaneously produced as it is by others. In fact their forced expressions are sometimes interpreted by our own mammalian vagal wiring as being "phony." Maybe, maybe not. Either way, they're truly giving it all they've got to give.

Individuals with autism spectrum traits can also be extremely sensitive to loud noises, bright lights, being touched unexpectedly, or other sensory input that puts the gut brain on high alert. Thus they typically have a hair-trigger panic button. At times it seems like they live within two emotional extremes: flat, calm, and emotionally uninvolved, or completely losing it—both emotionally and impulsively. Correspondingly, this stance can take form as painting the whole world with a similarly black and white/all or nothing brush: it's either really great or it's terrible; it's all good or all bad; there's one "right" answer and everything else is wrong; people are either for me or against me, and so on.

Further complicating their lives is their trademark difficulty with picking up on or caring about emotions of others. They may become more compassionate or otherwise appropriately affected once someone explicitly explains the cues. They may even remember such snippets of learning when they come across a similar situation. But meanwhile, they remain blind to many of the social cues everyone else takes for granted.

How they verbally express themselves is similarly less filtered by social considerations. What they say may come off as insensitivity or rudeness, rather than innocence. Anybody on the receiving end can get confused or even upset by it if they aren't aware of the underlying reasons. But for those with autism spectrum traits, others' hurt or angry reactions to their comments may seem to come out of nowhere. They end up feeling like they're constantly under siege for no good reason. Likewise, their innocence and blind spots make them more easily taken advantage of or lead astray by villainous types.

Going through life with such social experiences can make for additional mental health issues, such as depression, paranoia, and anxiety disorders. As self-esteem nosedives some may compensate for it by way of narcissism, grandiose thinking, sociopathy, or other maladaptive stances that help them feel more empowered and less vulnerable.

On the bright side, many autistic individuals have superior ability to understand and manage complex systems, so long as emotional intelligence isn't required. Furthermore, analytical IQ scores among those with high-functioning autism or Aspergers are at times above average, and can even be in the gifted range. These two factors explain why they fit so well in today's complex world of information technology, business and other math-involved systems, and engineering and design fields. Such analytical skills also explain why they are often able to learn on an intellectual rather than emotional level how to recognize and interpret what others may feel or think. They figure out ways to make up for missing intuition or instinct, as well as how to change their behavior to better fit in with social norms.

There really is a point to derailing so far into these autism and Aspergers weeds.

Imagine what it would be like to be this person—going through life blindsided by so many social realities, ones that even less advanced mammals may be able to sense. Perhaps you recognize some of the traits described above in certain loved ones, friends, coworkers, or public figures. They and others with these unique challenges especially struggle with cogjam-related fallout. They will have the most trouble figuring out what to do with it, as well as be more easily drawn into it.

The result of playing the game of life with this handicap is that we find a higher incidence of additional mental health difficulties among individuals who deal with autism spectrum conditions.[31] Effectively healing relationships with those so affected, especially in the midst of cogjam *sturm und drang*, requires extra understanding and respecting how these individuals truly differ.

The truth of the matter is: everybody has vulnerabilities. We all have our own quirks and unique chinks in our armor; they just don't necessarily have psychiatric labels attached. Regardless, we help reduce everybody's cogjam by respecting one another's vulnerabilities and hot buttons. And those living with organic brain conditions or other limitations deserve extra compassion, patience, and understanding, or at least as much as the rest of us.

PAST EXPERIENCE AND EXPOSURES

Once at an inpatient mental health facility, an odd-looking backpack was left behind in a waiting area. Nobody claimed it. Fearing an IED, staff scram-

---

31   Mukaddes, N. M., & Fateh, R. (2010). High rates of psychiatric co-morbidity in individuals with Asperger's disorder. *The World Journal of Biological Psychiatry, 11,* 486-492.

bled to evacuate patients. The fire alarm was soon blaring. All did what they could to keep their cool as the caregivers escorted their charges out of danger.

That is, everybody looked overstressed except the patients. They remained remarkably calm as they quietly and obediently followed their caregivers' instructions.

Why the difference? Querying after the fact revealed that it was not because these patients didn't recognize the potential danger, or its possible ramifications. They did. However for those who regularly live with delusions, hallucinations, disorientation, and major confusion, dealing with something like a bomb threat wasn't experienced as that much more stressful. It was just "today's disaster." Business as usual.

My account of this story is fictionalized, beyond all possible recognition of the original incident—except for the patients' reactions to crisis. They demonstrated well that past experiences and exposures have a dramatic effect on how people interpret and react to adverse events occurring in daily living.

In spite of how the above group handled immediate crisis, pre-existing mental health problems, even when mild, do have a negative impact on recovery after the incident. When my colleagues and I came across disaster survivors who reported already being under a therapist's care—or if not, seemed of a sort whose coping would likely benefit from therapy—we made sure they received closer scrutiny. Their resilience was already strained to manage everyday challenges. Sudden dramatic increases in stress like living through disaster take their chemical toll more quickly for them, often in the form of worsening pre-existing conditions.

This potential consequence is not limited to those with mental health diagnoses. Anyone whose ongoing lifestyle involves a lot of significant stress is at risk for difficulty coping, once disaster stress is added in.

We can expect such an outcome for cogjam stress as well. Impact may go in either or both directions. Those who already have stressful lives may have more difficulty with cogjam-fueled flare-ups, and those overstressed by cogjam may have more difficulty handling normal daily stress.

Little wonder so many new Middle East war veterans struggle to readjust, with such disturbingly high numbers falling victim to self-termination.[32] It's not just because of poor access to health care. Look at the stressful environment they've been coming home to. What they really need to be able to heal is access to everyday nurturing connectedness. If we think the cogjam environment is hard on us, imagine what it's like for them, with their gut brains still learning not to hover quite so intensely over the panic button.

---

32   Department of Veterans Affairs (2016). Suicide among veterans and other Americans: 2001-2014 report. Retrieved from http://www.mentalhealth.va.gov/docs/2016suicidedatareport.pdf.

CHILDHOOD LEARNING

Some individual differences in resilience can be traced back to experiences during the growing years.[33] Consider what a growing environment needs for a child to develop effective resilience:

- Exposures to natural challenges, in the context of the world they will one day live in
- Practice making personal decisions from early on, supported by caregiver coaching and feedback
- Regular opportunity to experience both positive and negative realistic consequences of coping choices

These elements are critical to learning what works, what doesn't, and what could be done differently in times of stress. In addition, children who develop strong resilience tend to be those whose growing environment is warm and supportive. The child both builds healthy attachments and trusts the guidance provided by those who care for them.

Some children, unfortunately, have learning environments that are not the greatest for resilience building. For example, an elementary school teacher introduced me to the concept of "helicopter parents." She was referring to ones who, for whatever reason, constantly hover. They shield their children from experiencing challenging life situations, perhaps even going so far as to make all of their decisions for them. When their children do come up against usual problems of living, these parents may intervene or otherwise keep them from experiencing natural consequences. Fine, if a child is about to run in front of a car; not so good if parents do their homework for them, or interfere with disciplinary consequences for picking a fight on the schoolyard.

Then there's that recent case of the "affluence defense"—pleading not guilty to a crime because of having grown up in an extremely privileged environment. The perpetrator's attorney argued that the teenager was not to blame for his actions because he never had the exposures necessary for learning right from wrong. Regardless of whether this is enough to get someone off the hook, there is some merit to the argument that the poor kid never stood a chance.

Parenting limitations can go in the opposite direction as well, such as using corporal or other extreme punishment after incidents like starting a schoolyard brawl. The fight or flight such interventions create encourages children to fine-tune avoidance behaviors, like lying or becoming guarded around parents, rather than take heed of corrective instruction that follows.

Conflict-ridden and abusive growing environments are well known for their links to adverse outcomes. For example, there's a huge mountain of evidence

33   Tsabury, S. (2017). *The awakened family: How to raise empowered, resilient, and conscious children.* New York: Penguin Books.

against using physical punishment to discipline children, a knowledge base that continues to grow.[34] Both boys and girls who are maltreated show more problems with thinking skills, especially boys.[35] Likewise, the emotional consequences of such early learning can revisit us in any stage of life, as the time-blind gut brain never gives up trying to bring it out in the open and get it resolved.

Then there are those parents who are under-involved or uninvolved. They don't coach their children, limiting themselves to an occasional rant or lecture when behaviors cause problems that can't be ignored. They don't step in when the child comes up against world situations he or she is not developmentally ready to take in hand. The child is left on his or her own to figure out how to cope, often turning to the most convenient herd for example.

All is not lost for such children. When it comes to resilience, the learning never stops. Adulthood offers many opportunities for learning how to better cope with adversity—including the golden opportunity cogjam places before us today.

POSTTRAUMATIC STRESS DISORDER (PTSD)

Currently the most well-known mental health consequence of disaster and other traumatic experiences is PTSD.[36] PTSD symptoms develop when people experience overwhelming threat to life or wellbeing. In terms of frequency, following a disaster major depression runs a close second. But many who struggle with unresolved trauma experience both.

In some ways, PTSD symptoms seem to contradict one another. Those affected tend to stay away from reminders of the event, such as avoiding trauma-related thoughts or external cues. They also may experience numbing, dissociation or spacing out, substance abuse, a sense of unreality, or other forms of disconnect from the world around them. Paradoxically, these same individuals also find themselves repeatedly re-experiencing the traumatic event through nightmares, flashbacks, and intrusive thoughts. As the two sides keep butting heads, the emotional merry-go-round can become extremely dizzying.

Anything about this sound familiar? It should. It's yet another skirmish among brain functions with competing agenda. One side supports a logical argument for shutting out feelings and memories related to the event: "Why dredge all that up? It's terrifying." But on the other side, the gut brain continues experiencing the original traumatic stress in a continual, timeless loop. It repeatedly tries to bring the emotional memory into awareness, and insist that

---

34 Gershoff, E. T., Goodman, G. S., Miller-Perrin, C. L., Holden, G. W., Jackson, Y., & Kazdin, A. E. (2018). The strength of the causal evidence against physical punishment of children and its implications for parents, psychologists, and policy-makers. *American Psychologist, 73*, 626-638.

35 Nooner, K. B., Hooper, S. R., & De Bellis, M. D. (2018). An examination of sex differences on neurocognitive functioning and behavior problems in maltreated youth. *Psychological Trauma: Theory, Research, Practice, and Policy, 10*, 435-443.

36 Bremner, J. D. (2016). *Posttraumatic stress disorder: From neurobiology to treatment.* Hoboken, NJ: John Wiley and Sons.

the threat be dealt with. This is most typically triggered when cues of the original traumatic event act as reminders.

Here's what's happening at the chemical level.[37] When trauma is prolonged or severe, adrenalin and cortisol excessively flow. Over time, the receptors of neurons important for memories and emotions become damaged by this chemical bombardment. The usual pathways for processing emotions become disrupted. This contributes not only to developing PTSD, but also to depression and other mental health conditions.

But those emotional memories haven't gone away, in spite of the disruption. They still reside in the shadows. When cues bring them back into the limelight, the logical brain and the gut brain are only able to scream at each other about it, using language that neither is able to understand. Inner brain structures end up further damaged by the new chemical surges caused by this inner argument. Thus, the stalemate. PTSD is now formally recognized as a type of brain injury, despite absence of an external blow or invasive disease process.

A variety of life pitfalls can cause trauma, and PTSD is not an uncommon diagnosis. You may already recognize the condition in someone in your support network. Cognitive behavioral therapies and other treatments help those with PTSD, allowing many to live normal lives—thus their underlying condition may not be noticeable. The good news for all of us is that the neuroplasticity that works so well for their recovery process can do the same for us, once we're ready to get serious about dealing with symptoms of cogjam.

This discussion poses another troubling question. Could cogjam eventually result in PTSD, as happens following other disasters or significant trauma? Given the many forms of anger floating around in our cogjammed society, I can't help but wonder if the more likely epidemic will be posttraumatic embitterment disorder (PTED), only recently systematically studied.[38] It occurs when people are so caught up in anger over past misdeeds and lack of restitution that it interferes with their daily lives. They simply can't let go of the outrage and other negative thoughts and feelings stemming from the unfair event.

I suppose either scenario is possible, at least as a hypothesis. Cogjam does involve the same stress chemicals bombarding us, just as precedes PTSD. Ironically, our current socio-political chaos does mirror being at odds with one's self in an emotionally dysregulated brain. And the social disruption of a cogjammed society certainly foils interpersonal attachments critical to avoiding or moving beyond PTSD and PTED. Only time will tell us of the long-term results of failing to intervene in cogjam.

---

37   Serin, J. E., & Nemeroff, C. B. (2011). Post-traumatic stress disorder: The neurobiological impact of psychological trauma. *Dialogues in Clinical Neuroscience, 13*, 263-278.

38   Linden, M., & Rotter, M. (2018). Spectrum of embitterment manifestations. Psychological Trauma: Theory, Research, Practice, and Policy, 10, 1-6.

CHAPTER 7

......

Cradle Beginnings

THE PREVIOUS CHAPTER described certain defense mechanisms and the roles they play when coping with hard times. Sometimes they work to our advantage. Other times, they may not.

When coping choices backfire, no matter the reason, we aren't purposely trying to be dysfunctional. We're only taking the best course of action we see for what we have before us. We make selections based on what we know how to do, at times choosing whichever coping tactic most quickly bubbles into awareness. We repeat a specific coping method only if at some point it worked out favorably, or in some other way quieted fight or flight.

As near as I can tell, we don't purposely use faulty logic, either. How much reasoning sophistication we apply to life problems appears to boil down to how much time and effort we invest into thinking it through, as well as the current contents of our reasoning toolbox.

If you find that your own reasoning practices have regressed some in the throes of cogjam, rest assured that it does not mean intellectual decay. It is only a retreat into the reasoning game plan that first got your young brain flourishing. Back at its beginnings, your brain was developmentally unable to do the types of reasoning needed to survive adolescence and adulthood. This is one of the reasons why human children need adult care and oversight longer than do the young of most other species.

But even as newborns we need ways to make sense of the world in order to learn, grow, function, and survive. We accomplished this end by using simplistic reasoning strategies, ones better suited for a brain starting from scratch. They were the right tools for the right job.

Here lies a refuge into which cogjammed thinking escapes during overwhelming spasms of fight or flight: dusting off and repurposing the simpler reasoning of an early day. Cogjammed conclusions and choices aren't because of stupidity, laziness, intentionally ignored logic, contrariness, or being evil. During earliest chapters of our lives, reasoning that potentially could produce unfortunate results made perfect sense. At times, it still does. Though problematic when misused, those early reasoning practices are still part of our inner repertoire.

Childhood reasoning skills emerge in concert with the limitations and advantages of developmental ages.[39] The progression of a child's cognitive development therefore can be used as a rough road map for tracking the reasoning advancements that brought us to the present.

THE INVITATION

I now invite you to revisit your own developmental journey—that stroll down memory lane I promised earlier. Before reading any further, if you have any, pull out photographs of yourself as an infant or toddler, preschooler, school-age child, and adolescent. If you have none, let your mind's eye picture what you looked like at each of those ages. What was going on in those heads? What do you remember? How do you feel as you view yourself at each age?

Embrace these inner children. They're still there, all right. The reasoning they use may have its limitations, and be annoyingly attractive to our overreacting gut brains. But those simpler cognitive maneuvers faithfully served our earliest learning. We couldn't have gotten to where we are without them.

Our younger brains also offer surprising nuggets of wisdom that can well serve us today, as we arm ourselves to do battle with cogjam.

INFANCY AND TODDLERHOOD

Imagine the plight of being unceremoniously shoved out of a warm, enclosed, safe environment and into a foreign land of instant chill, loud noises, bright lights, and drastically reduced physical support. Little wonder that upon

---

39 Bjorklund, D. F., & Causey, K. B. (2017). *Children's cognitive development and individual differences*, 6th ed. Los Angeles: Sage.

greeting the outside world, most newborns' first act of business is letting out a healthy squall.

That milestone marker shows us what's already built in at birth: the tactic of calling out in distress, the earliest possible example of fight or flight wiring. Even on day one, the gut brain is already on the job.

Classical conditioning. Classical conditioning, another function with close ties to the primitive brain, is also seen shortly after birth. Classical conditioning is most often explained using the infamous story about Pavlov's dogs.[40] He was studying their salivation patterns, and set a bell to go off at feeding time. After a while he noticed that his dogs salivated at the sound of the bell, even when no food was present. The sound of the bell had become a cue to salivate.

With humans, such stimulus pairings are most noted for their role in fear-based learning. Classical conditioning is what causes those with PTSD to internalize cues of their original traumatic experience. When they encounter those same cues anywhere else, they may re-experience the fear they'd had during the event, even if the present day situation is completely benign. For combat veterans, it might be the smell of sulfur. For a rape victim, it might be passing by a dark alley. For a cancer patient enduring multiple rounds of painful or otherwise traumatizing treatments, simply walking into a medical facility might be enough to set off a fear response.

Exploring conditioning ability in newborns is difficult, given their limited repertoire of willful behaviors. Most of what they can do is related to eating or other basic survival needs. Not to be swayed, researchers forged on with what little they had to work with. In doing so they successfully conditioned infants to produce such behaviors such as head turning, blinking, and sucking by repeatedly pairing them with specific sensations. They also found newborns capable of learning to recognize the smell of their mothers over that of other women.

The early logical brain. Classical conditioning happens at the sensing level, rather than the thinking level. Thus the logical brain's developmental status is not so critical to classical conditioning as it one day will be for other forms of learning. Which is just as well, since it takes many years for the logical brain to achieve its full potential. That's why our earliest conscious memories only go back to somewhere around two or three years of age. During the first few years, neurons making up the logical brain go through so much connecting, reconnecting, and pruning that most pathways to our earliest memories have disintegrated by adulthood.

The newborn logical brain first perceives the world as a scatter of disconnected pieces. Everything is new, other than whatever muffled sounds or other

40   Pavlov, I. P. (2003). *Conditioned reflexes.* Mineola, NY: Dover Publications, Inc.

outside stimuli were sensed inutero. Therefore coming up with some form of information processing is a must for making it on the outside.

This is where figuring out cause and effect enters the picture. Infant brains come wired with the ability to make such associations. For example, two-day-old infants have been taught to do things like suck on a dry nipple in order to get music to play.

And that's how the dance begins: interacting with the environment, and watching the results our behaviors produce. Bouncing legs makes the mobile wiggle. Squeezing the yellow ducky makes a squeaky noise. Smiling keeps the caregiver engaged longer.

Pieces of information are eventually grouped together into schemes. Newly gathered information is either added onto an existing scheme, or changes are made to schemes to make everything fit together. Prototypes get their start.

Physical maturation and learning unite, advancing fight or flight options: at first only being able to call out when in distress; later holding out both arms when wishing to be picked up; and eventually toddling in the direction of whomever the child perceives to offer safety. These examples of comfort seeking also show goal-directed behavior, the ability to coordinate schemes and actions to get a desired result. Even at this tender age, capacity for reasoning during stress was there for the taking. At a very rudimentary level, we were already thinking things through.

Early herd participation. Figuring out how to regulate behaviors and emotions in ways that get along with the herd is also an age-based process.[41] Just as with scientific reasoning, socialization begins in infancy and never really stops. Much of it comes by watching cause and effect: "When I do this, what does Mommy do?"

Role models also guide social learning, our herd orientation appearing early on. Infants as young as two weeks of age copy certain facial expressions. How parents so delight in that first smile, frequently turning up while the parents themselves are smiling at their infants. Their repertoire of imitated behaviors grows as they become more physically able to copy what they see others do.

Toddler behaviors show primitive understanding of the importance of getting with the herd's program. One example is how they sometimes try to meet others' expectations. I recently saw a good example of this while waiting in line at a local big box store. The woman in front of me was struggling to unload her cart and simultaneously keep an older toddler from climbing out of her seat. A store employee noted her plight and started a conversation with the little girl.

---

41   Santrock, J. W. (2013). *Child Development*, 14th ed. New York: McGraw-Hill.

"My goodness, look who's here! Why, I know you. You're that bottom-down girl. You always put your bottom down to help Mommy. And you help Mommy at home, too, don't you? That's what bottom-down girls do . . ."

The girl slowly sat, listening intently. She entered the conversation with an occasional nod or limited verbal response. All the while, she stayed in her seat.

The fancy social science term for the employee's ploy is "attribution of pro-social characteristics." In other words, she gave the child an inner label for who she was and how she behaved, in a way that let her know members of society viewed both as socially desirable. The little girl ate it up. Given that the store employee's message even overrode the ever-present drive to test Mommy's boundaries, social expectations apparently play a powerful role indeed.

Sometimes toddlers are able to tell the difference between something happening on purpose or by accident. When they do make this distinction, they are more likely to copy the behavior believed to be intentional. On some level they appear to think it through, and decide whether the observed behavior will help them be one of the gang. Apparently it's not enough for us to act like others. We also want to succeed like others.

Early herd instinct also encourages us to help like others. Children younger than two years of age have been found to show empathy and compassion toward others in distress, such as copying previously observed comforting behaviors. The early appearance of such behavior suggests that the desire to be part of the solution rather than part of the problem really is our true nature.

Learning to talk is the Muhammad Ali of imitation in action. However language needs to be presented within a social context to be meaningfully valued by the ever-observant infant. Exposure to recordings, television, and radio has only a limited effect on earliest language acquisition. So from a social learning perspective, even when very young we understand that words matter when interacting with others.

Organizing new learning. Language eases the job of noting the progress of a child's scheme building. Certain limitations to scheme-building reliably turn up in every child: overextension and under-extension.

Overextension is when a concept is applied beyond its accepted boundaries, much like the overgeneralizing that adults fall victim to. For example, at first all four-legged furry animals may be called "dogs." Likewise, boundaries of definitions may be too narrow, such as "juice" meaning apple juice, but not grape or orange. Thus we might think of under-extension as being an early version of "my way or the highway" thinking.

Does something else about this sound familiar? It's our old acquaintance single factor thinking, that practice that so often trips us up during adult reasoning. But it served its purpose well, back then. We needed simplified ways to categorize and bookmark the massive amounts of information we absorbed. Figuring out the greater complexities came later, in concert with brain growth and life experience.

As cogjammed thinking spectacularly reveals, dependence on overextension and under-extension is not buried as deeply as we would like to believe. Their hardwiring goes in so early that they may come to mind in a pinch more easily than newer sophisticated reasoning. The same as with other primitive brain influences that are present the day we're born: herd instinct, and tendencies to copy or follow after valued others; perceiving cause and effect or making other connections, even when there may be none. When faced with the hopelessly nonsensical, cogjammed brains find relief from confusion by returning to those earliest drawing boards, hoping that the previously tried and true will provide answers.

Awareness of the here and now. The most valuable lesson babies have for us has little to do with cognitive skills. It's something that buds and blossoms in a much less intellectual corner of the infant mind.

Have you ever thought about that urge of people to stop and stare when they spot a young infant? What makes babies so attractive to us? And when we let ourselves share in their innocent gaze, why do we often experience a sense of peace and contentment? I suspect something survival based is afoot. Perhaps the adult urge to connect increases the likelihood that an infant will be cared for.

But I believe there's more to it than that. A baby's experience of the world is precisely that: simple experiencing. They interact with whatever they encounter, without being bogged down by assessing and judging. They find joy and excitement in something as simple as repeating a certain action over and over, even when already knowing what the result will be. Simply shoving items off a highchair tray and leaning over to view the result may never cease to be a fascination.

A young child's play is about free experiencing, about being in the here and now, rather than analyzing and stalking after organized goals. There's something about joining with the infant's experience of world that is temporarily freeing for the rest of us. It's almost as if it activates a return to our own original here and now.

Sure, we adults still play. And we enjoy pleasant sensations as we do so. But how we go about it is not the same as the young child's carefree presence in the moment. For example, take playing on a golf course. We might toss up a blade of grass to check the wind and adjust our swing accordingly, hoping to get the ball close to the hole. We celebrate when we succeed, commiserate when we don't, and move on to the next stroke. The toddler, on the other hand, delights in simply running on the soft green grass. He takes in its sweet scent and sunny warmth, and drinks in the sensation of moving through the air, shunning any purpose or goals.

One of my undergraduate professors shared a related story. He'd attended a picnic gathering that included children of varying ages. They were running around together on a large lawned area. A softball was involved with what they were doing, but it wasn't the game of softball they were playing. There seemed to be loosely understood rules of some sort, but not anything the participants would likely be able to explain. Whatever the rules were, they made participation age-free. All of the children were having a great time with it.

Then the adults stepped in.

"Let's get a game of softball going!" They reorganized the children and joined in the fun.

However, all but the oldest children lost interest. The younger ones were soon drawn off to more stimulating pursuits. The free experiencing had ended.

This is a price we pay for intellectual advancement. We can lose track of simply enjoying the moment, and instead feel compelled to analyze, categorize, or pursue a goal. The here and now, and inner awareness of both it and ourselves, get buried. For as soon as we assign a label to an experience, it ceases to exist on an experiential level. From that point forward the logical brain reliably steps in to point out what it is we are experiencing. Cognition wins out over sensing. While this is an asset when trying to expose inner illogic needing to be stripped of its power, it is the wrong tool for promoting here and now connectedness. We so easily miss the boat this way.

Thankfully, that early inner awareness is still within us, nestled next to the joy of doing for the sake of doing. We just don't access it as frequently as we might in the midst of all the tasks, obligations, and general worries of the adult world that so often monopolize our attention.

Relief from cogjam patiently waits. This earliest-experiencing corner of our beings is more than willing to be enlisted to work to our advantage. Remember, the vagal system works both bottom-up and top-down. Just as the gut brain can make us revisit primitive thinking tactics, the logical brain can willfully redirect our experiencing back to this simpler way of being. And, it is a tool for combating cogjam.

Take another look at that photograph or virtual image of yourself as an infant or toddler. Did you ever imagine that so much ability and wisdom was already in place? You could do so much, and learn so readily, using both scientific reasoning and social connecting. You used the best tools you had for the job, and achieved your developmental goals. The proof: you are here now, reading this.

THE PRESCHOOL YEARS

Improved language skills of preschool-age children help pave the way to showing others who they really are. They also further ease the job of trying to figure out the reasoning strategies and limitations of young children.

Reasoning advances. Preschoolers begin trying to reason why things happen the way they do, without physically trying it out first. This is a huge step. They move from the simple cause and effect calculations of the infant, to predicting likely outcomes merely by thinking it through. However as they develop and test primitive hypotheses, they typically consider only one factor, and ignore many others that may be relevant. Conclusions drawn are often faulty.

Here's an example. A friend of mine was passing through a buffet line when a four year old squeezed in next to her. The girl perused the selections and zeroed in on a plate of peanut butter cookies.

"I want the one with the most peanut butter in it. That's . . . this one." She picked it up and sampled it. "I was right. This one has the most peanut butter." She dashed off, happily enjoying her cookie.

Her conclusion didn't take into account the fact that she hadn't tasted any of the other cookies, and therefore could not legitimately draw such a conclusion. As is typical for her age, her conclusion relied on intuitive sensing and blind belief, rather than logic. But the example does show a major advance in reasoning strategy: she developed a hypothesis, then attempted to test it.

Getting stuck on a single factor, such as tasting peanut butter in a cookie and over-interpreting its significance, affects other types of early judgment as well. For example, conservation is the ability to recognize that changing something's shape or configuration doesn't change its actual size or quantity. Preschoolers typically can't do this. If you pour a glass of water into a wide bowl and ask them if there's more water now, they will likely say yes. Their assessment considers only the obvious factor of greater width, without taking into account the corresponding difference in depth.

Preschoolers continue to make cause and effect connections, as do we all. But with so much new material getting packed into such limited knowledge bases, they often assume cause and effect simply because the two occurrences happened together, or share some other connection:

"I smelled this flower a lot. Now it's dead. I smelled it too much."

"I didn't drink all my milk. Mommy and Daddy are mad at each other. It's my fault they're mad."

In other words, in the preschool-age mind correlation equals causation—another of those reasoning blunders adults stumble into when hurried or stressed. But for the preschooler, these errant cause and effect assumptions are a vital training ground. Practice at making assumptions and then discovering the truth sets the stage for eventually considering other important factors.

Another limitation to preschool-age reasoning is egocentrism. This means that at first, young children assume others see, hear, or otherwise experience exactly the same thing they do. For example, they might point out the car window at a herd of cows and say "look at that cow over there," not considering that they need to mention it's the one with horns before others will know which animal they're referring to. They do better at taking into account others' perspectives when dealing with the familiar, and are more likely to err when new material complicates the task—the stress response striking again, not so different from adult reasoning errors.

I've observed a possible form of egocentric regression in adults when worked-up public figures explain their conclusions with statements like "it's obvious" or "everybody knows that." Such comments are often delivered with forceful, dismissive, or otherwise condescending overtones—a second indicator that the gut brain has grabbed the steering wheel. Yes, the conclusion is obvious to the speaker. No, it's not obvious to listeners, if they ask for clarification.

Theory of mind. By the end of the preschool years children have rudimentary understanding that others have thoughts and feelings different from their own. This is called theory of mind. Recognizing how others feel, think, or perceive is critical for empathy and altruism, as well as being able to behave in ways that fit in with the herd. Understanding multiple perspectives and thought-behavior connections will one day be crucial for problem solving in social situations.

Perhaps much of the insensitivity that pops up with cogjammed behavior represents regression to those early years, before we were fully able take into account others' feelings or thoughts in addition to our own. Likewise, cogjammed conversation is often devoid of respect for social rules that even most preschoolers know: that you take turns, don't interrupt people, and try to be nice. When cogjam takes control, we may temporarily overlook these.

All the same, putting recognition of others' inner experience on a back burner is an asset for the preschool-age mind when making sense of an overwhelming swell of information. Needing to factor in yet one more branch of information doesn't help a bit. But of course, ignoring the impact of behavior on others is the wrong tool when it interferes with tweaking social skills.

Emotional intelligence. Amidst the preschooler's advancing theory of mind and adventures with cause and effect, emotional intelligence buds. We become consciously aware of our own feelings. We learn the beginnings of how to manage them, recognize the emotions of others, and how to best relate to others. Modeling practices become more selective: we see the results others get from their behaviors and copy or ignore them, based on whether we believe they will get us what we aim for. We begin drawing conclusions about whom best to believe or imitate—early evidence of establishing leaders of the pack.

This is one of the reasons early childhood social exposures are so influential. Hooking up with unfortunate role models at this impressionable age costs us, detouring us onto a more difficult road to socialization. And, its early hardwiring means it likely continues lurking somewhere in the shadows of our adult reasoning, if alternative wiring hasn't had a chance to step in and take control. Taking pause to recognize and understand any such early learning helps us avoid having it shoved into the limelight when cogjam takes the reins.

Visualize your image of that little person who back then was you, so full of wonder and discovery. The world was unfurling before you. You opened up and welcomed its lessons with both native intuition and the beginnings of thinking things through. It was all starting to make sense, one way or another. The world was your oyster.

MIDDLE CHILDHOOD

Middle childhood moves us from the world of "can't do's" to "can do's," in terms of reasoning ability. The importance of thinking and logic over perception and intuition advances ever nearer to its rightful status.

Reasoning advances. Children begin to recognize that when making common sense judgments, logic in and of itself—the structure of an argument—is just as important as the actual details of the problem. Frameworks for sorting and storing information become more organized, and their understandings of the world become more orderly than those of preschoolers. They become better skilled at making mental comparisons, rather than needing concrete objects in front of them to successfully draw conclusions.

In spite of these advances, their scientific reasoning has a long way to go. While they are better at creating hypotheses, they still often forget to check them out before accepting them. Likewise, when looking for potential solutions for a problem, they do not yet perform the exhaustive search of formal science. They are more likely to try out a few solutions then give up.

School-related activities play a much greater role in their overall development. The academic setting quickly advances knowledge acquisition, building thinking-based and social skills alike.

Understanding the herd. Equally important to building reasoning skills is the school milieu's impact on social development. Learning how to function in a human village requires exposure to it within a manageable training ground, where children can practice and be mentored among large groups of others. The traditional classroom provides just such a setting.

Advances in brain development improve self-control, critical to both succeeding as students and getting along with others. They become better able to pick out what to pay attention to and what to ignore. Improving ability to take the perspective of others helps them better consider social context and others' feelings, as well as incorporate ideas that are different from their own.

Many of these improvements help them realize the importance of considering more than one factor. As brain development bolsters attention span, school-age children better shift focus among multiple pieces of information, without so easily losing track or missing the point.

For example, when my son was little I shared a funny story I'd heard. It was about a teacher who was having trouble keeping a particular student on task. He finally got the student redirected by first kneeling down and then asking him, "Want to buy a dead duck?"

I thought the story was hilarious, and that my son would think so too. But when I finished telling it he just stood there, hands in his pockets, staring at me as if expecting more.

"Don't you think that was funny?" I asked him.

He gave my question brief consideration. "So how much was the duck?"

Much of the school-age child's style of humor stems from new appreciation of there being more than one way to look at things. That's why they consider those books of riddles that adults find to be rather ho-hum to be such great stuff. Like, "Why did the man throw the clock out the window? Because he wanted to see time fly." Being able to activate such shifts in perspective is a new and wondrous discovery during middle childhood. Case in point: when I recounted the dead duck story to my son as an older child, he laughed not only at the story itself, but also at his original reaction.

Fitting in with the herd. These years bring major socialization advances. Children develop more realistic expectations of others, and adjust beliefs and behaviors accordingly. Likewise, they have more concerns about whether they fit in. They better recognize the necessity of social acceptance for succeeding in life. They become more selective in choosing buddies than they were as preschoolers, often gravitating toward those with similar interests.

They also become more selective about which members of the herd to follow after as favored role models. For example, they may recognize that a teacher has a better idea of how to do a complex math problem than a confused parent. It's not that children stop looking to parents as examples. Their ability to adjust perspectives is simply noting that everybody's abilities are not the same. They begin to recognize that different adults are experts on different things.

On the downside, this is when children begin to develop social anxiety. They want to fit in, and there will always be places where they do not. They don't realize it's only herd instinct at work, urging them this way and that in search of appropriate and secure placement. Such trials and tribulations are all part of the normal path to finding a niche.

At this age, perceived adult views of them can easily become self-fulfilling prophecies. Children may settle their identities into whatever valued others seem to tell them about themselves, regardless of accuracy or adaptive potential. Sometimes this can get in the way of following more productive paths of self-exploration.

The final product. Focus. Primacy of logic. Self control. Fitting in with the herd. These are the critical advances we welcomed during middle childhood. We use them to this day. Even way back then, we had figured out ways to tame the inner lizard when necessary. To varying degrees, we all exerted control over immediate impulses, placed less primacy on fight or flight feelings, employed logic, and crafted reactions or behaviors that helped us better fit in.

Do you remember an occasion when any of these factors influenced you as a school-age child? What first came to mind about my childhood was making myself practice the violin. I hated it. Nonetheless, self-control and willful focusing got me on task, fueled by the logic of practice makes perfect. Plus, the better I played, the better I fit in with the orchestra. So I chose to practice.

In terms of early fight or flight decision-making, I recall a bullying situation. A girl in my class liked to corner me and say nasty things about me—not tied to anything specific, just basic trash talk. It always left me feeling hurt and confused. One day the friend I usually sat with at lunch said this other girl wanted her to come and sit at her table. Not knowing about the bullying, my friend asked me to come along.

I was torn. No way did I want to sit through lunch with that bully. She knew full well it would make me uncomfortable. The invitation may even have been intended as passive-aggressive bullying. On the other hand, I didn't want to cause harm to my friendship with my usual lunch partner, who seemed pleased with the prospect of sitting at a more popular table.

At first I said nothing. I could only think of how awful going along with the offer would be. The only options I could think up were to go sit and endure the abuse, since my usual response of walking away would be harder to pull off; or to return fire with the armory of angry retorts I'd saved up over the last few months. Neither option felt good. Neither felt like me. Finally, I turned to my friend and simply said "No."

Understandably confused, she asked for an explanation. I did not relish the option of admitting I was being victimized. That would have meant yet another blow to already abused-feeling self-esteem. So after the repeated explanation of "I just don't want to sit with her"—along with a couple of undisguised tears—my friend agreed to sit with me instead. Interestingly, for whatever reason, not long after that episode the bullying ceased.

That's what I see in pictures of myself as a sixth-grader: a girl who was vulnerable, yet found the strength to focus, think something through, and impose her will when it fit in with her early values. She was able to feel hurt and threatened yet also come up with an acceptable plan of action, even when lashing out was the more attractive option. My eleven-year-old self successfully made use of training wheel skills for staying out of cogjam.

The situation would probably have had an even more productive ending if I'd told an adult about the bullying. There were also plenty of ways the situation could have gone south, in spite of how I handled it. Regardless, I still came out of the episode knowing I hadn't purposely poured fuel on the fire.

If children can avoid it, so can we. We can also have confidence in and find comfort in our own ability to do so.

When is the first time you recall your better judgment playing out over impulse? Think hard, it may take a while. We don't typically examine childhood memories from that particular angle. In fact, only as I penned this chapter did I recognize that the bullying incident represented something more than a case of playground victimization. It illustrated how I was becoming a person, expressing who I was, and moving toward the niche in the herd I wished to fit into. The niche, by the way, that I eventually found.

What might memories of your own early experiences be whispering to you?

ADOLESCENCE

During the teenage years, we move ever closer toward reasoning as we will in adulthood.

Formal logic blossoms. Adolescents have the ability to abstract. In other words, they can consider a problem in abstract terms, completely devoid of the specific content, and still come up with a correct conclusion.

For example, if you tell a preschooler that Joe is taller than Jim, and Jim is taller than John, at the very least the child must mentally visualize the three boys to be able to compare them and arrive at the conclusion that Joe is taller than John. The school-age child is able to figure it out by thinking through a representation like Joe > Jim, Jim > John, therefore Joe > John. The adolescent can take it one step further, evaluating the problem as an abstraction: A > B, B > C, therefore A > C. The answer would be the same regardless of what A, B, and C represent. Over time adolescents add numerous A and B manipulations to their reasoning arsenal.

Ability to abstract allows advancement in scientific reasoning. The adolescent not only becomes able to consider and combine multiple relevant factors, but also to see that multiple hypotheses can be drawn from the same set of facts. Their scientific reasoning capacity therefore becomes more like that of the adult. However their continuing shortcomings are similar to those found in cogjammed decision-making:

- Single factor reasoning, such as working extra hours to save money for college, even though it is beginning to get in the way having study time needed to earn good grades
- Insufficient search for options—going for the impulsive, or first viable option to come to mind, rather than thinking through other possible options and their merits
- Persistence of irrational beliefs—unwillingness to let go of an assumption, even as evidence piles up against it
- Misapplying probabilities, such as deciding that a one in ten chance of contracting the HIV virus means it probably won't affect the teen; or combining and applying statistical conclusions in ways that support the preferred perspective, but are not logically valid
- Short-sightedness, typically overvaluing the immediate consequences of a decision and undervaluing possible long-term consequences

Yes, adults make these same mistakes. What changes for adolescents is that at this stage they are now developmentally able to do better, as do savvy adults.

Herd adjustments. Adolescents' realization that they can reason similarly to an adult is pretty heady stuff. It gives rise to new forms of egocentrism. In their glee and pride they may insist that their unique conclusions are valid, even if they've not yet tested them in the real world. If it's logical, it must be right, and people ought to conform to it.

Such idealism commonly leads adolescents to band together behind various causes, perhaps saving the world with sit-ins, picketing, and other demonstrations of loyalty to "obviously" logical causes. These flights into limited reasoning do have their developmental place. Such egocentrism and idealism helps bolster adolescents for the scary task of separating from parents, and getting comfortable with functioning on their own.

Upon recognizing their new abilities, adolescents also may develop "personal myths" or "invincibility fables." They attribute more uniqueness or superiority to themselves than is really there. While this can and often does create problems, it also helps build confidence for being able to move toward independence. They feel freer and more comfortable with seeking out their rightful place in the herd. They learn to consult their values and do what they believe is right, rather than go along with school-chum, family-based, or other sub-herd pressures. Personal myths eventually dissipate as they become obsolete.

When I was a teenager I recognized that excelling at academics was my only likely ticket to moving beyond humble beginnings. However I lived in a house filled with noisy younger children. One Sunday afternoon while I was attempting to get through a massive mound of homework, my siblings kept carousing by. I gathered up my schoolwork and resettled in my bedroom. However, it was a shared bedroom. It didn't take long before their frolicking passed through there as well. Finally I stuffed things into a bag, put on my coat, and told my mother I was going to find a quiet place to study. She told me not to, insisting I could study at home.

Today, I do not recall why she didn't want me to leave. What was more salient at that moment was the pivotal crossroads I saw before me. I wanted higher learning, and I needed the grades to get into a good university. Yet I would likely end up with neither if I continued to go along with expected family herd practices.

I left the house anyway, and walked a mile or so to the local library. As it was Sunday, plenty of others were there. But this gathering was peaceful, and so warm and cozy. Simply walking through those glass double doors made me feel at home in a way I'd never before experienced. I immediately knew I was onto something. To this day I still get that cozy, peaceful feeling while perusing the stacks.

Of course, there were consequences for having left home without permission. But I considered them well worth it. My adolescent willingness to buck the herd and find my own way eventually lead me to where I am today. And, it likely plays a significant role in my willingness to look at what's going on around us and develop healthy alternatives to letting cogjam rule.

That ability to buck herd influence lives on within each of us, hopefully in a place where it doesn't make our lives or those of others unnecessarily trying. It can be reenlisted today, if we're seeking that extra oomph to buck influences that promote cogjam.

MOVING FORWARD

Take out or visualize those snapshots of your evolving child selves. What occurred to you about your own early values and self-concept? Have you rediscovered anything about yourself that got lost during the turmoil of coming of age? Or perhaps you remembered something about yourself that you didn't like, that you decided you would try not to do again. You wanted to grow up. You wanted to become, to succeed.

It doesn't need to be something as dramatic or definitive as my experience of finding peace and belonging simply by walking into a library. It might be relatively minor, a brief incident when you had an "ah-ha" moment. Perhaps you missed its significance as it happened:

- Recognizing faulty logic, pointed out by someone else or stumbling upon it on your own
- Realization that there is more than one way of looking at the same problem
- Adopting a new strategy or skill while playing a game, that turned out to be valuable
- Figuring out for yourself that a plump white-bearded man could not possibly fit down a chimney on Christmas Eve
- Feeling touched by a playmate's act of compassion or kindness, such that it made an impact on how you viewed friendships

It could also be something considerably more abstract, such as a set of new feelings that you have difficulty putting into words.

When I was about twelve, my large family piled into the station wagon for a trip to the coast. After hours of winding travel in cramped quarters we stopped at a byway. Though hidden by sand banks dotted with stirring beach grass, we could hear the ocean in the distance. We spilled out of the car and scattered over the banks, the faint roar of crashing waves beckoning from beyond. As I climbed toward the top of the last mound, the surf's roar crescendoed.

A sudden blast of cold salty air practically stole my breath away. Then it was there: the sea, belted by an immense band of sand, exquisitely smoothed by the elements. I ran down to the beach, arms outspread and embracing it all, my long hair flinging in every direction as I skipped and danced. It was exhilarating.

But it was more than serendipitous enjoyment of nature in all its glory. I felt a previously undiscovered connectedness—with the sea, with the human experience, with the world in general. I realized I was part of it, in a way I had never before understood. It was so sensual, so here and now, and so benign. It blotted out any lingering angst over the family dynamics that evolve in a packed car.

After returning home I made multiple attempts at writing poetry to describe my visit to the sea. It was the only way I could think of to recapture and somehow hold onto those precious, timeless moments. In retrospect, I believe part of my spiritual self had awakened—a big part of what has spurred me on to seek answers to our current socio-political dilemma.

Whatever early bit of growth you recall, hold it dear. Make it your anchor—not necessarily the content of what you learned, but how the experience helped you become you, as such experiences did for all of us before cogjam.

CHAPTER 8

......

On Stuckness

INSANITY: **DOING SOMETHING** the same way over and over, and expecting a different result.

The proposed origins of this oft-quoted definition range from Einstein to Alcoholics Anonymous to ancient Chinese proverbs. The current definition of insanity is more clinically and legally oriented than historical meanings. By today's standard, the old saying refers more to what we call being irrational. If you keep approaching a problem the same way, even though you aren't getting the results you want, for some reason your learning curve has gone flat.

Many things can get in the way of benefitting from everyday lessons, and thereby not letting such learning have its due. But if you've made it to this chapter, chances are pretty good you're ready to at least consider how well your reasoning handles cogjam, as well as potential options for changing course.

So far, what have you learned from what you've read? Here are main points to keep in mind:

- Body chemistry behind fight or flight and social bonding creates emotional urges, that at times encourage us to do things that violate our better interests.

- While the logical brain is capable of overriding such urging, misused reasoning strategy can get in the way of it successfully doing so when we're highly stressed.

- We built our repertoire of reasoning strategies as infants, children and teenagers—and those skills are still there, even if at times we may feel as if we've lost them.
- Moving beyond cogjam requires recognizing the above, as well as choosing the right reasoning tools for the job.

The first step for letting this new knowledge help you reduce cogjam and build a better life is deciding you're willing to take action on it. But—what if you find that you want to change things for the better, but struggle with stuckness? Read on.

CHANGE AND THE INNER LIZARD

Change is scary. If you don't believe me, just ask your gut brain.

We're more comfortable with routine. It's so familiar. We feel at home with the familiar, and don't need to put out much effort toward thinking what to do next. It often happens seemingly automatically. We also don't need to worry about what might happen should we try out the untested. Thus another old adage: "Better the devil you know, than the one you don't."

Yet change is the rule of our existence, rather than the exception. Buddhist philosophy spells out its pivotal role: in life there is change, and with change there is always some form of suffering. However personal growth is the product of seeking answers as we adjust to change and suffering.

This is not to say we should purposely seek out suffering so we can better experience growth. That's more like masochism. We don't need to make suffering happen. There's plenty of change and suffering spontaneously entering most everybody's lives, as is so well demonstrated by our current cogjam saga.

Rather, we embrace change and suffering when it finds us during our journey's natural flow. We use it to spur on new and better ways of experiencing, striving, and coping. What we get in return is a continually revised sense of stability, as contradictory as that may sound. We constantly readjust our equilibrium to better roll with the punches and potholes.

Enter the gut brain. This is the last thing it wants to hear. All we have to do is think about making a major change and juices begin to spurt. Anxieties follow; the brakes engage: "Hold it right there. What in the world do you think you're doing?"

This is what stuckness is about: once again, letting the fear response call the plays. And as it bounds out onto cogjam's center field, it carries with it the entire playbook:

Fight. "Change is bad. Absolutes are good. That logical brain is clueless. Get him out of here." "Who says I need to change? Point them out. Let me at 'em." "Those bad guys are the ones causing problems. They're the ones who need to change."

Flight. "Keep to yourself. Opening your mouth is too risky. Doesn't matter what you say, people are still going to pick a fight with you." "Don't look at me. I don't have an opinion." "What socio-political problem? It's always been like this." "I think we're through here." "Enough with this cogjam falderal. The book that trashes [insert preferred bad guy here] is a lot more stimulating. Let's dive into that little gem. That'll tell us who the bad guys really are."

Freeze. "I don't get it. What's going on?" "Do I go with the scary new, or get clobbered for sure by the tried and true? Scary, or clobbered. Scary, clobbered. Scary, clobbered . . . (*tilt*)."

In spite of gut-brain biases, change does not necessarily mean chaos. Nor does it need to be scary. After all, it's part of the natural flow. Change goes on regardless of whether we choose to pay attention to it. Even more important, if we don't recognize the primacy of change, it may mean the light has not yet dawned on us that we're already coping with it. Quite handily, at that.

Willingness to go along with change varies in part with the mightiness of an individual's gut brain. If your inner lizard is really into eating his Wheaties, change is more uncomfortable for you than what many others experience. Therefore those with conservative political views tend to have more difficulty moving toward change than those whose views are more liberal.[42]

From what we know about preferences represented by conservative or liberal stances, we would expect this difference. It might even explain why we find more liberal views on the US west coast than most other parts of the country. Their pioneer ancestors' inner lizards were less likely to complain about taking on a venture so crazy as heading into an unknown wilderness and starting over from scratch.

However, the drawback experienced by conservatives does not mean their strong fear response is a sign of personal inferiority. In other circumstances, having an inner lizard on steroids is a major advantage. It only becomes a problem if excessively allowed to override the logical brain. In fact, after studying fight or flight's role in politics and religion, one researcher reported that based on what he found, his own centrist stance saw fit to be a little more conservative.[43] What we're seeing here is simply another element that affects choosing the right tool for the right job, even if genetically influenced factors make overcoming cogjam a thornier battle for some than for others.

---

42 Jost, J. T., Glaser, J., Kruglanski, A. W., & Sulloway, F. J. (2003). Political conservatism as motivated social cognition. *Psychological Bulletin*, 129, 339-375.

43 Haidt, J. (2012). *The righteous mind: Why good people are divided by politics and religion.* New York: Pantheon Books.

And, keeping this in mind well assists us all, as we seek to engage compassion toward those with alternate views.

REWIRING THE BRAIN

In decades past scientists believed the brain didn't change much after we reach adulthood, other than decline caused by aging, illness, or physical damage. That's why they were so amazed when Phineas Gage recovered from his extraordinary brain injury. They'd thought that by adulthood we were hopelessly stuck with permanently fixed structures, formed by whatever grew or got programmed in during child and adolescent development. It was all the better we were expected to ever be.

Today we know this is not true. For example, in some regions of the brain new neurons seem to generate out of nowhere when needed. In addition, throughout our lives new learning appears to correspond with new synaptic hook-ups within the neural web. Likewise, synapses strengthen or weaken, depending on how often they are used. This experience-based adaptability of the brain is called neuroplasticity.[44]

Neuroplasticity works both to our benefit and our detriment. Since it is a value-free biological process, it doesn't distinguish between healthy and harmful learning. It only enters the data, reinforces whatever keeps getting used, and weakens or disables the rest.

PTSD is a good example of neuroplasticity working against us. Overwhelming fears and their ongoing stress chemistry eventually damage receptors of neurons that process fear, potentially bringing on a host of ills. Neuroplasticity can also program in dysfunctional thoughts, behaviors, and emotions based on unfortunate learning experiences in daily living.

On the plus side, neuroplasticity is the reason we are so capable of changing it all for the better. We are always able to learn. We are always able to build new connections. That is why we are so resilient. We can move forward no matter what type of earlier stress or trauma has interfered with healthy brain integration.

Future chapters present a smorgasbord of approaches for rewiring cogjammed habits, be they behavioral, emotional, cognitive, or interpersonal. For now, the most important nugget to keep tucked in a near pocket is neuropsychologist Donald Hebb's catch phrase: "Neurons that fire together wire together." We can make this work for us. The key to getting unstuck, whether from cogjam or other problematic thoughts and behaviors, is getting our brains to introduce neurons to each other frequently enough for change to take place.

---

44   Doidge, N. (2016). *The brain's way of healing: Remarkable discoveries and recoveries from the frontiers of neuroplasticity*. New York: Penguin Books.

FERRETING OUT ROOTS OF RESISTANCE

We don't all get stuck for the same reasons. Therefore we each need to identify the unique specifics of what in particular seems to interfere with our forward progress. The roots of stuckness slip into numerous hiding places, and many of them aren't obvious. Given the gut brain's preference to avoid fearful unknowns, we tend not to examine our stuckness very often.

If you have or had PTSD, or are currently working through a trauma-related issue, the roots of your stuckness may already be familiar traveling companions. Or, they may be buried so deeply that you have yet to ferret out the cause of your symptoms. Trauma-based cognitive behavioral therapy, mindfulness techniques, and certain somatic therapies are all helpful in identifying and addressing persistent mental health issues fueled by past trauma.

If your symptoms are significant, I recommend working through stuckness and other cogjam-related issues with your therapist. Your primitive brain might be correct in its preferred approach. It keeps you stuck because you're not ready. Your resilience needs more time or bolstering before you take on symptoms of this newer trauma.

Most of us, however, don't need a therapist to face cogjam head on. And we don't need to look far to find motivation to do so. Being stuck is in itself uncomfortable, even distressing for some. Feeling trapped in this mess is definitely no fun. Our resilience is ready and waiting, fully capable of freeing us from stuckness, one way or another.

Here are some common reasons why people get stuck, and ideas for how to address them.

Inner discomfort. "I don't like looking at this from such a personal angle. I guess thinking about it from the standpoint of what others are doing is okay. But not what it may mean for me. It doesn't feel good. I might even discover I'm doing something 'wrong.' That never feels good."

Of course it doesn't feel comfortable. That's the gut brain, stepping in to remind you that change is scary, and that you can't allow yourself to be vulnerable.

The logical brain processes opportunity for change differently. When given the opportunity, it is more likely to approach stuckness and alternative options with tactics like assessing potential outcome, such as the costs of changing versus not changing:

Costs of changing:

• Changing requires effort; it's easier to do nothing.

• It means taking a risk, and I might not succeed at first. Is my ego up to that?

- Some people might be confused if I start acting differently. What will others think? How will they react? It may mean needing to change how I fit in with the herd.
- Learning and figuring out how to use new skills takes time and practice.

Advantages of changing:

- I won't feel so trapped. Realizing I have the freedom to change is liberating.
- Nothing is likely to change if I handle cogjam the same as always. Like Ghandi said, I need to be the change I want to see.
- Some of my relationships are getting so strained that trying something different probably won't hurt anything. It can only get better.
- Some good may come of trying new ways to deal with cogjam. The new skills I pick up may help with handling other social and emotional challenges, too.
- I will learn more about myself.
- Some of what I learn might rub off on others.
- Any opportunity for posttraumatic growth is priceless. I shouldn't squander it.

The pros and cons of staying stuck versus changing vary from person to person. You probably can think of other factors that fuel resistance or desire to pursue change. And, your gut brain most likely has something to say about each and every one of them.

Yes, listen to your gut brain. Windows to feelings will open. Listening, though at times uncomfortable, may be how you discover exactly what it is that you really want or need.

But remember that feelings related to a decision are only something to acknowledge and consider. They are a source of information, rather than what should make the decision for you. Base your choice on what makes the most sense. Will you feel worse about doing something new that fails, or doing business as usual and living with cogjam stress indefinitely?

Obsessing. "I won't need to worry if I just do...X, Y, Z." Actually, there's no need to worry about it even if we don't do X, Y, or Z. Worry solves nothing. We do need to plan. But planning is something else entirely.

Obsessing is about investing more time and energy into thinking about a problem than is necessary or productive. It is not solution oriented. Obsessing either dwells on the past: bad feelings about what happened, stewing over what others did, how you might have failed, what you wish you'd said or done, an opportunity you missed out on, and so on; or is wrapped up in tallying everything that could possibly go wrong in the future.

It keeps us stuck because the time and effort wasted on obsessing interfere with directly addressing the situation. The gut brain certainly welcomes constant reminders of fear, perhaps even feels stronger or more in control because of them. But for most of today's fears, its compass is out of whack.

Besides, neither the past nor the future is within our control. The past is over and done with; there's nothing we can do to change it now. We can make plans for the future, and a certain amount of advance planning is a good thing. But many additional factors influence what the future brings, things we can't know until they happen. Nobody has yet succeeded in crossing a bridge before first coming to it. Final solutions come into being as we think things through in the present and face fears directly.

Confusion. "I just don't get it." So much is happening. So much contradictory information gets tossed in every direction. Everybody's and anybody's beliefs are under attack. How do we bring enough order to this gush of "facts" to move forward?

True, much of what we're hearing these days doesn't make sense. But it doesn't necessarily need to, for the rest of us to travel our personal journeys. However we do need to sweep aside the litter, and get it out of the way of where our journeys lead us.

Instead of being distracted by the nonsensical, establish a steady focus. Take time to examine your stuckness and how it affects you, rather than let yourself be overwhelmed by socio-political *sturm und drang* or how others handle their reactions. You don't need to have everybody else figured out in order to move forward. Only within ourselves is change truly under our power, no matter what course of action the rest of society chooses.

Rigidity. "I've always been this way. It's who I am." What you do is never who you are. Who you are is a completely different paradigm, stemming from sensations, preferences, inclinations, and other elements of how you experience all that is life. What you do is only behavior. Yes, you are more likely to choose behaviors that fit with your inclinations. But that is only a choice, a behavior in itself; it is not who you are. You have the option of ignoring rather than going along with an impulse. "Who you are" has control over that. You can change usual behavior, and still be you.

Some confuse rigidity with stability. Stability is comfortable, and certainly desirable over chaos. But it's not an either/or proposition. Nor is rigidity about having a stable life framework to depend upon. Rigidity is about refusal to change how we think or behave, even when staying in place creates instability in our lives.

Willingness to learn and grow is how we established our lives and world-views in the first place. That process is and always should be nonstop. As the world changes, corresponding consequences follow. These take place regardless of whether we choose to learn from and adapt to them.

Flexibility and openness to new experiences are the opposite of being stuck. There is so much we miss out on when we cling to rigid ways.

Take a moment to check in with your child selves. Remember how flexible you once were, so ready and willing to sponge up new learning and experiences? That's what you may need to re-welcome: that early fascination, excitement, and willingness to discover.

At times we discover something hardwired rattling around inside that's getting in the way, such as unfortunate coping behaviors picked up during trying times. But hardwired does not mean unchangeable. All rewiring requires to begin its mission is our willingness to try something different.

Black or white thinking. Absolutist beliefs are the very foundation of stuckness. Since any concept taken to the extreme is unworkable, black and white thinking leaves no wiggle room for problem solving. A perspective or solution is judged as either good or bad, right or wrong, or some other unshakeable absolute. Therefore when we impose it on ourselves, all problems are automatically defined in unsolvable terms. Why even try to get unstuck? There will always be something new to violate the agenda. May as well give up now.

Only you can choose how you reason. Choose to acknowledge reality's gray areas. They offer more options for success.

Active avoidance. Busy lives provide plenty of excuses to not challenge cogjam head-on. We throw ourselves into our work, take on excessive exercise regimens, disappear into the boob tube or video games, or limit social lives to Facebook. A few drinks and other overindulged pastimes and we forget about whatever we wish were different. Or, we get over-involved in others' lives, telling them how to fix things instead of looking at what we ourselves can do. Unfortunately, the mere act of pushing it out of awareness can make the discomfort even worse.

Trauma alert: One of the ways people experience past unresolved trauma in the present is by going into a freeze or even "feigned death"-type response when certain stresses arise. This is not necessarily a maladaptive form of avoidance. Your gut brain may be shutting you down because you are already overwhelmed. You may not even be consciously aware of the past traumatic incident that spawned it. If you find yourself often coping by way of emotional shutdown or numbness, therapist support is highly recommended before getting too far into addressing your cogjam symptoms.

Hostile dependence. Hostile dependence develops when we unwittingly put ourselves at the mercy of those we hold responsible for whatever angers us. Or, we convince ourselves that someone else needs to change in some way before we can be happy. They don't, of course; and our anger predictably mush-rooms as they repeatedly fail to meet our demands. In the case of cogjam, the previously listed causes of stuckness can all come together to create hostile dependence:

- *Discomfort:* "Look at this mess. It's infuriating. And scary. I'd rather cover my eyes. Besides, it's the other guy's fault. He/she is the one who needs to get with the program, not me."

- *Obsessing:* "I need to keep worrying, as long as so-and-so is so messed up. There's nothing I can do about it. He/she is the only one that can make things better."

- *Confusion:* "How can those people believe in what they're saying/doing? They all need to make more sense before I can move forward."

- *Rigidity:* "Taking control is not who I am. I'm a follower, not a leader. I will always be that way. So there's nothing I can do about it. Others should be fixing it."

- *Black and white thinking:* "The other guy is the one in the wrong. I'm the one in the right. And there's only one right answer: my way, or the highway."

- *Active avoidance:* "I need to invest time into things that are worthwhile, like my job or family. I can't help it if so-and-so's behavior is such a distrac-tion. It's his/her fault that staying on task has become so much harder."

Those who are the most profoundly stuck, no matter what the problem, are usually those who've entered a state of hostile dependence.[45] The belief that others must change is paralyzing, yet the gut brain is more than happy to go along with it. After all, hostile dependence identifies a bad guy to aim at: "Fire away!"

GETTING UNSTUCK

You do have power over stuckness. You need only seek it out and embrace it. Following are a list of steps that can help you free yourself:

- First comes deciding you want to be unstuck. This sounds like a ridiculous thing to ask. Who would want to be stuck in this confusing and emotional mess? However there's secondary gain afoot among many who stay in freeze mode, such as worries over fitting in with the herd as they know it, or avoiding new risks. The arguments against change listed earlier illus-trate these. Consider both pros and the cons of changing, and decide for yourself whether you've had it with foundering in quicksand.

---

45   Aldrich, K. (1966). *An Introduction to Dynamic Psychiatry.* New York: McGraw-Hill.

- Forgive yourself for getting stuck. It's a common condition. We all find ourselves there on occasion. What you have encountered is that you are human. Welcome to the herd! Come on in, the watering hole's fine.
- Consider your initial motivation. What led you to pick up this book? What were you hoping it would tell you? What particular nuggets did you hope to find, that for you would be especially meaningful? Knowing your own heart makes for easier focusing on the prize.
- Be willing to face the fear or concern that has you peering out from beneath the bushes. Avoidance keeps you stuck because you don't get that chance to find out you really do have what it takes to get through life's uncomfortable challenges. You are resilient. You can handle it. Look at everything you've handled so far, and yet are still alive and kicking. You're stronger than you think.
- Keep your eyes on the goal. You are an agent of change, regardless of whether you choose to activate that strength. You don't even need to know exactly what you want to change about life with cogjam, other than wanting its impact on your life to be over with. At this early stage of setting up a personal game plan, what carries you furthest is simple willingness to try something new. It frees you to say yes when the next "ah-ha" moment shouts "Bingo!" Discovering that you can change for the better is in itself freeing.

MORE CARROTS FOR THE END OF THE STICK

If you need additional motivation to forge onward, consider the many rewards people say they've gained from posttraumatic growth:

- Increased self-confidence, as they tap into strengths they never knew they had.
- Greater comfort with who they are.
- Greater compassion—for both themselves and others, and discovering other pieces of inner wisdom that reside at a deeper level.
- Greater comfort with uncertainty.
- Rewarding changes in life direction, as they pursue newly discovered passions and abilities.
- Their eyes finally opening to who they really are.

Philosophy of life in general changes with posttraumatic growth. People report being more able to live each day to its fullest. They appreciate little things along the way, instead of feeling overwhelmed by the bigger picture. They feel more able to experience the here and now, and are less likely to sit around and stew over the past or future. Some say they are no longer so afraid of their own mortality. In general, they reassess what is really important in life, and in doing so reap greater rewards.

Most important to the cogjam predicament, posttraumatic growth promotes positive relationship changes, regardless of whether healing particular relationships is an ultimate goal. People who experience posttraumatic growth often say they no longer take friends and family for granted. Difficult times have a way of revealing who our real friends are. People realize how important relationships are to them, and feel closer to loved ones. Going through the unimaginable together creates deeper bonding. Some report feeling more comfortable with intimacy in general than they had been before the traumatic experience.

Improved capacity for giving and receiving social support calms the collective acting out of our gut brains, and helps heal divisive community. Yes, cogjam brings us widespread stress and even trauma. But by doing so it also sets in motion the potential for valuable lessons—here, for the taking. We need to adopt sufficient self-compassion to let us take advantage of them.

CHAPTER 9

......

Self-Compassion

ONCE IN ELEMENTARY school I was sitting in the gym amidst a large gathering of chattering girls. We quieted as our group leader gave instructions for the next activity. She told us to pair off. Girls quickly clasped hands with nearby friends, myself included.

But there were an uneven number of participants. One girl was left sitting on her own. The leader said the activity would still work out if one of the pairings had three girls, and asked for volunteers to take her in.

At first nobody moved, or spoke. I do not recall the actual thoughts entering my mind before making my next move. However I do remember my feelings.

The girl without a partner looked so down and dejected. Her body literally sagged as seconds quietly ticked by. Something about it hit me like a gut punch.

I scooted up to where she sat and wrapped my arms around her. Our twosome became a threesome. It felt like the right thing to do, or what was needed to "be nice." That's all the more I thought of it at the time.

Looking back, I recognize this incident as an act of early compassion. I was able to empathize with the girl's plight, and sought to comfort her. I related to how she must have felt. In my young life I'd had my own share of being left out, such as being last chosen for playground teams, or unable to participate due to lack of a bicycle or other key equipment.

I'm certainly not alone in such early experiences. All but the most extraordinarily fortunate have gone through similar childhood trials and tribulations. But on this particular occasion, I happened to be first in the room to both note the unfolding scenario and be physically near enough to act on it.

Take a moment and consult your own child selves. What is your first memory of acting with compassion? It could be something similar to this incident, when you included someone who had been left out. Or perhaps you saw a person going without, and shared something you would rather have kept for yourself. It could even be a kind word or gesture offered to someone who looked hurt or feeling down.

Compassion comes built in. As mentioned in Chapter Seven, compassion is already observable among toddlers. And even those living with challenging mental health conditions are seen to demonstrate compassion toward others.

Self-compassion, on the other hand, is a more complicated story. Moving beyond cogjam does require a certain amount of self-compassion. A good deal of the turmoil stems from how hard we sometimes get on ourselves. Unfortunately, Western culture has its ways of unwittingly training out compassion for the self.

Here's an example of how it occasionally shows up in my own life.

The road to psychologist credentials is a steep one, and very competitive. That early obsessive drive to get grades acceptable for university entrance persisted into my college years, since getting into graduate school was even more demanding. The competition didn't end there. After the doctoral degree came the national licensing exam. Passing it required months of independent study. The year I earned my license, only the top forty percent of test takers in our state passed. But I'd made it, by golly. Victory, at last.

However it came with a price. Making it in highly competitive fields can turn us into tough taskmasters. Self-criticism and demanding nothing less than getting to the top can be effective motivators for lofty goals. However they also take their toll. Self-esteem suffers collateral damage. For if we don't make it to the top or otherwise fail to reach our goals, we are tempted to judge ourselves as substandard. We question whether we are "good enough."

Much of this muddle is specific to Western culture, especially the self-esteem concept. Our herd tendencies lead us to judge both ourselves, and each other. It's part of the social orientation plan. We assess who measures up to acceptable standards, including ourselves, and how to fit in accordingly. After all, we do need to fit in with the herd in certain ways to get along in life.

The gut brain respects this survival angle of measuring up to herd expectations. If what we're doing doesn't feel like it too respects this need, it sounds the alarm. It seeks an offending object or entity to attack, in this case our own self-esteem. As the gut brain snaps the whip the willful brain cowers, seeks coping, and tries to figure out how to do better.

Self-criticism and self-compassion are inherently at odds with one another, which perhaps explains why this chapter was one of the hardest for me to put into words. I suspect it has something to do with the book publishing world being as gruelingly competitive as that of academic achievement, if not more so. I get plenty of opportunity to note that my old taskmaster hasn't hung up the whip.

Old habits do die hard, so it seems. But I also found that hiding out for a spell in this particular chapter was especially soothing. Perhaps you will discover the same.

DEFINITION

Self-compassion means offering ourselves the same caring and concern that naturally emerges when we see others suffer. Each of us is in the best position to know when we could use a little compassion. Given the personal failures, inadequacies, and unfortunate happenstances that color our lives, there's no shortage of opportunity to practice self-compassion.

It's not a form of self-pity, or judging ourselves to be weak or substandard. It's about acceptance of the human condition. It's also about willingness to self-accept, to truly be one of the herd, in spite of built-in kinks and quirks.

Kristen Neff proposes that self-compassion is made up of three facets: self-kindness, common humanity, and mindfulness.[46] All of these must be drawn in when practicing self-compassion.

- Self-kindness is the ability to be warm, gentle, and understanding toward yourself when encountering pain or personal shortcomings, rather than ignoring them or becoming self-critical.

- Common humanity acknowledges that personal failure and other forms of human suffering simply show that you belong to the human race. We're all in the same boat. Common humanity is our joint interconnectedness in the experience of being alive and all it entails—the good, the bad, and the cogjammed.

- Mindfulness is holding here and now experience in balanced awareness, rather than stuffing bad feelings or blowing them out of proportion. We open up to thoughts and feelings surrounding inner pain with acceptance, which can then be worked through. Mindfulness recognizes that momentary thoughts or feelings are not "who we are." Thoughts and feelings are only passing experiences, eventually replaced by others, no matter who

46 Neff, K. (2011). *Self-compassion: The proven power of being kind to yourself.* NY: HarperCollins.

you are. Such a perspective helps keep the gut brain from picking a fight with self-esteem when things go south.

For those to whom these are completely new concepts, these may sound like a pretty tall order. They may even bring to mind terms like "navel gazing," "kumbaya moments," or other tongue-in-cheek phrases.

If this describes where you sit, hang in there. You see, self-compassion is about finding and comforting an inner self that's been waiting there for your attention all along. That inner self will appreciate your efforts, no matter how novel doing such a thing may be. It could be that actually experiencing self-compassion and its benefits will do more to advance your understanding of what it is and why it is important than any pathway I recommend for your journey.

WHY IS SELF-COMPASSION SO IMPORTANT?

We all know people who rant and rave when frustrated, especially in these cogjammed times. They may even turn their anger and criticisms our direction, if we look like convenient targets. Left to their own devices, our gut brains go on high alert during such attacks. Therefore for the logical brain to more easily step in, gut-brain reactions need a bit of derailing.

Compassion is excellent for this purpose. Feeling furious or defensive does not coexist well with feelings of empathy and compassion. One or the other will have to give. We get a choice over which we will let hold center stage.[47]

Other-compassion and self-compassion are intertwined, just as self-criticism and other-criticism are close traveling companions. Except, we're typically harder on ourselves than we are on others. This is useful to remember while suffering through others' unreasonable outbursts. Such individuals likely feel even worse than you, as objects of their own self-directed anger.

Having been aware of this for many years, it is now one of my first thoughts when sitting through others' rants. My gut brain grumbles mightily. But at the same time, I hear my logical brain say something like "Yes, this is horrid treatment they're dishing out. But just imagine how much harder they are on themselves. What it must be like to live in that head . . ." Keeping in mind their likely inner status always pulls up some degree of compassion, no matter how offensive the ranting. A future chapter describes at length how we can take such compassion and run with it when seeking solutions for cogjammed relationships.

Likewise, self-compassion is a balm for our own cogjam underpinnings. We need to find ways to tell our inner lizards "there, there, now" when they feel

---

47   Wolpe, J. (1968). Psychotherapy by reciprocal inhibition. Conditional Reflex: *A Pavlovian Journal of Research and Therapy*, 3, 234-240.

trapped or otherwise pressured to fight, freeze, or flee. A future chapter delves further into mining the logical brain, as well.

For now, here's the key takeaway: given that compassion toward self and toward others is so utterly interconnected, getting a handle on both is sound strategy for overturning influences of cogjam.

BENEFITS OF SELF-COMPASSION

In addition to potential for combating cogjam, research in general has piled up in favor of self-compassion practices. Self-compassion is related to many corners of wellbeing in our lives.[48]

Attitude/worldview. Those who are self-compassionate are generally happier and more optimistic than those who do not practice self-compassion. They are more satisfied with their lives, and grateful for what they have. They have less difficulty taking initiative when it is called for. They can risk being curious, and are more willing to give in to curiosity and explore the unexplored. They experience greater wisdom, personal competence, and self-determination, and are better able to keep things in perspective. They are less self-critical, which contributes to less fear of failure and lower likelihood of procrastination. In general, they tend to function better in their day-to-day lives than do those who are not self-compassionate.

Interpersonal life. The intertwining of self-compassion and compassion for others walks hand in hand with the benefits self-compassion brings to relationships. Those who are self-compassionate feel more connected with their fellow human beings. They are more agreeable and less opinionated, and willing to consider alternative points of view. They are conscientious about fulfilling their responsibilities, and take responsibility for problems caused by their own actions. In relationships with significant others, they report greater levels of satisfaction and attachment security than those who are low in self-compassion. They are more likely to apologize and strive to repair relationships their behavior may have damaged, and are more likely to forgive when others err.

Emotional wellbeing. Those who are self-compassionate experience more positive feelings. Since they have the ability to self-soothe, their emotional resilience is stronger. They are more willing to face unpleasant thoughts and feelings, rather than suppress or ignore them, allowing them to cope better with adversity than those who are not self-compassionate. They are less susceptible to depression, anxiety, stress, and ruminating behaviors. They are also less likely to develop traits and behaviors akin to psychopathology, such as unstable sense of self-worth, distorted self-perception, narcissism, directing

48   Neff, K. D. & Germer, C. (2017). Self-Compassion and Psychological Wellbeing. In J. Doty (Ed.) *Oxford Handbook of Compassion Science*, Chapter 27. Oxford University Press.

anger or violence toward whoever appears to threaten their egos, or making unrealistic comparisons of themselves to others.

Physical health. Self-compassion promotes better self-care. Those who are self-compassionate are more likely to experience body appreciation rather than body shame, which encourages following through on health needs. Following trauma, they are less likely to experience PTSD symptoms. They have been found to better cope with chronic pain and serious conditions such as HIV, spina bifida, and breast cancer. Self-compassion can serve as an asset for overcoming substance abuse. Important to our purposes, it has a positive impact on physiological response to stress, most notably lower levels of that dastardly cortisol. Perhaps less cortisol is why those who practice self-compassion tend to have more effective immune systems.

All of the benefits described above are certainly desirable. And it's easy to pick out the ones especially useful to the mission of reducing cogjam:

- Lower levels of cortisol, resulting in less handicapping of the logical brain
- Lower stress levels, and improved ability to cope
- Greater connectedness and caring toward fellow human beings
- Less critical and angry behavior
- Less defensiveness, and greater tolerance for diversity of perspective

WHY THE RESISTANCE?

Within mainstream Western cultural attitudes, self-compassion tends to get banished to the corner like some misunderstood stepchild. It is often confused with self-centeredness, self-indulgence, self-coddling, or approval of errant behavior. Actually, it is none of these.

Admitting need for comfort also violates the belief that strength requires invulnerability. Therefore, we shouldn't admit to having hurts that require compassion. Likewise, we overvalue the importance of personal independence and self-sufficiency. This gets in the way of noting the occasional need for compassion from others or the self.

The gut brain certainly prefers a self-perception of strength over one of weakness. Take for example my own overzealous taskmaster, who keeps stepping in and violating the intended spirit of this chapter. It prefers to meet goals by cracking the whip as I write, rather than providing encouragement or support.

It's not that having an achievement orientation is in itself maladaptive. The problem is how easily the achievement orientation can go overboard. It leaves us awash in this unspoken inner message that we must criticize and be hard on ourselves if we are to meet important goals.

Then there's the self-esteem hype we've gone along with for the last few decades. Research has indeed shown us benefits of good self-esteem. Many of them are similar to those found with self-compassion. That probably has a lot to do with why use of a self-esteem yardstick went unchallenged for so many years.

But eventually research clarified that adopting a self-esteem mindset brings along for the ride a number of nasty side effects. These include perfectionism, becoming overcritical, inaccurate self-perceptions, and conditions of psychopathology that are more akin to problems found among those low in self-compassion.

These side effects develop because the self-esteem concept is a system of self- and other-judgment. It places a contingency on self-worth: if we don't measure up to the perceived standard, we lose faith in our self-worth. We tell ourselves we shouldn't have good self-esteem if we don't succeed.

A self-compassion mindset, on the other hand, is judgment-free. All people are valued and cared about, simply because they are human beings. All are deserving of compassion, regardless of whether they succeed in a particular effort.

So if we don't try to measure up to a standard, how do we succeed at anything?

Setting aside the self-esteem mindset does not mean no longer trying to meet goals or do our best. What moves in to take its place is a deeper and more personal level of motivation: passion-fueled striving. We go after important goals because we care about them, rather than out of fearing what our gut brains or others will do to us if we fail.

Our personal goals are often intertwined with our passions. We fail to notice this when focused on dodging the whip, just as a child may lose inner motivation to behave when focused on fear of corporal punishment. Letting go of the self-esteem mindset better frees us to set and achieve attainable goals—ones that actually matter to us, rather than go after the latest trend or be satisfied only with perfection in everything. Likewise, we do not judge ourselves poorly if a goal proves too lofty. Instead we comfort our disappointments and encourage ourselves to move on toward the next effort.

From a research perspective, whether those who are highly other-compassionate are also highly self-compassionate is not clear-cut. What I'm about to suggest seems counterintuitive. All the same, I can't help but wonder if those who practice very high levels of compassion toward others are also in some way handicapped in their ability to practice self-compassion.

Back on the disaster trail I noticed that disaster workers were less likely than others to accept disaster assistance for themselves, even when they clearly needed it. In fact, the suffering of other survivors was often their excuse for neglecting their own wellbeing. They kept putting others' needs first, even when doing so became detrimental to providing services.

Likewise, there's that reputation physicians and other medical professionals have for being horrible patients. For some reason many are not comfortable with finding themselves on the receiving end of what they so caringly give to others. In Western culture compassion for others is both viewed as desirable, and valued for its contribution to a functioning society. Self-compassion, for various reasons, has not been so readily included in that bargain.

Of course, the evidence I just presented about those who demonstrate exceptionally high levels of compassion is entirely anecdotal, rather than based on scientific inquiry. But it does support the wisdom of approaching all things in moderation. We succeed by seeking a balance, developing compassion for both ourselves and others. Anything taken to the extreme can turn into something absurd, including adopting a perfectionistic stance toward compassion. Everybody benefits from compassion, and none deserves to be deprived—including ourselves.

Any new task goes better when broken down into its component parts. The same goes for self-compassion. The following describes how its main elements—self-kindness, common humanity, and mindfulness—each contribute to experiencing self-compassion.

THE PRACTICE OF SELF-KINDNESS

Self-kindness may be difficult for those whose daily lives are consumed by heavy-duty acts of kindness toward others, such as parenting, caregiving, emergency work, and providing health services. Feelings and expression of kindness become more wired in as something to do for someone else. Self-kindness can get lost in the shuffle.

What does being kind to ourselves look like? The easiest way to imagine it is considering ways in which we are kind to those we care about.

Suppose a close friend of yours hits a rough patch. He had a job interview. Even while it was ongoing he recognized he was royally botching it. He has just heard he will not be getting the job. He'd so had his heart set on that position. And now he'd gone and blown it.

For each of the following pairs of approaches, which option would you choose for responding to your hurting friend?

- Option 1: You become supportive and sympathetic toward how he is feeling.

  Option 2: You point out exactly how badly he messed up, so he's sure not to miss something.

- Option 1: You remind him that everybody makes mistakes and that nobody's perfect.

  Option 2: You remind him of other times he's screwed up that exact same way.

- Option 1: You show continued unconditional acceptance of your friend, in spite of it all.

  Option 2: You laugh at or chastise him for having been such a loser.

- Option 1: You encourage him to continue following after his passion and look for a similar job.

  Option 2: You tell him that given his track record, he may as well forget about ever getting such a position, and to look for something less challenging.

- Option 1: You let him know you're truly sorry it didn't work out.

  Option 2: You tell him what he should have done, if only he'd had his head on straight.

The Option 2 approaches are almost laughable, right? That's because most people are too thoughtful to even consider subjecting someone they care about to such grotesque insensitivity. Yet the second options are what we so often do to ourselves when we feel hurt or are coping with a personal failure. We judge ourselves harshly, at times even disparagingly, all the while stuffing or ignoring the pain that's eating us alive.

Self-kindness means treating ourselves exactly as we would treat a treasured friend. We comfort and soothe, provide encouragement, and express unconditional acceptance. You don't need to be feeling kindly toward yourself as you do it. It's about how the hurting self within you feels when offered words of kindness. Self-kindness is a behavioral choice, not a feeling.

Think about how you might comfort a child who is upset or hurt. Self-kindness stems from that same natural tendency to nurture. We already use it in other contexts. It simply needs to be redirected inward, rather than outward.

Consult your past child selves. What did they like to hear when hurting or frustrated? Better yet, are there old hurts floating around in there that never got comforted?

As I draft this, an example of my own comes to mind. When I was about ten our teacher took us out onto the playground to show us how football is played—girls included, a rather avant-garde move for the early sixties. Most of us girls were clueless about the game.

She positioned us to start, then provided ongoing instruction as the game proceeded. As you might well imagine, with over twenty kids out there and many never having played or even followed football, the game was mostly a confused free-for-all. Being the smallest person in the class, I found it especially intimidating. Nevertheless at one point the ball ended up in my hands, with team members hurrying me along—in the wrong direction. The teacher stopped play and repeated certain instructions, including the rule that a two-handed touch was required to end a play.

I was standing toward the back, still holding the ball. A member of the opposing team swiftly turned toward me and obediently delivered her version of a two-handed touch, which was actually a double stiff-arm jab to the shoulders. I landed on my tailbone in a most undignified manner. Fortunately I was not physically injured, though definitely a bit sore.

But the greater injury was to my feelings. How could someone sucker punch me that way? And get away with it, without any consequences. Then, she and everybody else were too preoccupied with the teacher's latest round of instructions to help me up. Nobody seemed to care about what had just happened to me. Not even the teacher seemed to have noticed my plight. And here I'd been trying so hard to do what was expected of me, in spite of my challenged size.

That afternoon I walked home with a neighborhood friend who was football savvy. I started to tell her about my experience, hoping to gain some form of sympathy. But she immediately stopped me. She said she already knew all about it. Her class had been watching us out the window. She barely contained her laughter as she shared a play by play of how entertaining the lesson had been for the spectators.

I was crushed. In retrospect, yes—watching us neophytes scramble around with a football had to have been hilarious. And my friend, in her innocence, was actually trying to cheer me up by sharing what had made it fun for her and her classmates. But that was definitely not what I needed at that moment.

As I look back, a few twangs of resentment continue to rattle around. Perhaps not so surprising, since after my friend's reaction I was loath to seek sympathy from anyone else over the incident. Instead I swallowed my feelings, buried the memory, and moved on. Until it peeked out just now, popping into the present within this developing context.

I apply self-kindness by revisiting that hurt in the here and now. What would have soothed my injured ego, way back when?

I consult my ten-year-old self. "What would comfort you? What would you like to hear somebody say?" Her answers:

"Are you okay? I'm glad you didn't get banged up."

"That wasn't very nice. She shouldn't have done that."

"I'm sorry your feelings got hurt."

"You have every right to be upset. I'd be upset, too, if that happened to me."

"Hooray for you, for trying so hard in spite of how intimidating that was."

"There, there, now. Have a good cry. You deserve it."

And it works. I feel moved as I offer my ten-year-old self these nuggets of self-kindness. I don't go along with the good cry idea, but the other answers do soothe. Those twangs of resentment over something that happened a half-century ago no longer seem so near.

So much like how I put my writing taskmaster in its place, when it starts cracking the whip. Rejection letters, writer's block, toxic reviews, word-processing program challenges, and the like are part and parcel of a writer's life. But rather than letting frustrations get me down on myself, I offer self-kindness:

"Yes, this is frustrating."

"You try so hard. Good for you."

"You've gotten a lot of things published. There's no need to be so self-critical."

"Your drive to complete this project shows your passion, that this matters to you."

"Remember to take care of yourself, too."

"Every day is a new day."

"You *are* a writer, because you write every day. Don't cave to suggestions of otherwise."

Note that I don't tell myself I should be satisfied with failed efforts, that achievement doesn't matter, or that I should stop trying to follow my passions toward challenging goals. Nor do I criticize myself for being self-critical. Instead, I comfort and soothe my bruised ego and go on. I don't need self-criticism to find motivation. I stay on task because I'm doing something I care about. My taskmaster gives up and returns to its rabbit hole. Healing wins.

COMMON HUMANITY

We all drift along in this same boat. We're all flawed, make mistakes, have our share of personal quirks—and at times, we all suffer for it. We lose sight of this when we get wrapped up in comparing ourselves to others and assessing status in the herd. We see our shortcomings as evidence of not being "normal," that somehow human suffering is an abnormality experienced by ourselves alone.

In truth suffering, personal challenges, learning, and growing are all part of the normal human experience. They bring us closer together, if we let them. You've probably seen interviews with disaster survivors who've lost almost everything, yet are coping admirably. In part this is driven by their sense of shared humanity. They readily point out to reporters how others have it worse. Or, that they are grateful just to be alive, which may not be the case for others' status. They are aware of the greater picture. They are in touch with common humanity, even while still living in dire straits.

In the past I've joked that the three topics mental health professionals should never bring up with colleagues in polite company are CISD, EMDR, and the Great Pumpkin. To further the cause of illustrating the value of common humanity, I am about to violate this long-standing tongue-in-cheek edict.

Critical incident stress debriefing (CISD) started out as after-incident gatherings firefighters held for working through emotions after especially difficult responses. It seemed to work for them, as well as for certain other emergency response teams. Heavy-duty promotion of the practice lead to its use with almost any collection of traumatized individuals. Satisfaction surveys taken by participants afterwards were spectacularly positive. A success story, right?

Not exactly. Mental health professionals stepped in for a closer look. Outcome studies were performed to control for placebo, confirmation bias, and the like. The results: they typically found CISD to have either no benefit for preventing lingering trauma symptoms, or to produce even more such symptoms, in spite of participants stating they liked the actual experience.[49] The worsening symptoms may well be because forcing the timing, rather than waiting until the person's resilience is ready to face trauma, throws off the natural healing process.

But what about all those satisfaction surveys? Most likely it was not the CISD protocol itself that made the experience feel good. It was probably due to the social support such groups provide, and the key role social support plays in recovering from difficult experiences.

Such healing stems in part from common humanity. This is why support groups arranged for so many different issues prove successful. They let us see that we are not as alone and isolated as difficulties may leave us feeling. We're all on the same Spaceship Earth, facing similar perils. But we're also all finding our way past them, in part by joining the trek of common humanity.

The value we so often place on individuality and independence can get in the way of enjoying the rewards of common humanity. We may assume we exist only as ourselves, alone. This construct works for some contexts, such as establishing responsibilities for specific roles we fill. But on a deeper level, are we really so separate? How much of who we are is more the product of a long history of genetic and environmental influences, chance encounters and expe-

49   Jacobs, J., Horne-Moyer, H. L., & Jones, R. (2004). The effectiveness of critical incident stress debriefing with primary and secondary trauma victims. *International Journal of Emergency Mental Health*, 6, 5-14.

riences, and the like—eternally-evolving actualities we get little if any control over?

Self-acceptance and understanding blossom when we recognize and respect how we fit in with common humanity. None of us is perfect, or ever will be. Our imperfections merely qualify us as members of the human race.

MINDFULNESS

Simply stated, mindfulness is setting aside the past and future in favor of experiencing the here and now. It's about being open and receptive to the present moment. Mindfulness notes the thoughts or feelings entering awareness without judging, avoiding, or otherwise processing them.

"This mindfulness business is all new to me," many say. "How do I even know if I've achieved it?"

Donald Altman put together quite a list of ways to describe a mindful state.[50] Perhaps you can relate to a few of these (Reprinted with permission from *The Mindfulness Toolbox* by Donald Altman):

- Opening to the moment
- Noticing the truth of change
- An open-hearted acceptance of this moment
- Living in the *what-is* as opposed to the *what-if*
- Getting freed from habit and reactivity
- Acceptance and letting-go
- Focusing on the moment
- Changing the history channel
- Loving awareness
- Tuning-in
- Moment-to-moment awareness of the breath
- Stop, look, and listen
- Non-dual awareness
- Unplugging
- Finding the center
- Prayerfulness
- Leaving the busy mind by dropping into the body
- Awareness that doesn't take sides
- Inner hospitality

50 Altman, D. (2014). *The mindfulness toolbox: 50 practical tips, tools & handouts for anxiety, depression, stress, and pain.* Eau Claire, WI: PESI Publishing & Media, pp. 3-4.

- Cultivating a neutral, detached awareness

Mindfulness is a key element of self-compassion. We must first acknowledge and be willing to face our pain to be in a place to recognize when we would benefit from that caring touch. Since our brains are organized to avoid pain, we often choose to ignore it. Likewise the "keep a stiff upper lip" mindset can have us burying hurts, especially if it fits in with herd expectations. Also complicating the issue are those times we really do need to ignore pain in order to address an immediate crisis.

But leaving inner pain ignored indefinitely is associated with a host of physical and mental ills. Healing past hurts requires bringing in sufficient mindfulness to understand our reactions, and move past them. Facing lingering symptoms of past trauma can be part of how we achieve posttraumatic growth.

You may have already experienced mindfulness, but did not realize that was what it was. Sometimes it steps in on its own, such as when we're taking a quiet walk through the woods, listening to waves crash against the seashore, enjoying the sensations of soaking in a hot tub of water, or watching the first snowflakes of winter float down and blanket all. The majesty and dignity of the natural world does have its way of directing our attention to the greater picture of existence. Mindfulness can also find us when we're lost in meaningful conversation, or have had a true meeting of the minds with a fellow human being. Prayer and other moments of faith can bring on a state of mindfulness.

Mindful awareness came so easily when we were infants and young children. That ability is still there. But as adults, beyond those serendipitous moments, achieving mindfulness takes some degree of active effort. After all, over our entire lives our logical brains have been pointing us away from it in order to better zero in on thoughts.

The next chapter looks in greater depth at bringing about mindfulness and self-compassion, as well as other techniques that can help heal the inner fallout of cogjam.

CHAPTER 10

......

Soothing the Inner Lizard

NOW'S THE TIME to roll up our sleeves and get serious. What exactly will we do to start whittling away at symptoms of cogjam?

Given that the stress response is able to step in at any moment and overwhelm other mental efforts, our first task is building personal strategy for reassuring an alarmed gut brain. No matter how convinced we are that we need to change course, the rest of the world will only change on its own time schedule. Socio-political unpleasantness will continue on its merry way, no matter what we do with our own processing of it. This, our gut brains cannot ignore. So we need solid strategy for how to survive the long haul.

How do we calm the fears, anxieties, anger, frustrations, and other disconcerting feelings stirred by cogjam? What do we have to offer our inner lizards that might convince them they're safer than they say they are, and that they have our permission to remain basking on their sun-warmed rocks? The answer is a little different for everybody. Here's how it started out for me.

I spent most of my adult life "taking off like a house afire," as my grandmother used to call it. Like most mothers, my dashing around arose from the need to multitask. During early adulthood I juggled caring for multiple children and household responsibilities with volunteer work and finishing graduate school, then with building a private practice, teaching, and other professional activities. By middle adulthood my life had morphed into chasing off onto disaster assignments, then getting myself home quickly enough to catch up on writing projects. I accomplished most everything I did by rapidly moving from one task to the next.

Then along came Bandit, a small English setter. Bandit could have served as poster child for gratuitous anxiety. Throughout his thirteen years in our home he was ever on the lookout for impending doom. No matter how minor a perceived threat, we could count on his whining and yelping to let us know he was sure he was about to die. And, where the best hiding places were. Late in his canine years, we learned that a brain tumor likely played a role in his inability to let down his guard.

As so often happens in a world of silver linings, Bandit's unfortunate condition played a key role in the maturation of my mindfulness practice. Whenever Bandit noticed others' quick movements, he interpreted them as evidence of dire threat looming ahead. Therefore he, too, would get up and begin dashing around. And for some reason, he believed the best course of action was to throw himself into the moving person's legs.

After numerous mishaps I figured out that I could not jump up from my computer and dart off to check the pot roast or answer the door without also tripping over a panicky spotted dog. In self-defense, I learned to slow down when relocating myself from task to task.

It was difficult at first. Beyond the ongoing need to multitask, we live in a fast-paced society. Everybody rushes around, for a variety of reasons. I'd become accustomed to doing so as well, supposedly to keep up. It was an entrenched habit. Forcing my body to move slowly between points A and B felt like being dumped in a foreign country. How was I to occupy my mind during such slow passage?

Valuable lessons arose nonetheless. Strangely, I found that tasks got done just as efficiently with my body moving more slowly. The greater lesson, however, was what bubbled up from within. My longest-standing and perhaps only formal "slow the show" hardwiring already on tap was practicing mindfulness. It stepped right in to fill the void.

Simply physically slowing down brought me more into the present. I came to realize that hurrying kept me future-focused—always mentally preparing for what I was about to do next, rather than truly experiencing life as it happened. Those brief interludes when I did no more than move at a snail's pace brought the rewards of awareness in the here and now: the quiet music playing next door, the beautiful sunny view out the window, the softness of the carpet beneath my feet, sounds of children carelessly cavorting out in the neighborhood, or even my good fortune in being able to pursue the work I love.

I studied writings of numerous meditation masters over the years, and practiced many of their teachings. But it was living with a small spotted dog that ultimately brought mindfulness into day-to-day existence, rather than restricted to whenever I had time to meditate. Bandit forced me to *slow down*. That was when I began truly noticing everything I was missing.

Perhaps this means I also owe him for setting the stage to sort out the cogjam effect. For this is where my cogjam journey first got rolling: being mindful of what I and those around me were *experiencing* regarding everything happening at that moment. I was open to recognizing the pain and trauma lying beneath the divisive behavior and faulty reasoning. Rather than getting wrapped up in my own fears, defensiveness, and opinions, I became better able to notice and experience the here and now realities of what cogjam places before my eyes.

In summary, mindfulness created an opening in my crowded inner agenda, and gave my logical brain wider berth to step in and explore possibilities. This is how mindfulness can serve anybody as a platform upon which to build a strategy for reworking cogjam.

NUTS AND BOLTS OF MINDFULNESS

Modern society is fast-paced, not only in activity level but also in thought lives. The gut brain is perfectly happy to reinforce such a habit. The sooner we recognize threat, the more quickly we can guard against physical harm, personal failures, potential conflicts, and other mishaps. However for healthy emotional balance we can't ignore the slower, re-stabilizing influences of simply letting go and experiencing the lessons of the present. Mindfulness is a way of hitting the reset button, and getting us back to taking in what slips by unnoticed during a rush.

Mindfulness is associated with a long list of mental health benefits. Not surprisingly, many of them are similar to the ones found with self-compassion:[51]

- Decreases in emotional reactivity
- Greater ability to regulate emotions, such as tuning out upset and focusing on solutions
- Less rumination
- Fewer negative feelings
- Less anxiety and depression
- Improvements to memory and attention
- Greater cognitive flexibility

51   Davis, D. M & Hayes, J. A. (2011). What are the benefits of mindfulness? A practice review of psychotherapy-related research. *Psychotherapy*, 48, 198-208.

Interpersonal relationships benefit as well, as evidenced by:

- Higher relationship satisfaction
- Less conflict
- Greater empathy
- Less overreacting during conflict
- More effective communication of emotions
- Better social awareness

PTSD symptoms—arguably the most debilitating of ailments to rear their stubborn heads following trauma—can be lessened with mindfulness practices, even for those who've been through military combat.[52] If mindfulness can remedy the trauma of war scenarios, imagine how much more it might have to offer for those of us coping with cogjam stress.

However for many, re-finding what was so easy for the taking as infants may take a bit of rewiring. So first, let's nail down a few of the concrete biological underpinnings of what we're about to tinker with.

In review: When the polyvagal system notes threat it activates stress chemistry and behavior, working both bottom up and top down. Since neurons that fire together wire together, reactions we practice while aroused are reinforced at the neurological level. Those reactions are therefore more likely to be repeated. Top-down activity drives the logical brain's stepping in and exerting its will in ways that also can have a lasting effect. So as our brains change, so do our minds; and as our minds change, so do our brains. By actively promoting mindfulness, we can redirect frenzied wiring so that we slow down and more adaptively focus during stress.

An intriguing line of research explores how the body physically benefits from practicing mindfulness. As already mentioned, immune system functioning appears to improve and inflammation may lessen. Furthermore, mindfulness is associated with a longer lifespan. Such findings are supported by recent discoveries of what's happening within individual cells.[53]

Here's how it works.

Most cells of the human body have a nucleus. That's where the chromosomes holding our genes are located. Telomeres are caps located on the ends of strands of chromosomes. Their job is to repair damaged cells and replace those that need replacing. The longer a telomere is, the better it does its job.

Stress has a relationship with telomere length. While a mindfulness orientation is associated with having longer telomeres, chronic stress and threat

---

52   Seppala, E. M., Nitschke, J. B., Tudorascu, D. L., Hayes, A., Goldstein, M. R., Ngyuen, DTH, Perlman, D., & Davidson, R. J. (2014). Breathing-based meditation dereases posttraumatic stress disorder symptoms in U.S. military veterans: A randomized controlled longitudinal study. *Journal of Traumatic Stress, 27,* 397-405.

53   Epel, E., Daubenmier, J., Moskowitz, J., Folkman, S., & Blackburn, E. (2009). Can meditation slow rate of cellular aging? Cognitive stress, mindfulness, and telomeres. *Annals of the New York Academy of Sciences, 1172,* 34-53.

reactivity are associated with shorter telomeres. Many unwanted physical conditions are also more common among those with shorter telomeres, such as cardiovascular disease, diabetes, vascular dementia, arthritis, and chronic pain. That even basic longevity may be toyed with by never-ending cogjam stress is a sobering thought, indeed.

Fortunately, mindfulness has the ability to lessen these effects. It does so by encouraging the release of an enzyme called telomerase. Telomerase helps lengthen and strengthen the telomeres, thus extending the lives of our cells.

And the cell-level story doesn't end there.

A while back I consulted with a Native American colleague about her work on the reservation. She said one of the most pervasive symptoms she came up against was anger. It wasn't necessarily a kind easily traced to specific incidents, but a collective ongoing anger.[54] She described it as an insidious feeling of "no voice," which was in fact the status of Native Americans after Europeans moved in and began calling the shots. She said she'd also seen this anger turn up among those who were only part Native American, or whose families had left behind both the reservation and their cultural heritage generations ago.

How could that be? This brings us to the topic of epigenetics.[55]

We used to figure that genetic traits were pretty much cut and dried—developing or not developing, based on dominance or recessiveness within particular pairs of genes. We now know that telomeres also affect this process. They change gene expression in ways that adapt to environmentally based conditions and experiences. These adjustments aim to support survival during such conditions.

Environmental input like stress affects telomere activity, such that the stress-related gene expressions are passed on. In this manner stress can determine which gene expressions affect the next generation, even while still in the womb. The next generation inherits whatever helped survival in the previous generation's world—until new adaptive adjustments take place.

Therefore intervening in cogjam is not just about us. There are ramifications for the health and wellbeing of future generations as well, no matter what kind of physical world situation we leave behind for them. The good news: we are able to be better stewards of our collective gene pool. We contribute to a better world simply by finding ways to make life a little easier for our inner lizards. Like, taking advantage of mindfulness.

54 Lehrner, A., & Yehuda, R. (2018). Trauma across generations and paths to adaptation and resilience. *Psychological Trauma*, 10, 22-29.
55 Lester, B. M., Tronick, E., Nestler, E., Abel, T., Kosofsky, B., Kuzawa, C. W., Marsit, C. J., Maze, I., Meaney, M. J., Monteggia, L. M., Reul, J. M. H. M., Skuse, D. H., Sweatt, D. J. & Wood, M. A. (2011). Behavioral epigenetics. *Annals of the New York Academy of Sciences*, 1226, 14-33.

PATHWAYS TO MINDFULNESS

Possible pathways to finding mindfulness are endless. Exploring it from the self-compassion angle is a good fit for healing the effects of cogjam, since self-compassion brings added benefits of soothing and encouragement to an era of pervasive hurting. However everybody differs, and so does what works best for any given individual's learning or application style.

Unfortunately a bit of competitive sell job mentality flutters about in some of these fields. If you've looked into different meditation and mindfulness techniques you may have run into claims such as "our system is better researched," a secretive "this movement is exclusive/the most ancient," or sometimes even a cult-like "this technique is better/deeper/the only good one."

So be it. However be assured that such claims can't dictate what's right for you.

Besides, scientific investigation is about establishing probabilities, not absolutes. Some techniques may well show effectiveness for a greater number of research participants in one group than in another. But like all scientific research, this doesn't give us a black and white answer. In the case of comparing meditation techniques, there are typically plenty of people in both groups who show greater benefit than some in the alternate group. The statistical gyrations usually only highlight base rates or averages. Individual differences are typically controlled for, rather than spotlighted to show what is most likely to work best for whom. Only we can figure out what best works for ourselves.

So in addition to the self-compassion approach, this section includes discussion of several other methods for finding and reaping benefit from mindfulness. They all share three important features. They:

1) slow down the pace of thought,
2) create focus other than adrenalin- or oxytocin-fueled pressures, and
3) open a space in our inner experience for new ways of thinking, feeling, and healing to settle in.

In other words, each in their own way, the following mindfulness enhancers help regain influences of logic and heart that may have been overcome by the effects of cogjam. You may want to review this entire chapter before deciding which method you would like to try first. Whatever works for you is the right answer.

In preparation for beginning any of these practices, find a quiet comfortable setting where you can safely and effectively let down your guard. Take a few moments to relax as you can. Beginning with a practice you already use for slowing rushes of thoughts and feelings can be especially valuable. It allows opportunity to scaffold onto existing hardwired learning, which can become an anchor for the new strategy. Remember: "neurons that fire together wire together."

COMPASSIONATE MINDFULNESS

Self-compassion helps overcome cogjam by setting up an inner space of self-caring, which both emotionally comforts and arranges a platform for new learning. Compassionate mindfulness is also useful during bad moments, be they cogjam-related or otherwise, because it can transform those bad moments into moments of self-kindness.

In review, the three core elements of self-compassion are self-kindness, common humanity, and mindfulness.[56] While immersing in your "relax as you can" moment, take the following steps, using whatever comforting words feel right to you.

- *Self-kindness*: Note that you are struggling. Validating your inner experience creates room to step back and evaluate the situation, rather than emotionally react.
- *Common humanity:* Remind yourself that struggles in life are normal. They are a part of being human, of being alive. They only show that you belong with everyone else.
- *Mindfulness:* Offer yourself words of kindness. Pause in that place, and allow yourself to fully experience the consequence of receiving kind words.

It's that simple. The process doesn't judge, criticize, or let the gut brain take over. Instead, the focus is moment-to-moment awareness. You acknowledge any percolating pain or anxiety rather than bury or ignore it, which would only distress the gut brain further. Rather than ruminate or catastrophize over adversity, you reawaken the inner experience of being part of a greater whole. You understand that we all endure and deal with occasional pain, but the amount of suffering is optional. You give yourself a deserved hug or pat on the back for allowing yourself a moment of compassionate mindfulness.

Think of an incident when cogjam got the better of you. Perhaps you felt misunderstood, and were saddened by the distance it created between yourself and another. Or, you lashed out or said something stupid that later you were ashamed of. Or, your impatience with the illogic of an argument has you about ready to burst. Stepping back and reworking such past experiences turns them into valuable teaching moments for the present.

Let's try out the self-compassion strategy with the following example.

A politician, pundit, or other public figure has just said something that you find insensitive, offensive, shortsighted, or just plain outrageous. Here's one

56   Neff, K. (2011). *Self-compassion: The proven power of being kind to yourself.* New York: HarperCollins.

way compassionate mindfulness might be used to calm your gut brain's reactivity:

- *Self-kindness:* "Yes, this is painful. It breaks my heart to see what these comments do to everyone, myself included. It's so hard to deal with all the confusion and conflict they create. I'm struggling."
- *Common humanity:* "Pain during adversity is normal. I hurt because I care, about both myself and the greater whole I am a part of. Others also hurt right now over these comments. The pain shows me I'm a member of the human race, that I belong."
- *Mindfulness:* "May I feel the kindness of these loving reassurances, and appreciate the comfort they offer."

Can you think of how this approach might be used during or after your own cogjam moments? Try writing it out using your own words, and you will have a new tool to pull out that is a good fit. Feel free to revise as needed. In fact, it's that ongoing revising that sums up the concept of posttraumatic growth.

Silently repeating a loving kindness meditation afterwards can further duration of your awareness in the here and now. If preferred, a meditation like the one below can be spoken out loud:

May you be safe.
May you be healthy.
May you be happy.
May you live life with ease.

Note there is no insistence that the politician's comments should not happen. There are no accusations that the person who makes such comments is somehow "bad" or "wrong." There are no tantrums about how unfair it is. Instead, we rewire the unpleasant experience with gentle awareness, reassuring and quieting the gut brain's fears. Doing so helps break up the logjam blocking the flow of productive ideas, ones that might help us better deal with a cogjammed world.

TRADITIONAL MEDITATION PRACTICES

Structured meditation practices had their beginnings around four or five thousand years ago, mainly in China and India. Many different approaches combined concentration, specific movements, and breathing techniques to seek improved overall wellbeing. They were generally grouped together under the single term "qigong" around the 1950's.

Originally, qigong-like practices appear to have been considered exercise regimens. Over the many centuries, it was slowly shanghaied and infused into arenas such as religion, martial arts, and medical healing. Today's many popularized versions of and uses for meditation stem from these early beginnings. Greater mindfulness can result from pretty much any of them, regardless of the specific technique's supplemental goals.[57]

Describing how to perform the many different practices currently available would take us well beyond the scope of this book. In fact, it would require an entire encyclopedia. So instead, I've clustered them based on common features. I provide brief descriptions and/or simple instructions for trying them out. Hopefully this summary gives you a general idea of what's out there, and will help you decide if there's a particular meditation practice that appeals to you— which you can investigate further as you please.

Mindfulness meditation. Though all meditation practices increase awareness of the here and now, mindfulness meditations identify this particular state as the ultimate goal. The practitioner focuses on thoughts, feelings, and other experiences as they pass. The idea is to simply observe them, without analyzing or judging. It requires very little training, and is one of the most popular meditation practices in Western civilization. It's easy, pretty much anybody can do it, it's nonsectarian rather than tied to a particular religion, and resources on the topic abound.

Currently gaining popularity is an eight-week course known as mindfulness-based stress reduction (MSBR).[58] It was developed in the late 1970's to address stress- and pain-related conditions. Its teachings combine mindfulness, yoga, and body awareness in ways that reduce severity of stress-related symptoms. In addition it aims to help practitioners experience greater day-to-day serenity, joy, and nonjudgmental awareness, as well as increase ability to use inner resources for stress management and healing. It is often used in medical settings to promote relaxation, stress reduction, and greater feelings of wellbeing.

Mantra meditations. Those who practice mantra meditations achieve mindfulness by focusing on a collection of sounds or words. By repetitively saying them aloud the practitioner falls into a rhythm, which helps with clearing the mind and letting go of stress. The Buddhist tradition has long used "Om" as a mantra. However other mantras can work out, regardless of whether words have specific religious meanings. The words need only be meaningful or otherwise useful for the individual practitioner.

Transcendental meditation. If you like structure and discipline, are willing to invest time and money, and don't mind a lot of formal training and practice, transcendental meditation might be right for you. It emerged in the 1960's,

57   Gauding, M. (2005). *The meditation bible: The definitive guide to meditations for every purpose.* London: Godsfield.
58   Kabat-Zimm, J. (2013). *Full catastrophe living: Using the wisdom of your body and mind to face stress, pain, and illness,* rev. ed. New York: Bantam Books.

founded by Maharishi Mahesh Yogi.[59] The Beatles and other celebrities of the era popularized its practice, and it remains popular to this day. The focus of this technique is on an individualized mantra, which serves to let the practitioner step back from his or her flow of thoughts and achieve a "unified and open attentional stance."[60] Training aims to establish an ongoing daily regimen of 20-minute sessions, twice a day.

Transcendental meditation began as an offshoot of Hindu beliefs, and for many it remains a faith-based practice. When this is so, the method's primary goal is seeking enlightenment. However transcendental meditation is also taught for secular purposes, and as such is effective for increasing mindfulness. There are many books and online resources describing this method.

Spiritual meditation. If you already practice a certain faith, you are in luck. Most organized religions to some degree incorporate practices such as prayer and/or meditation. Wiring in greater mindfulness is easier if there's already a network in place to hook it up with.

Hinduism and Buddhism are probably most known for incorporating meditation into spiritual seeking. However writings of Judeo-Christian faiths and others also mention meditation as a way of getting closer to God.

Spiritual meditation can be practiced without adopting a particular religious stance. Religion serves as a vessel, a personal receptacle we choose because we sense it best holds the spirituality flowing within us. One size does not fit all. We each decide what best resonates with our spirituality, even if it turns out to be something not thought of as religion-oriented. The critical element is that our spiritual practice connects us to something greater than ourselves, be it defined as God, enlightenment, the Divine, nature, the universe, or the interconnected oneness of common humanity. Following are some simple instructions.

- Begin by sitting in silence.
- If you have one, engage your personal prayer/meditation.
- Focus on the silence and stillness.
- As your mind settles, let it wander to a particular prayer or spiritual question that has meaning for you.
- Simply listen as you concentrate, without judging what comes to mind.

Answers often arise. Some experience answers as coming from the outside, such as a message from God. Others feel like answers come from somewhere deeper within their own being, or from a corner of our joint shared spirituality. Regardless, the emergence of answers suggests that you have established

59   Roth, B. (2018). *Strength in stillness: The power of transcendental meditation.* New York: Simon and Schuster.

60   Dakwar, E., & Levin, F. R. (2009). *The emerging role of meditation in addressing psychiatric illness, with a focus on substance use disorders.* Harvard Review of Psychiatry, 17, 254-267.

greater mindfulness. Sufficient clutter has cleared for additional perspectives to move in.

Movement-oriented meditations. Not all meditations require that the practitioner remain still. Eastern philosophy has spawned many movement-based regimens, some very popular. Eastern methods still with us today seem to have evolved similarly to the way of Western folklore, with benefits of certain practices noted after centuries of successful field trials. As with acupuncture and acupressure, only in recent decades have they been put to the test of scientific rigor.

The following practices are found to offer benefits similar to what can be attained by other techniques for increasing mindfulness.

- Hatha yoga involves holding poses that require varying types and amounts of muscle effort and agility, with mastering body and mind as its goal.
- Contemporary qigong practices go through motions designed to encourage "qi"—life energy—to enter and more freely move throughout the body.
- Certain forms of T'ai chi involve dance-like movements that aim to create harmony between body and mind.
- Movements for Chakra meditations intend to open up "chakras"—spiritual/energy centers in the body—as a start-up to meditation sessions.

These brief descriptions are undeservingly simplistic. But they are additional options in the quest to find the mindfulness method that is right for you. Personally, I like the economy of getting both mindfulness and exercise into my day in one fell swoop.

Drat. There's that multi-tasker. But again, to each his or her own.

MINDFUL MOVEMENT, AS IT HAPPENS

Several years ago my dentist advised me to use an electric toothbrush. I pooh-poohed it at first. When it comes to technology, I'm notoriously old school. I knit with two sticks and a string, and have never considered trying a knitting machine. I was probably the last one in my doctoral program to write a thesis without a computer, and I'm always slow to update software. Even though I enjoy cooking, I have little interest in fancy-pants kitchen accessories like super-deluxe mixers and choppers. So it wasn't until the electric toothbrush became the only answer to my dental problem that I finally caved.

I absolutely despised it. Its high-pitched whine was annoying, all the more so while it was in my mouth. The sensations were just too similar to a dentist's drill. Besides, the vibrating bounced it around and made it difficult to control, which was mildly painful for some of my more sensitive teeth. The vibration also caused a lot of salivating, which meant more frequent need to stop and spit in the sink—or if not moving quickly enough, ending up with a sudden splatter of toothpaste-laced drool dotting the bathroom mirror or the front of my shirt.

"Just do it and get it over with," I would tell myself. "It only takes two minutes. You can handle it." But this mindset only fueled more hurry and annoyance.

One day as I stared at myself in a bespattered mirror I was sufficiently frustrated to step back and think it over. "All right. You're a psychologist. You know plenty of strategies for dealing with the super-annoying. What've you got up your sleeve for this one, Doc?"

And there it was again, my old friend mindfulness.

Instead of fighting the experience, I immersed myself in it. In the place of resenting its annoying features, I inserted thoughts of what the electric toothbrush was doing for my pearly whites—which I deserve to hang onto, the same as everyone else. I reminded myself that what I was doing was an act of love, not torment.

I slowed movement of the instrument and became purposeful, rather than hurried. I imagined each tooth caringly cleansed, my challenged gum line enjoying gentle massage. I focused on other non-irritating sensations, like the polished smoothness of newly cleaned teeth and the toothpaste's minty zing. I noted how my hands held the toothbrush, and how I might turn it this way or that for optimum control and effect.

It worked.

Time now passes more quickly when I brush my teeth. I still don't appreciate the sound, the vibration, and the excess saliva. But I don't mind it as much as I once did.

Furthermore, letting myself drift into mindful tooth brushing brought unexpected bonuses. Over time my more sensitive teeth felt less pained, perhaps in part due to rewired sensory connections. And these days after I brush my teeth, I actually feel more relaxed and less hassled than whatever state I was in beforehand. That's how mindfulness helps in general—in this case, delivering me to a less bothered corner of my mind, as opposed to jumping aboard my primitive brain's tantrum train.

Mindfulness can be built into any form of movement. Following are a couple of more usual examples of cultivating mindfulness during movements that take place in everyday living.

Mindful walking. Moving from point A to point B uses up a healthy slice of our days. Introducing mindfulness into the simple activity of walking therefore easily fits in with daily routine. It has the added benefit of wiring mindfulness to a common activity, so that calm awareness might be more easily accessed in times of need. For those who prefer more diligent practice, mindful walking as a regular 10-minute meditation exercise is an option.

1. Begin in a standing position. Stand straight without stiffening, arms relaxed at your side.

2. Set your bearings: Orient your awareness to the surrounding environment. Adjust your gaze slightly downward, so that you are still aware of what's in front of you but are less distracted by it.

3. Notice various sounds, sights, and smells—sensing, but not judging or labeling them. Note the solidness of your feet against the ground, the temperature, and air movement.

4. Walk at a slower pace. Pay attention to the sensation of your feet lifting and falling, and the changes in your feet as heels, balls, and toes leave then return to the ground. Incorporate these sensations into your overall environmental awareness.

5. Your mind will occasionally wander. This is normal. When it happens, gently and nonjudgingly lead it back to the sensations of leisurely walking, noting each individual footfall.

6. When it's time to stop, remain still for a moment. Consider your state of awareness. Focus on any new feelings as you transition into your next task or activity. The longer you hold onto newly heightened awareness, the more opportunity it will have to wire in.

Mindful eating. Currently our culture crams so many activities into single days that eating is rushed. Or we multitask it—eating while viewing a screen, steering a vehicle, or participating in a power lunch. Since we can't fully focus on two things at once, the experience of eating typically comes out the loser, ignored in favor of whatever other task holds our attention. Since we don't fully process the sensation of eating, our brains don't stop complaining that we need more. We end up either overeating or feeling deprived.

Like mindful walking, mindful eating can be introduced by way of simple adjustments to the usual. For example, as I draft this I am simultaneously chowing down my morning bowl of fruit and cottage cheese (my apologies for the less than optimal role modeling). If I were trying to increase mindfulness by way of my eating practices, I would:

• Sit at the table while eating.

• Get rid of distractions like the laptop, TV, radio, and pileup of task-related materials scattered across the table.

• If a family member joined me, arrange to converse before or when finished eating.

• Adopt a slower eating pace than my usual habit.

- Encourage slower eating by putting down my eating utensil between bites, picking it up again only after swallowing.
- Let my mind wander, settling only on sensations centered on the eating experience: the sight, smell, taste, texture, and temperature of the food; how my body feels as I consume it; the self-kindness represented by the simple act of nourishing my body; the quiet companionship of whoever else is near; the peacefulness of sitting in contented silence; and mere experiencing.
- Consider all the different people who contributed to getting this fruit and cottage cheese to the table, such as farmers, ranchers, pickers, cooks and other processers, packagers, truckers, and grocery store personnel; and appreciate that the final product is an actualization of mutual supportiveness within common humanity.
- When finished, thank myself for the opportunity for mindfulness.

For some, a different meal or snack time works better for trying this experiment. It makes no difference when or where you do it. Regardless, many find they eat less when practicing mindful eating. It gives the body enough time to catch up and tell us we're satisfied.

Mindful eating can also be practiced as a freestanding exercise. Select a small piece of food, like a nut or raisin—which you are about to get to know extremely well. Take your time with the following steps, stretching out the full experience to last at least five minutes:

- Examine the morsel carefully. What does it look like? What shape, colors, or other visual features does it have?
- Close your eyes. How does the piece of food feel as it sits in your palm or between your fingers—smooth or wrinkled, hard or soft, warm or cold?
- Does it have a smell? How would you describe it?
- Take a bite of it, even though the food item is small. Let it sit in your mouth for a moment before chewing, noticing the feel of it, then the taste, focusing on one sensation at a time.
- Chew very slowly, again focusing on individual sensations. What does it feel like between your teeth, and on your tongue? What changes in texture do you notice as you chew? How does it taste? Do your saliva glands respond, or other bodily sensations?
- Slowly swallow the food, and pause to notice the change in sensations. Consider the nourishment it brings to your body.
- Take your second/last bite of the morsel. Repeat the process, remembering to focus on one sensation at a time. When thoughts wander, gently return awareness to a specific eating sensation.
- When finished, take a couple of slow deep breaths and open your eyes.

Note the changes in your awareness of the here and now, and give it a few moments to settle in before starting another task.

TAPPING TECHNIQUES

Energy psychology offers another intriguing path to mindfulness.[61] Tapping techniques "tap" into the same energy system in our bodies as do acupressure and acupuncture (sorry, the pun was just too tempting to resist). Like acupressure and acupuncture, scientifically demonstrating how it works—or even if it works—is not easy. In recent years the mechanism behind these techniques has been hypothetically tied to the primo-vascular system, a network of clear microscopic channels spreading out and over the body's internal organs.[62]

In brief, the practitioner taps on a series of nine meridian points on the body while mentally focusing on a current source of stress. This is believed to release chemistry that sends calming messages to the stressed part of the brain.

Tapping techniques aren't a form of therapy or a cure for mental illness, at least at this stage of the game. Nor is it best to think of them as a cure-all. They are more for using mindful focus to relax, and working through whatever is causing stress at the moment.[63]

BREATHING EXERCISES

Breathing exercises are varied and vast in number. They are the simplest exercises to perform, and easiest to incorporate into day-to-day life. Many meditation practices begin with a brief breathing exercise, so that breath can serve as the focus to which a wandering mind might return. In addition to promoting mindfulness, breathing exercises are an excellent way to reduce stress and anxiety in the moment.

If you've watched infants sleep, you may have noticed that we first accommodate incoming air more with tummies going up and down, and not so much expansion of the chest. As the stresses and strains that come with maturation settle in, our diaphragms habitually tighten. A tight diaphragm alters how we breathe. We end up expanding mainly our chests, compensating for the restriction caused by the stiff belly. This leads to shallower and quicker breathing. It also requires more energy and effort.

61   Feinstein, D., Eden, D., & Craig, G. (2005). *The promise of energy psychology: Revolutionary tools for dramatic personal change.* New York: Penguin Books.

62   Soh, K-S., Kyung, A. K., & Kyu, Y. H. (2013). *50 years of bong-han theory and 10 years of primo vascular system. Evidence-Based Complementary and Alternative Medicine,* Volume 2013 (2013), Article ID 587827, http://dx.doi.org/10.1155/2013/587827

63   Ortner, N. (2013). *The tapping solution: A revolutionary system for stress-free living.* Carlsbad, CA: Hay House, Inc.

Once again, the polyvagal system's top-down mission can step in and be of assistance. We overcome this stress symptom—as well as get closer to mindfulness—by directly and willfully instructing our diaphragms to loosen up. Once relaxed, the diaphragm sends the feedback that all is not so tense as the gut brain had us believing.

The following exercise is called diaphragmatic breathing.[64] It can be performed while lying down, sitting, or standing. If sitting or standing, do so in a straight, upright position rather than slouched.

- Place a hand on your diaphragm.
- Slowly breathe in through your nose for about four counts, pressing your diaphragm against your relaxed hand.
- Breathe out through pursed lips, again about four counts, letting your diaphragm fall and relax.
- Wait a couple of seconds before inhaling again, focusing on the sense of calm moving into your diaphragm.
- Repeat the first four steps.

If you adopt diaphragmatic breathing as a formal exercise, practice it about once a day for five to ten minutes. Once you get it down, you can improve its effectiveness by imagining yourself breathing in calmness and breathing out tension. Some find that placing the other hand on their chest helps them better track where the breath work is taking place.

Whatever you sense, it comes from within, from a higher level of functioning than gut-brain reactions. You are taking control of—or perhaps giving rightful control back to—a vital natural function. You are listening to what your body tells you, shaping your breathing to increase here and now awareness, and bringing benefit to your overall wellbeing. It is opportunity to note inner experience other than chemical by-products of threat or conflict. Many different exercises combine structured breathing with specific physical regimens, such as systematically tensing and relaxing muscles, yoga stances, or qigong movements.

Diaphragmatic breathing is so basic and simple it can be introduced anywhere, any time—such as while having an argument, taking an important test, just before giving a speech, or during any situation where excess anxiety becomes an impediment. It can even be done in secret, like in the middle of an emotionally charged meeting. Few would likely notice.

64   Altman, D. (2011). *One-minute mindfulness: 50 simple ways to find peace, clarity, and new possibilities in a stressed-out world.* Novato, CA: New World Library.

RELAXATION EXERCISES

Many relaxation exercises have turned up over the last half-century, far too many to mention by name. However one deserves special attention.

Herbert Benson developed *The Relaxation Response* around the same time transcendental meditation got rolling.[65] Back then mainstream culture viewed transcendental meditation as fringy, or just plain weird. Terms like "meditation" and "mindfulness" became hopelessly intertwined with it, such that any practice connected with those words often found itself dismissed as flaky or somehow ungodly.

Dr. Benson's choice to use the term "relaxation response" to describe a practice that achieves the benefits of mindfulness was a stroke of genius. Relaxation and mindfulness do intertwine. But he avoided getting mixed up with the stigma by putting the goal of relaxation on center stage, and leaving other mindfulness benefits situated in the wings to enter as they would. At least, that was my take on it.

Everybody can relate to the need to relax. Thus the popularity of relaxation exercises took off. Many adaptations churned to the surface in the wake of the originals, producing similar results.

Typically the practitioner sits quietly with eyes closed, systematically relaxes all muscles, and focuses on natural breathing. With each breath the practitioner mentally rehearses a word—such as "one" or "peace"—which can also be used for getting back in focus when thoughts drift. Sessions usually last 10-20 minutes.

REWIRING FOR HAPPINESS

Perhaps you still find the whole mindfulness thing to be just so much hocus-pocus. If so, having something more concretely defined to hang your hat on might work better. One such focus is aiming to achieve a specific emotional outcome—like happiness.

Rick Hanson developed such a technique, drawn from current understandings of brain science and positive psychology.[66] Dr. Hanson reminds us that thanks to the negativity bias, bad memories are like Velcro, while good memories are like Teflon. We survived natural selection in the wild by always being keenly aware of potential threat. While it did contribute to survival, it also predisposed us to focus more on bad feelings than good.

---

65   Benson, H. (1976). *The relaxation response.* New York: HarperCollins.
66   Hanson, R. (2013). *Hardwiring happiness: The new brain science of contentment, calm, and confidence.* New York: Harmony Books.

However, we can help our neural systems bypass some of this bias with a little self-directed brain change. Experiencing a state of happiness is fueled by certain neurotransmitters:

- Dopamine, helping equip the brain to experience pleasure and reward
- Seratonin, producing a calming effect
- Oxytocin, important to feeling pleasure in social bonding
- Endorphins, lessening pain and stress

Deep states of relaxation, such as those occurring during mindfulness meditation, release these neurotransmitters. Once released, prolonging focus on the good/relaxed feeling reinforces the happiness wiring, which makes it more likely to activate in the future.

The steps to hardwiring happiness use the acronym HEAL:

H–Have a positive experience
E–Enrich it
A–Absorb it, and
L–Link positive and negative material.

Following is a basic description of these steps.

Have a positive experience. Assess where you are right now, what you are aware of. What do you note that produces good feelings? It doesn't matter what it is, only that you feel good when you think about it. And it's not enough to just think about it. You need to actually feel good as you think it, so the neurotransmitters get released. It could be something external, like a picture on the wall that brings fond memories, the sun's warmth, the colorful beauty of a vase of flowers, a favorite song being played on the radio, the yummy smell of cookies baking, or the comfort of the chair in which you sit. It could be something purely internal, like memories of a happy time, thinking about a rewarding relationship with a significant other, gratefulness for being warm and fed, or feeling encouraged by guidance in this book that brings you hope.

Enrich it. Stay with the feeling for at least five to ten seconds. Enjoy it; let it fill your mind. Note any bodily sensations that may go along with thinking about it, such as certain muscles relaxing. Look for ways to ramp up the sensation, such as thinking of specifically what it is that makes you happy, you personally. Once again, the neurons that fire together will wire together.

Absorb it. Imagine and sense these feelings becoming part of who you are, how you experience your existence. It may help to think of it as something precious to place on a mental shelf, there to be had again when it suits you. Or, that it is something you are drinking in, filling you to satisfaction. Encourage the experience to feel as if it is now a part of you.

Link positive and negative material. This step is optional, and is more difficult. But it could prove valuable in the face of cogjam. The idea is to introduce a memory of something negative, and hold onto both the negative feelings and the more positive feelings at the same time. For example, if your positive experience involves closeness to others, introduce something that distances—like how you feel when you read hostile tweets or posts. Let the positive overcome it, comfort it, or set it aside.

The value of the last step is that it wires greater primacy to good feelings, which makes them easier to access the next time your gut brain reacts to hostility. In theory, it could wire in as part of your natural reaction to such exposures, rather than something you must search for. However, if the negative keeps taking over the experience, discard it and go back to experiencing the positive. Some other example might work better for you for practicing the step of linking to the negative.

MUSCLES FOR THE INNER LIZARD: BUILDING RESILIENCE

Perhaps none of these options sounds like something you can relate to. Never fear—there are other ways greater here and now awareness can get a foot in the door.

A less direct strategy is to bolster the effectiveness of our resilience. Better emotional resilience increases ability to cope with any disaster, in addition to dealing with the stress of everyday life. Resilience turns clearing mental debris into an easier task. The American Psychological Association offers several guidelines for strengthening resilience, which are adapted below:[67]

- Nurture your interpersonal life. A strong social support network does much for soothing the bumps and bruises of daily trials and tribulations.

- View crises as challenges, rather than insurmountable problems. You can't stop stressful events from happening. But you can change how you react to them.

- Accept that change is a part of life. Consider the counsel to be found in the prayer of serenity—accepting what you cannot change, acting on what you can change, and exercising wisdom in recognizing the difference between the two.

- Take decisive actions with those personal trials and tribulations you truly can do something about, rather than avoiding them or wishing them away.

---

67   American Psychological Association (2006). *The road to resilience.* Retrieved from http://www.apa.org/helpcenter/road-resilience.aspx.

- Set and move toward realistic goals. Rather than focusing on what can't be done, focus on steps you can take—even very little ones—that bring you closer to your goals.
- After a struggle with any adversity, seek out positives in yourself. What strengths are you now aware of? What post-adversity growth do you see?
- Foster a positive self-view. Adversity feels less overwhelming when you have faith in your ability to handle it.
- Keep adversity in perspective. Rather than blow an unfortunate event out of reasonable proportion, consider the bigger picture and longer-term outlook. This too will pass.
- Be optimistic. Pessimism solves nothing. Optimism encourages solution finding.
- Take care of yourself, both body and mind: eat right, get sufficient exercise and rest, avoid unhealthy practices like substance abuse, make time for activities you enjoy, and honor the needs of your feelings. You deserve to be cared for, the same as anyone else.

SUMMARY

This chapter covered a wide sampling of the many ways to bring mindfulness into your life. Techniques may be simple or complex. They may be tied to your religious practices, or not. They may be incorporated into something you already do during the day, or as a set-aside exercise. Mindfulness can be the primary goal of a technique, or a side benefit attained during a particular practice. There really is something for everybody.

However the most important element is how effectively a particular technique brings you into here and now awareness. Mindfulness allows you to step back, and see how your gut brain may affect not only your behavior, but also beliefs and choices—our next topic.

CHAPTER 11
......
Recalibrating: Healing Fractured Science

RECENTLY I ATTENDED an informative and entertaining continuing education workshop. When we broke up for the noon hour another attendee asked if I would like to have lunch with her. I had no need to rush through the meal and squeeze in other tasks, so I accepted her invitation. We were in the middle of stimulating conversation when our sandwiches arrived.

The plate set before me was piled high with French fries. Not just any fries. They were those wonderful flavor-packed ones—the kind that's first been dipped in some kind of seasoned coating. Then gently and perfectly deep-fried until brown and crispy on the outside, yet delectably soft in the center. They were piping hot, too, clearly not left to sit around and get limp. And yes, nestled next to them was a generous, eagerly awaiting container of sweet, red ketchup.

I reveled in my continuing serendipity, scooping up ketchup and gobbling down fries as I conversed with my lunch companion. Before I knew it I had polished off almost the entire pile.

Now for most people, giving in to such an indulgence might only mean needing to eat more reasonably the rest of the day in order to make up for the splurge. For me it was a different story. The status of my diabetic condition could handle a small portion of fries without my blood sugar levels complaining. But consuming an entire plateful was a definite no-no. My blood sugar did indeed spike—not drastically, but to a level I try to avoid.

This story is an example of thinking things through, or then again not thinking things through, when opportunity arrives on the doorstep. In the preceding example my logical brain took time to clear the last minute lunch date, noting nothing else more important before deciding. That particular choice was appropriately considered before chosen. My choice to consume an entire plate of French fries, on the other hand, did not consider important consequences—even if a more impulse-driven corner of my brain was in seventh heaven: "Have at it! Damn the torpedoes."

This is the difference between spontaneity and impulsiveness, at least in terms of avoiding life complications. Spontaneity has been through the sifter of common sense. Impulsiveness just does what it feels like, without realistically considering potential consequences.

Making ourselves think things through before speaking or acting is *so* not in the moment. Yet unquestionably, in some circumstances the amount of thought we put into a choice is critical. Lack of foresight before acting can even destroy the coveted joy of the moment.

We need not completely give up spur of the moment opportunities. As with everything else, any concept taken to the extreme becomes absurd. But we do need to stop and think first, when doing so is in our best interests.

The French fry story also illustrates what so easily steers us toward cogjam missteps. My visceral experience of being immersed in stimulating conversation at an enjoyable workshop temporarily overwhelmed my better judgment. Everything felt so pleasurable. I couldn't resist giving in to the *esprit de corps*. Only after the damage was done did I take note of my dietary blunder.

How much more easily this happens during angry discourse—blurting out retaliations that feel satisfying in the moment. Then realizing after the fact that we made the situation worse, rather than moving closer to resolving it. We get caught up in our emotions, and in doing so pay the price.

Lessons in self-compassion and mindfulness are a good beginning place for changing the course of cogjam. But all the here and now awareness and compassion in the world will not make much difference if our behavioral choices do not also enlist the logical brain's gifts for solution-finding.

Likewise, we need to take a long and hard look at exactly what is floating around in these logical brains of ours. What schemes came into being between the days we were born and how we see things today? What beliefs did we adopt, that currently guide our common sense? We often aren't completely aware of what they are. They just prod us every now and then from behind the scenes.

However examining and addressing faulty beliefs in itself can bring the calm needed to manage cogjam.

Figuring out what's actually back there can take a bit of digging. And it's not just about examining and challenging faulty beliefs. Sometimes it's also about truly listening to what the gut brain is trying to tell us.

HOW TO USE THIS CHAPTER

One of the lessons that jumped out at me during the journey of writing this book is how much easier it is to notice others' reasoning missteps than recognize our own. I shouldn't have been all that surprised. It's only another version of that subjective/objective bugaboo. We never completely do away with subjectivity about ourselves, or about anything else we care a lot about. In fact half the job of psychotherapy is helping clients calm gut-brain interference long enough for their logical brains to step in and point out answers that were there all along.

I also realized that as our logical brains process opinions being expressed by others, we have the advantage. As the view is shared, the speaker is simultaneously dealing with subjective gut-brain input. That has its own brand of logic, which at times bypasses common sense.

Our own gut brains may very well get into the act after hearing the message. But as we first take it in, we are in the more objective position for seeing the quality of the logic, or its lack thereof.

What does it mean for us, then, as we decide how to use this information about cogjammed reasoning? No doubt while you were reading earlier chapters, plenty of examples of others' blunders came to mind, with comparatively few of your own. That is to be expected, given the subjectivity/objectivity bias.

But it also presents a major stumbling block that must be cleared. If you're on the receiving end of someone's reasoning errors, your gut brain may insist on retaliating: "Tell him what an idiot he's being! It's my way or the highway." Unfortunately, pointing out others' challenged logic may only convince their gut brains to ramp up the fight—once more, cogjam on the loose.

The solution? *Compassion.* Remind yourself that they're dealing with an inner lizard, the same as you are. Keep in mind how others' errors are so much easier to recognize than your own—yet we all succumb to them. In fact, sometimes we discover that the other guy or gal is right. Consider the compassion and forgiveness you offer loved ones when they are hurting or have erred. Refocus those attitudes and feelings toward your inner lizard's perceived adversary.

Therefore take care to think of this chapter material more as a set of guidelines for advancing your own thought life, rather than fixing someone else's.

What pieces of fractured science have been hiding out as stowaways in your intellectual journey? Or, how might you get back to the more effective analysis you once brewed, before cogjam dipped a spoon in the pot?

This doesn't mean we completely ignore others' problematic thinking, or refrain from evaluating it. Far from it. We track it for multiple reasons:

- Gaining understanding of the reasoning behind why others feel or react as they do
- Figuring out what, for us, may be cues that trigger our own gut brains to overreact
- Recognizing when someone's fear response has bubbled to the surface, and that sensitivity will be needed
- Guarding against herd behavior gone awry, and letting others' faulty reasoning or behaviors rub off on ourselves

For your own moving forward, reaffirm your dedication to an evidence-based mindset. Choose to take best possible advantage of the common sense your brain was designed for. Ask yourself this simple question: To what extent am I using the right tool for the right job?

The first step before any purposeful change can happen is figuring out what could use a change in course. As you go through this discussion of healing fractured science, begin taking mental or written notes of which issues seem most significant to your own journey with cogjam:

- A specific reasoning error you want to do less of
- A seeming absence of thought before acting, or a reliance on copying herd behavior
- An automatic behavior you would like your logical brain to intervene in more often
- An attitude that might be adjusted, simply by looking at things differently
- Better understanding of loved ones
- Learning new techniques or solutions, ones that help you better access all those useful nuggets awaiting in your logical brain

WHERE SCIENTIFIC METHOD AND "SAY WHAT?" COLLIDE

In review: science is not a bunch of people in white coats running rats through mazes, or a specific field of study, or incomprehensibly complicated research write-ups, or other stereotyped representations. Science is a tool, a system our brains are designed to use. It's our best method for processing information that relates to factual reality.

What have you learned about whatever typically guides your reasoning? What successes or blunders have you realized? Following is a brief review of major concepts already introduced. It may help jog your mind about what you would like to do either differently or more of.

Chapter Three concluded with takeaways for how the tool of scientific method helps us decide what to believe. Obviously, we don't stop and analyze every speck of dirt to the *nth* degree. Some issues matter, others don't. Some do matter but can be put on hold until we know more. The following suggestions represent what to consider when information is important enough to make sure we're getting it right.

- *"Consider the source."* How reliable is the individual who shares the information? Does he or she know where it came from? Does this individual typically provide information that is later verified, uses reliable sources, does not give contradictory messages, leaves emotional reactions out of decision making, tends to look at both sides of an argument, and/or otherwise appears to be level-headed, thorough and conscientious?

- *"Consider more than one piece of information when applying a conclusion beyond its original context."* Is it something that happened with only one person or in one instance, or in a single or completely different context, where other factors are likely to apply? Do multiple sources support this fact, or just one? Does it logically fit in with other things you know?

- *"Never forget to look for possible disconfirming data."* Is the answer you've found the one you'd hoped to find? If so, that's all the more reason to check it out before settling. What evidence supports the opposite of your position? Have you possibly accepted a hypothesis without testing it, or otherwise checking out your assumption?

- *"Rather than paranoid rejection or jumping in with both feet when coming across new information, practice healthy skepticism."* And then, don't immediately leap onto the bandwagon of any disconfirming data that feels irresistibly attractive. Take a measured approach. Process the whole picture, especially when it involves something important.

Chapter Four described common reasoning errors, and how they fit in with cogjammed thoughts and behaviors. Have you seen yourself succumb to any of these ill-advised practices at just the wrong moment?

- *Rationalization*—starting with a conclusion then looking for data to support it, rather than seeking objective information and then drawing a conclusion: "Fred talks on the phone all the time while he's driving, and I've never seen him have problems. Therefore I can answer this incoming call right now and not suffer consequences," or "we must act as [country of choice]'s adversary; they pose a potential military threat" (when a good relationship with the other country offers potential benefits, should diplomacy seek them).

- *Denial*—deciding that an important problem doesn't exist or is not an issue for you, when it really is: "I'm not addicted to nicotine; I've quit smoking many times," or "refusing to negotiate with those on the other side of the aisle is an effective approach to government" (then the government shuts down over inability to negotiate a budget).

- *Single factor thinking*—making decisions or drawing conclusions based on a single factor, rather than considering other important factors that may apply. "My hammer is great for pounding things. Therefore everything is a nail," or "[insert person here] was very loyal and helpful on the campaign trail, therefore he is competent to handle most any position in government (when the person at hand actually has little if any training or experience in the relevant fields)."

- *Overgeneralization*—assuming that a trait or opinion often found in a particular group represents overall traits or opinions of everyone in the group: "[insert political party here] are all the same," or "if they're not in favor of our way to handle the healthcare problem, they're against healthcare in general."

- *Black and white/all or nothing thinking*—interpreting information only in extremes: "People are either good guys, or bad guys," "you're either for me or against me," or "our group is made up of good guys, therefore everything they support is good; the people on the other side are all bad, and therefore anything they propose is tainted by ill intent."

- *Fundamental attribution error*—blaming people for undesired outcomes or circumstances, rather than the complex situations that create them. "Those guys holding office right now are the ones who caused the current problem; we should hold them responsible" (when it took generations of decisions and actions to arrive at this place).

- *Correlation as causation*—believing that if two things occur in the same time or place, one caused the other, especially if it's the answer you're looking for: "I wore my lucky shirt during the last Super Bowl, and my team won; it'll do the same this year," or "crime went down while our party held the reins of government, so policies we put in place are responsible for it" (when crime rates had been going down every year for some time, or it's accountable for by factors in place long before the party took control).

THOUGHTS AND BUCKING THE HERD

Herd influences also affect thinking processes, as the following example illustrates.

I signed onto the field of disaster mental health around the time that mission first came into being. Little was there to guide us. We knew how to help people who were in the middle of mental health crises, or struggling with a pre-existing condition. But back then the science of trauma psychology still had training wheels attached. What was best to do for everyone else immediately post-disaster was a relative unknown.

The protocol of the relief organization I traveled with was relying largely on the ill-fated critical incident stress-debriefing (CISD) format. I took the required classes along with the rest of my professional colleagues, and off we galloped into the wilds of disaster world. At the time, I did not question what was presented at those trainings. They felt like commonplace continuing education gatherings with the usual set of peers. Naturally, I assumed my trusted colleagues wouldn't put forth material that didn't have valid backing. Only much later did we discover that the protocol had gotten into the system without appropriate scrutiny by the field of mental health.

Something about it never did feel quite right. Collections of distressed people randomly gathered into groups are rarely all in the same stage of recovery. How an adversity is currently affecting them usually varies widely, even when they're reacting to the same incident.

Furthermore, the prescribed debriefing ritual flew in the face of the first rule of intervention: namely, begin wherever people are at. Trying to roll a CISD-like template into their midst felt like shoving a square peg into a round hole. Or, it took the process into directions other than what the protocol intended. I did strive to do what was best for individuals, regardless. But afterwards I'd feel semi-guilty for having deviated from herd protocol.

My "ah-ha" moment waltzed on-scene shortly after the events of September 11th. My first assignment for that disaster was at operation headquarters. One of my duties was to provide debriefings for those who were finishing their commitments and about to leave the operation.

One afternoon I met with a young man who also had been working with disaster mental health. He'd spent considerable time in the trenches, exposed to many severely traumatized people and tragic stories. As we stepped into the closet-like debriefing room, anybody could see he was an emotional wreck. As I closed the door he halfway crouched in his chair, pale, visibly shaking, and hesitant to establish eye contact. He appeared on the verge of shutting down altogether.

We began with usual introductions. I don't recall much of what we ended up talking about. But I well remember that as he struggled to get words out, an enormous red light was flashing in every corner of my gut. The spotlighting sensation was similar to that one I'd had all those years ago as a teenager, when I'd been faced with the decision of whether to go study at the library and succeed, or do as I'd been ordered to do and fail.

You see, we health professionals vow to do no harm. Thanks to years of experience with helping hurting people, my gut had become wired to alert me to potential for doing harm. That red light was blazing out the message that getting someone who was this emotionally overwhelmed to go even deeper into feeling-related material was a really bad idea.

I abandoned all thoughts of the debriefing template. I interacted with the worker as I would for someone of his emotional state in any other setting. By the time we finished he had stopped shaking, and had a little more color to him.

But as he got up to leave, he gave me a curious sideways glance. "That wasn't the usual debriefing plan."

I smiled at him. "No, it wasn't, was it? You can still go do that when you're ready, if you decide you want to." In retrospect, most of his anxiety may have stemmed from foreknowledge of what he was about to go through—and that the standard protocol of the day was something he definitely was not ready for.

My logical brain did not catch up with my gut brain about this episode until I returned home, and began the process of sorting and settling all that had been stirred up by that difficult and chaotic assignment. Realization sprouted in the form of a flashbulb-like memory of an early mentor, back in graduate school. He was sitting at the head of our seminar table wearing his trademark cozy cardigan and sunny smile, sharing intricacies of psychodynamic therapy in his gentle, grandfatherly style.

"Challenge people only when they're ready," he was explaining. "Do not take them places where they are not yet able to defend themselves."

That's when it hit me.

The herd had led me astray. Unintentionally, of course. All the same, it was clearly roaming toward the edge of a cliff. Maybe, just maybe, it was time to change course.

Fortunately, many other mental health professionals were coming to a similar conclusion. We banded together, did necessary research, and recalibrated disaster mental health practices into something of benefit for survivors and disaster staff alike. What disaster mental health practitioners do now looks very different from what went on during our earliest efforts.

But for me the conflict became crystal clear because I first listened to a signal from my gut; then introduced common sense to investigate why going with the status quo might not be the best choice. And when that red light began flashing, I didn't impulsively jump up from my chair and run off screaming—which my gut brain happily would have supported. Instead I mentally stepped back and considered what my gut was telling me. I came up with an alternative plan, consistent with both hardwired professional wisdom and the true needs of an emotionally fragile disaster worker.

I suspect the gut brain always senses the real picture before the logical brain climbs aboard. It operates faster than the speed of conscious thought. But that doesn't mean it should automatically be awarded primacy. It's not a foot race, where winner takes all. It's simply the order in which information coming from within typically appears. As happened for me during the debriefing story, mapping out appropriate next steps requires that common sense join hands with gut instinct, no matter which type of information appears first.

Bucking the herd also requires examining ourselves from the perspective of what truly drives our choice before going along with it. Sometimes going along with the crowd is a good idea, such as the concept of doing no harm. Other times, it isn't.

Chapter Five covered a number of problems that stem from indiscriminately following herd leanings. Escaping cogjam requires at least a little bucking of this tendency. It means risking doing something different, or going with a notion we feel in our gut and hear in our logic to be sound, even if it means we have to work upstream. Or, it could mean a need to change herds. There are surely others out there who see things similarly to you, just as I found among my mental health colleagues. But you may need to seek them out. They're often at watering holes other than the ones you and your current herd frequents.

Is there something you know you have done mainly because others do it? Perhaps something that didn't quite feel right. Or something you've never thought all the way through, but at the time were willing to settle for. You're concerned that it may contribute to cogjam, rather than better our lot. Re-evaluating and adjusting that particular issue may be your starting point for change. Consider the following:

- What do you, and maybe those around you, really need to do to reduce—or at least not perpetuate—conflict, ill will, and bad feelings?
- What actions or changes might make things better, for them and for you?
- What can you alter about your own herd participation that might contribute toward reducing socio-political strife?

Our personal choices are our journey alone. The herd merely benefits or pays a price, based on the choices of its members.

THE ROLE OF VALUES

We never stop seeking the guidance of role models, mentors, and leaders, both formal and informal. Sometimes they are brought into our lives by chance—such as our parents, other children who lived in the neighborhood, whatever teacher we happened to get for seventh grade science, or our first boss. Others are people we observe then choose to emulate, using them as our guide for a life well spent. Most often we continue to imitate or get the most guidance from those who have values similar to our own.

Regardless of whether people become our role models by chance or by choice, sometimes those we look up to fail us. They are, after all, fallible human beings, the same as ourselves. Or in addition to shared values, they hold ones that are very different from our own, which we may not notice until a situation gets out of hand. Or they have an ax to grind that doesn't mesh with our own lives or personal goals. It's easy to get caught up in the agenda of chosen leaders, mentors, role models, and the like if we are not selective about which of their beliefs or behavioral styles we adopt as our own.

So knowing when to buck the herd requires at least some awareness of personal values—a huge topic in itself, for which we will barely skim the surface. But for the task at hand, begin by considering the values you hold that you're most aware of. Perhaps you realized the existence of an especially important value while reviewing a particular childhood "ah-ha" moment.

For example, Chapter Six described examples of some of my own early leanings. Valuing "being nice" spawned an impulse to include a girl who felt left out. Valuing nonviolence resulted in my choice to walk away from bullies, rather than shoot similar barbs their way. Valuing academic achievement led to choosing to leave home and study at the library, even though I knew there'd be a price to pay. Instead of doing like others, emerging values slipped in and won the day.

For each of these moments, some level of thinking it through brought out what, for me, were the most important guiding lights. That's what bucking herd leanings requires: thinking situations all the way through, rather than looking to what others do or what you think they want and following without question.

Cogjam behavior regularly violates what most of us think of as our higher values. That's because gut brains are relatively unconcerned about values, other than avoiding harm and protecting loved ones. There's nothing wrong with those particular goals. The problem is that higher brain functions are the primary drivers of the less selfish values, as well as of those that join us with common humanity. The needs of gut and logic must balance out. This often takes conscious effort.

Consider the following values, ones to which most people aspire: compassion, kindness, honesty, integrity, love, nonviolence, fairness, inner harmony, respect for self and others, and wisdom. Even though these values are typically highly placed in our priorities, cogjammed behavior violates them among the best of us. Cogjam can smother our guiding lights, sending us blindly into thoughts and behaviors more likely to divide community and fracture science than promote our true values.

Did your own example of failing to buck the herd violate something you value? Which value did it violate? What other values seem promoted by your herd that differ from your own? How might you step away, if a similar situation arose? Critiquing past experiences is excellent strategy for increasing chances of being more true to yourself in the future.

Again, bucking the herd does not mean teaching yourself to ignore the herd altogether. On the contrary: it means seeking greater awareness of it and recognizing when it appears to be leading to the edge of a moral cliff, then actively choosing a different path.

WAYWARD SCHEMAS AND COGNITIVE DISTORTIONS

Schemas are those patterns of thinking we first began putting together during childhood and adolescence. They are usually not specific thoughts, but rather core beliefs lying beneath the surface of our thought lives. They hold substantial sway over what we do or believe, and how we take in and process new information.[68]

The schemas creating the most grief in the realm of cogjam are those that have to do with how we view ourselves amidst others—the human "ways of the world," so to speak. If our schemas have been over-influenced by unfortunate early experiences or exposures, we may hold a few ill-founded beliefs that override any conclusions the logical brain might provide. Such beliefs are known as "cognitive distortions." And when our thinking is distorted, unpleasant feelings and ill-advised behavior often follow.[69]

Fortunately, there are ways of addressing this very common human predicament.

"You can't keep the birds from flying overhead, but you can prevent them from nesting in your hair." An elderly fundamentalist shared this bit of wisdom with me several decades ago, well before the cognitive-behavioral movement had gotten into full swing. That's because it's common sense. Bad things hap-

68   Young, J. E. (1990). *Cognitive therapy for personality disorders: A schema-focused approach*. Sarasota, FL: Professional Resource Exchange.
69   Burns, D. D. (1980). *Feeling good: The new mood therapy*. New York: HarperCollins.

pen in the world. And bad thoughts about them arise. But we don't need to let them sit there and fester.

To deal with cognitive distortions we first must gain awareness of them, and acknowledge that they're there. Then we point out to them that they're mistaken, and let our logical brains fill them in with more realistic readings. If we exercise this type of control over such passing thoughts, we also better control how we feel during difficult times. And when we feel differently, we behave differently. With enough practice, new wiring overrides cognitive distortions.

Some of the most common distortions were mentioned in terms of botched interpretation and application of scientific findings: all or nothing thinking, overgeneralization, confusing correlation with causation, and jumping to conclusions. The following example illustrates how these distortions might affect feelings and behaviors in a difficult situation.

A major election is about to take place. Jenny is upset with long-time friend, Dee-Dee, because she supports a different candidate. It's a hot political season, and the election almost always finds a way into conversation. Dee-Dee gets heated up whenever she talks about her position. When this happens, Jenny feels attacked or intimidated. Lately after their get-togethers, Jenny walks away feeling hurt, frustrated, or otherwise unsettled. She considers walking away from the friendship all together.

Here's how these four cognitive distortions could be blowing Jenny's feelings and behavior out of proportion, and how she might argue with them:

- *All or nothing thinking*—seeing things as all good or all bad, or completely successful or not successful at all: "If we can't even agree on this, we can't agree on anything. I may as well give up on this friendship," or "if we don't see everything the same way, then we're not really friends."

  Countering argument: "Actually, we have lots of things we agree on. And why should we need to agree on everything, anyway? We're friends because we like each other, care about each other, and share many common interests and values."

- *Overgeneralization*—losing overall perspective by focusing only on the single negative factor happening in the here and now: "Dee-Dee always gets angry when we get together. It's all there is to our relationship now."

  Countering argument: "This too shall pass. Politics will move on, and so will the angry rhetoric. Besides, we have a great time together when today's politics don't find their way into conversation."

- *Confusing correlation with causation*—assuming that because two things happen in the same time or place, one must cause the other: "Politics weren't this messed up before Dee-Dee's candidate got involved. It's all

LAUREL HUGHES | 151

his fault. She should get a clue."

Countering argument: "The cause could be the other way around: with politics being so messed up, someone like Dee-Dee's candidate actually has a chance of winning."

- *Single factor thinking*—jumping to conclusions on the basis of a single piece of information: "Dee-Dee is angry with me over having a different opinion. It must be how she truly feels about me in general. She's really not my friend."

  Countering argument: "One swallow doesn't make a spring. And nobody agrees about everything. Being upset over this one issue doesn't necessarily reflect her overall feelings about me. Check out that hypothesis before accepting it."

In addition to these four types, Jenny might fall victim to any of these additional forms of cognitive distortion:

- *Personalization*—seeing herself as responsible for a negative event, when she has little or nothing to do with it: "Dee-Dee only gets so upset because I argue with her. It's my fault. She's better off without me as a friend."

  Countering argument: "She's responsible for her own feelings, just as I am responsible for mine. Others don't 'make' us feel things; how we process what they say or do is responsible. We have control over our interpretations of the world around us. If I feel like I need to blame something, I can always blame cogjam—then take what control I can over my corner of it."

- *Catastrophizing*—blowing a particular situation out of all reasonable proportion: "This is the worst thing that could possibly happen. What will I do if Dee-Dee's no longer my friend?"

  Countering argument: "I've been through a lot worse than this. And I clearly got through life somehow before Dee-Dee and I met. Yes, she is my best friend right now, and I would be sad if our friendship ended. But it wouldn't be the end of the world. Besides, I have other friends. And I can make new ones, too. I'll get by fine either way."

- *Labeling*—using emotionally loaded extreme designations to describe herself or others when they fail or somehow disappoint her: "Time and time again, I fail to get her to agree with my position; I'm such a loser," or "no matter how many times I point out the obvious, she still doesn't see things my way; what a dimwit she is."

  Countering argument: "People can't be categorized that way. Not gaining the upper hand on a particular issue doesn't describe overall character for either of us. We are who we are; our beliefs and behaviors are simply beliefs and behaviors. We regularly adjust them from time to time, but we're still who we are, regardless.

- *"Shouldistic" thinking*—insisting that something should, must, or ought to align with a certain value or belief; and if it doesn't, there are dire consequences: "We must see things the same way in order to be friends."
  Countering argument: "Nobody died and made me God. Dee-Dee can see things however she wants. And I can believe whatever I want to believe. It's a free country."

Note that it would be highly unlikely for Jenny to experience all of these cognitive distortions, though some do tend to overlap. Regardless, only Jenny knows which ones fit in with her particular state of mind. That's what we each need to examine when finding ourselves in similar difficult situations:

- How do we feel while dealing with them?
- What are we thinking that excessively promotes negative feelings?
- How do we act when we think and feel that way?
- How might we alter feelings and likelihood of undesired behavior simply by changing our thoughts?

This is the task before us. We need to ferret out thoughts that make the situation worse for us, and perhaps for others, than it needs to be. Then we take action to counter the cognitive distortions, before we react in ways we later regret.

Fortunately there are numerous resources out there that address adjusting our thought lives. Perusing the self-help shelves of your local bookstore will help you become more familiar with them, and which one might work well for you.

ADJUSTING EXPECTATIONS

Not long after the events of September 11th, I heard a journalist interview some men who had immigrated to the United States as "Lost Boys of Sudan." They were well acquainted with disaster, having been orphaned early and driven from their war-torn homeland. They were now functional adults with productive lives, in spite of their tumultuous early beginnings. How had they coped so well? What was their secret?

Their answer was not what the journalist expected. They told him that when the 9/11 incidents happened, they were as horrified as everybody else. However a week later they were surprised to find that everyone still seemed as upset about it as they had been the day it happened. Yes, this was a terrible thing that had taken place. But it was over and done with; it was old news. The adult "lost boys" had accepted its reality, and were continuing about their lives. Expending extraordinary effort to cope had not been necessary.

Their lesson to us is this: how we handle and move beyond hurt during adversity is altered by our expectations. For men who had spent boyhoods enduring tragedy after tragedy, it was a part of their world. It was expected. Survival meant accepting tragic events when they happened, grieving them and beginning the healing process, and continuing to go on.

For those of us who have always lived in the United States, expectations were different before then. Until the last couple of decades, our lives did not include seeing much mass tragedy in our very midst. Hostile outrageousness, whether mass casualty or cogjam oriented, is more difficult and stressful than adversity we've already come to recognize and accept as a normal part of life.

Our gut brains, as usual, react with aimless clanging and flashing red lights: "It simply can't be so! There's too much vulnerability at stake. I won't tolerate it, and that's all there is to it." But the gut brain can't actually do much about it, beyond saving our skins while escaping dire threat. Once that's over with, the gut brain's style of handling adversity only gets in the way.

Difficulty with admitting vulnerability and other unrealistic expectations created work on the disaster trail, too, beyond incidences of those refusing to leave the paths of approaching floods or hurricanes. Their target of choice? That would be us, the disaster workers. About ten days to two weeks into any operation, we could count on hearing complaints about the performance of disaster relief organizations and agencies. Expectations that others could immediately step in and meet seemingly any possible disaster need were common.

Because of this misperception, many survivors didn't bother to adequately prepare for disaster. When aftermath relief resources didn't work out as they'd counted on, gut brains cried out in protest. The good and the bad were clearly delineated: "Disasters are the all bad. Relief agencies are the all good. Of course they can always make sure nobody is left wanting." But when relief agencies don't meet this lofty goal, gut brains shuffle them off to the "all bad" side of the equation: "Let 'em have it!" Shouldistic thinking wins.

And fire away they did. We'd hear complaints at shelters, emergency aid stations, and service centers about those things we could not do, or over not giving what other agencies were actually responsible for providing. News media reliably reported on any perceived or real shortcomings of relief operations, since by then reports on the disastrous incident itself were wearing thin.

The old hands of disaster knew how to let such criticisms roll off their backs. Hearing such complaints was expected. You could practically set your watch by it.

For the newbies, however, such feedback could be devastating. On average about 80 percent of disaster volunteers are working their first and only disaster operation, one of the reasons why situations occasionally did get bungled and need to be fixed. But look at it from the perspective of the newbies: they'd left their homes and loved ones, used vacation time or had lost pay, perhaps traveled great distances, taken on tasks they may have never before attempted, were working 12-14 hour days, and had chosen to live in hardship conditions—all for the purpose of helping survivors. Why was the community lashing back, when all they were trying to do was help them in their time of need? Their expectations were dashed into smithereens. We mental health workers at times stepped in to clean up after the residual debris of such violated expectations, for survivors and workers alike.

We stand in a similar space today with cogjam. In addition to adjusting our early-learned schemes and core beliefs, cogjam recovery requires a little expectation recalibration. What should we realistically expect, based on what we've experienced to date?

The field of psychometrics offers an avalanche of measures that aim to predict human behavior. However none of them is so reliable as a measure that has been around since the dawn of humanbeinghood, something we all know and use regularly.

The most reliable way to predict what people are going to do in the future is simply by looking at what they've reliably done in the past.

This makes a pretty easy job of establishing expectations relating to cogjam. What have we seen going on in our society? Based on such observations, in the future we can realistically expect that:

- Politics and public figures will continue to occasionally say and do things that we find insensitive, divisive, evasive, illogical, offensive, or otherwise outrageous.

- Comments that stir up socio-political strife will continue to be part of social media, news broadcasts, conversation at the water cooler, or anywhere else people gather.

- Our gut brains will continue to react to such commentary, and insist that we must strike back or in some other way act to protect ourselves.

However, we've also seen that:

- Change is the rule, rather than the exception.

- The logical brain can override the overzealousness of the gut brain and herd instinct.

- People are capable of changing their thoughts and behavior, including whatever expectations they have adopted.

- Many individuals have already made self-adjustments that help rein in cogjam.
- We are resilient, even in the face of disaster aftermaths like the events of September 11th.

Ratcheting down the expectation that something like cogjam just shouldn't be, or that it is otherwise outside the norm of daily reality, helps quiet gut-brain reactivity.[70] That's because habituation moves in. Even though the gut brain may not like that it's there, it will accept cogjam as an expected feature of the background—not needing immediate attention, and perhaps even to be ignored all together. It's one of the reasons why so many people have already minimized cogjam in their lives. They've accepted that it's there, and they take measures to avoid or not contribute to it.

SYSTEMATIC PROBLEM SOLVING

Let's say we've done enough quieting of the gut brain and clearing out of distorted thinking to gain a suitable handle on objectivity. This sets the stage for working on complex problems in focused and structured ways, a practice that often gets derailed when we are too worked up.

The following detailed steps represent a typical problem solving strategy. It is both systematic and objective. Jotting down your responses, rather than just doing it in your head, increases the ease of staying focused and objective.

- *Define the problem.* Exactly what is it that bothers you? A conflict? A situational circumstance? A person's behavior?
- *Separate out sub-problems.* Problems often cluster, but can only be systematically resolved one at a time. You can always go back to the sub-problems later, if they still exist after you've addressed the priority issue.
- *Describe how you feel while the problem is playing out.* How does it affect you? In what ways might it be getting in the way of dealing with the issue? How might you set aside that feeling, in order to remain objective?
- *List possible causes of the problem.* There are often multiple contributors to any given problem. Taking a look at the many factors that may have lead to the problem's existence often exposes potential solutions.
- *Generate a list of possible solutions.* Come up with as many solutions as you can think of, even those that seem ridiculous. Write them down, regardless. If they come to mind, they are possibilities your gut brain might tap into if you have not yet outed them as absurd.

---

70   Kahneman, D., & Miller, D. T. (1986). Norm theory: Comparing reality to its alternatives. *Psychological Review*, 9, 136-153.

- *List advantages and disadvantages of each option.* Now is the time to review and evaluate in depth each suggested option. Looking at pros and cons of the crazy ones can bring a little humor into the process, never a bad thing for stress. Sometimes we discover a favored option is unrealistic only after we've fully examined both its pros and cons.

- *Select the option that presents the most positives and fewest negatives.* The perfect solution is a rare bird. But the solution doesn't need to be perfect. It only needs to be better than the likely outcome of continuing with the problem still in place.

- *Create an action plan.* What, specifically, will you do or say? When? Where? With whom else, if other people are involved?

- *Establish how and when you will evaluate the success of your plan.* Did you achieve your desired result? Was the option doable, but there were things you hadn't thought of that got in the way? Or was it doable, but didn't achieve the desired result? Was the problem only partially solved? For any of the above, you can always go back to the drawing board—and remember to apply what you learned during the first try.

While working with state government I attended trainings on goal setting for programs designed to address specific social problems. The principles involved spelled out another critical component of problem solving, one often forgotten while we're caught up in what we're fighting to achieve.

The trainers introduced two separate concepts, serving as platforms for whatever our particular agencies were trying to accomplish: the vision statement, and the mission statement.

First came the vision statement. What final outcome did we want see—that is, not what was likely to ever happen, but what would it look like in the best of all possible worlds? In other words, ideal outcomes like "nobody will be left homeless," or "there will always be plenty of good foster parents to go around," or "services will meet all special needs of those in senior residential facilities during disaster," and so on.

Next came the mission statement. It describes outcomes consistent with the vision statement that could actually be possible for an agency to achieve. What efforts will get the agency closer to meeting the goal reflected by the vision statement? For helping the homeless, the mission statement could be something like "to increase affordable housing" or "to streamline the social services that transition the homeless into jobs and housing." Or it could be even more global, such as "to reduce the number of homeless people on the street," with the other two options set up as goals within the overall mission.

Naturally, we would prefer to eradicate homelessness all together. But problem solving is about planning for and going after the possible, rather than demanding that our efforts get us nothing less than a perfect world. That's gut brain reasoning again—insisting that either your efforts are a complete success, or they are a total failure. Social problems only get better in increments. We need to celebrate these increments, and find satisfaction in what we can actually contribute toward, rather than insist that our efforts make things perfect before they're worthwhile. We need to appreciate that the glass is half full, rather than catastrophize every time we see it half empty.

Therefore there would be nothing wrong with adopting a personal vision statement of "wiping cogjam from the face of the earth." However if we make that a goal to achieve rather than an ideal to aim toward, we are doomed to disillusionment.

On the other hand, we can do plenty to reduce the interpersonal strife and confusion stirred up by socio-political posturing and put-downs. True change will rise from individual increments of reducing the daily misunderstandings and frictions that keep cogjam alive and well. Change happens one person, one incident, one relationship, one support network, or one community at a time. While some have already begun this critical work, there's still plenty out there to do.

What can you adopt as a mission? Where do your possible increments lie? Seeking objectivity and solving problems in systematic ways increase chances of achieving your mission, wherever you see yourself placed in this effort. The final chapter will share more on this.

As you move forward, remember to keep in mind that science does not tell you what to do. It only tells you what is most likely to happen if you do it. Only you can decide if what you objectively observe around you is important enough for you to dive into creative solution finding.

CHAPTER 12

......

Breaking Counterproductive Patterns

B ACK IN EIGHTH grade gym class, girls' basketball didn't look the same as the game played most everywhere else. Teams were made up of two half-court sub-teams, with a group of three playing defense at one end, and another threesome on offense at the other end. Furthermore, we were only allowed to bounce the ball up to three times before we had to either shoot or pass the ball. Random assignment rotated team members after each basket, so that everybody in the class had a chance at both defense and offense. For kids our age there was an additional catch: some of us had started our growth spurts, while others had not. This created a hodgepodge of built-in advantages and disadvantages.

Unfortunately, I was among those in the class who were latest to bloom. Thanks to having younger brothers, my family home had a basketball hoop in the driveway. I had ample opportunity to practice shooting baskets. But the extraordinarily limiting rules of girls' basketball pretty much hamstrung how much strategy might be applied.

One day the inevitable happened. At both ends of the court, the tallest class members were on defense and the shortest on offense—myself included. For about five minutes the ball went back and forth, up and down the court, with not a single shot attempt getting close to the rim. The taller girls on either side simply circled wagons below the basket, moved along with the shooter for the obligatory three bounces, and easily batted away whatever headed upward.

The entire class was getting frustrated or annoyed. Plus, those of us who were out on the court were beginning to wear down. As our offensive threesome once again headed toward the basket, I wracked my brain for anything else we might try, other than repeat the doomed pattern.

Breaking pattern—yes. That had to be it.

I ended up with the ball. As I turned to dribble left, I scanned the lay of the land. The Great Wall of China we'd been trying to chuck a ball over anticipated my next moves, or so they thought. They were shifting left along with me, expecting a shot after the third dribble.

Now was my big chance. I slowed, bounced the ball a second time. A sliver of an opening cleared out to my right. I quickly spun and leaped, letting go a one-armed lay-up with all the muscle I could muster. The ball made it to the top of the rim and teetered. Finally, it slowly rolled inward.

Cheers burst out. Even a couple of the tall girls from the opposing side thanked me for getting that sorry rotation over with. Our team eventually won that game. We were ecstatic. Team members congratulated one another as we headed for the locker room.

I stopped for a drink at the water fountain. As I rose and wiped my mouth I discovered a surly looking member of the opposing team staring me in the eye. And blocking my path.

"You won by luck, not skill." She continued to stand there, arms folded, glaring at me.

At first I was stunned—less about the poor sportsmanship than the absurdity of her comment. Nobody else in the game had tried the fake-out routine. Nobody else had thought up a successful way to break pattern. And for once I'd actually done something worthwhile in gym class, a rare feat for someone of my challenged size and athletic prowess. I wasn't about to let her rain on my parade.

And I was already primed for breaking pattern.

I burst out laughing, as if she had just told me a hilarious joke. "Yeah, I know. Isn't that great?" I turned away and headed to my locker, leaving her every bit as stunned as her comment had done for me.

Ending cogjam is a process of breaking pattern. It's about intervening in that eons-old back and forth defensive posturing when it's at its most dysfunctional. We have the power to take control over its direction at any moment, simply by finding a different way to respond.

What do you usually do when others are purposely offensive, or otherwise target you with their anger? How can we defuse those situations, rather than let a ready and willing gut brain dictate our defense?

BREAKING PATTERN

Right now is *our* big chance: to use what we've learned about our own thinking to more effectively interact with others. This is the arena in which cogjam plays its dirtiest.

Thus far focus has mainly centered on stabilizing our own inner selves during cogjam moments. Our inner beings do reap benefits from positive changes in relationships, as well. But with the right adjustments, how we act amongst fellow herd members steers us away from unnecessarily provoking others' gut brains. This contributes to their more easily letting their logical brains rule, further helping interpersonal healing.

Breaking counterproductive interpersonal patterns first requires giving our usual inner ways a quick self-check. The following nuggets are summarized from earlier chapters—concepts that can help us get our better thinking on line. We don't necessarily need to have all of these down pat. Zero in on those specific areas that you recognize typically play roles when you have trouble keeping your cool, or can't stop feeling overwhelmingly vulnerable.

- *Slow down.* Slow your thought processes. That way you know your gut brain hasn't completely taken over. Taking a slow deep breath, or slowing your physical movements or rate of speech, can help you better focus.

- *Introduce here and now awareness.* Let in a bit of mindfulness, using whatever strategy or cues best help you get in touch with it. Be especially mindful of the greater perspective or the global situation. You're not just taking care of the issue at hand. The interlude is also about the relationship you have with this individual, about your own self-respect, and about your contribution to common humanity.

- *Identify your inner experience.* Do you feel hurt by what the other person is saying? Confused? Angry? Hurt? Frustrated? Annoyed? Threatened? Impatient? Exasperated?

- *Acknowledge inner feelings.* Step back and reassure your gut brain that yes, you hear the threat it's screaming its lungs out over, and you're going to do something about it. The gut brain eases up a bit once it perceives that the message has been received. Offer your inner lizard a word of kindness, and thank it for pointing out the problem.

- *Engage compassion:* Perhaps you best tap into sense of compassion by first connecting with self-compassion. Or, you find it by thinking of the compassion you feel for someone you care deeply about. Or, by getting in touch with feelings of universal compassion, such as compassion for all of common humanity. The right answer is whichever works best for you. Inadvertently blurting out harsh words in the heat of the moment is less likely while you're experiencing compassion, no matter what issue is causing consternation.

- *Apply corrective measures to cognitive distortions.* If you hear yourself saying things like "he shouldn't say things like that" or "this is horrible, I can't take it," remind yourself otherwise. You can take it. In today's cogjammed society you've likely endured considerably worse. If you continue to have too much trouble letting go of cognitive distortions that raise your ire, you may come out of the situation better by using one of the quicker and dirtier techniques about to be suggested, ones that typically shorten the exchange and require less of you.

- *Choose not to respond.* If you can't simmer down at all, put off meaningful discussion for another day. Nod, or say nothing. Or find a reason to excuse yourself from the person's presence. Take a deep breath and move on.

Also remember to avoid personalizing alternate opinions as criticism of your own views. That will tear you down faster than anything. Everybody's opinions differ somehow, no matter what the topic. So before buying into your inner lizard's insistence that an exchange represents a personal attack, give the other person opportunity to clarify what he or she is saying. You may discover that your gut brain is jumping the gun.

Likewise, having an opinion that is different from someone else's doesn't make you wrong, stupid, or ill informed. It's just another opinion. Opinions may be based on objective facts, but the opinions themselves are subjective. Of course, this doesn't stop the name-calling practices of those in the world that like to assign negative labels to those who disagree with them. But that's their reasoning or behavioral blunder to correct, not ours.

REACTING TO ANGRY PEOPLE

Just as we each have our own way of handling anger, we also have differing comfort levels for trying this or that with any given person or situation. As you review the following suggestions, think of times when specific others in your life have become combative. Which of these options feel comfortable for you? Which tactics might have proven worthwhile in those past situations? Especially if you deal with a recurring argument, and are highly likely to get another crack at handling it. It doesn't hurt to practice ahead of time with an empty chair, while looking in the mirror, with a trusted friend, or in any other setting that helps you get more comfortable with breaking pattern.

"But that isn't me. I don't act like that. It's being phony." Actually, it is you. It's a corner of your logical, willful self that you have yet to recognize and get used to, a direct contrast to unquestioningly going along with whatever resonates with your gut. In the process, you will likely discover your own unique style of replacing gut reacting with logic. It's been there all along, waiting to be brought to light and allowed to sparkle.

Dodge the bait. Sometimes there's more to an altercation than two clashing opinions. Some, for many unfortunate reasons, purposely try to punch others' buttons. They bring up a topic because they know, consciously or subconsciously, that it will get the other person riled. That's gut brains at work. They're exploring possibilities of objects to attack, in hopes that their half-blind shotgun-pattern approach will nullify a threat they sense lurking out there somewhere.

Often others recognize our sensitive areas more easily than we do ourselves. Are you aware of your own hot buttons? What topics tend to pump up your gut reactions?

Think of times when keeping your mouth shut has been especially difficult for you. For example, you surely have opinions about our current socio-political climate. What issues do you hold especially dear, and what's happening with them? That's just the sort of place a hot button likes to hang out.

Once you locate your hot buttons, you are in a better position to recognize when they're being punched. That's the time to step in and exercise control. Slow down, become mindful of what you are feeling and acknowledge it, and give your logical brain opportunity to come up with a way to break pattern.

Sometimes doing no more than sitting and saying nothing reveals there was no need to respond in the first place. The purpose of others' angry or frustrated comments could turn out to be only letting off steam, not a desire to discuss the issue. Or, it represents a "gotcha." By goading someone else into reacting, they feel like their own anger is vented vicariously, or that they take some control over their own feelings of vulnerability.

By now you probably also know other peoples' hot button locations within this socio-political drama, at least for those in your daily lives. Do yourself a favor. Just don't go there. There's no need. They'll bring up such topics themselves if they truly want to talk about them. Instead, examine why you are feeling tempted to punch somebody's buttons. Why are you really angry or threatened? Will punching the other person's buttons really do anything worthwhile?

Listen, rather than react. I once consulted at a residential facility for vulnerable populations, which included a number of individuals dealing with mental health challenges. I knew of one crotchety resident by reputation before we ever had the chance to meet. He constantly made disparaging remarks about "those #@%& humans." According to his rants, you couldn't trust a one of them.

Naturally a number of residents—and a few staff, as well—were put off by his rhetoric. Arguments and altercations sparked on a daily basis. Because of his limitations, nobody was having much luck talking with him about it.

I decided to hunt him down during the lunch break and introduce myself. I found him seated alone, scowling, hunched over his meal and muttering to himself. True to form, the first topic he brought up was "those #@%& humans."

I sat there and said nothing, ever attentive as he rambled on. Every now and then he would look up, as if expecting me to jump in. I only looked back at him, continuing with my best show of interest and goodwill.

Finally, it came out.

"Wolves. I'd rather be with wolves. All the while I was with them, not once did they get nasty out of nowhere, the way humans are. Except once. When I got charged at. Made a mistake, that time. I got between a male and his mate while she was in season. But that's the only time."

"You used to have wolves?"

An hour-long monolog followed as he described a previous life, one in which he had cared for semi-domesticated wolves. His stories were fascinating. As he went on, his enthusiasm blossomed, underscoring how much he missed those "good old days." And he clearly relished having the opportunity to talk about them.

When our conversation ended, he was no longer so slouched and angry looking. I gave the staff a few pointers, and the altercations at the facility decreased. Nonetheless, the last thing he said to me when I left the facility was "those #@%& humans." But this time there was a twinkle in his eye as he said it.

Gut brain reactions to cogjam issues get in the way of understanding what people are really trying to say, just as it did for staff at that facility. Once the inner alarm sounds, if left unbridled, defensive mode takes over and clouds the picture.

The field of eyewitness testimony studies this as something called "weapon focus."[71] If a bad guy enters the scene with a gun or other weapon, adrenalin floods the chemistry of those who feel threatened by it. Their narrowed survival-based focus zeroes in on the weapon, the most deadly element of the situation. However in doing so standers-by often don't notice other important details—like what the bad guy looks like.

This is one reason for inconsistency in eyewitness testimonies. It's not necessarily because of poor memory or purposeful fabrication. The standers-by

71 Loftus, E., Loftus, G. R., & Messos, J. (1987). Some facts about "weapon focus." *Law and Human Behavior*, 11, 55–62.

never picked up on key details in the first place. After the event, memory fills in the blanks of representations with whatever makes the most sense, which may be complete fiction.

My adventure with trying to get a chat group to understand what I was saying about civil protest could also be a case of weapon focus. With everybody so sensitized, any comment even suggesting possible deviation from standard practice turned loose the inner lizards: "Sound the alarm!" The haste of anticipatory self-defense had them introducing all sorts of inferential leaps. Only with extreme persistence did I finally get my point across, in spite of the fact that all of us already held the same general perspective. Even Deepak Chopra, world-renowned and well-respected spirituality and health guru, reports not being able to open his mouth about socio-political topics without being told he believes something he does not.[72]

That's how misguided our listening skills can become. Thanks to narrowed focus, cogjam keeps sweeping them into the dustbin. Therefore the value of retrieving and dusting off listening skills is not only so the other individual can feel heard. It's also so we can better decipher what is actually being said.

Political rants also tend to end more quickly if we sit and listen without responding. That interested ear may be all others really need to calm themselves and refocus, no feedback required. Not letting our personal agenda interrupt can help us learn a thing or two as well, such as why certain people feel so strongly about their positions. Our own views rob us of this if we let them jump in and change the course of conversation.

After others seem to have said all they need to say, there's always the option of finding a diplomatic way to change the subject. There's no need to throw fuel on dying embers. Having your own strong opinion does not mean you always need to express it. Especially if in the ongoing situation, doing so is not likely to get you anywhere.

Active listening. Active listening goes beyond listening as the other person vents. It is "active" in that whatever you say or do eases expression of what he or she is trying to say. The goal of active listening is to increase understanding, rather than compare differing positions. The listener holds personal or other opinions at bay, so that the speaker can feel like his or her position has been heard. After all, that's what the speaker's gut brain is fighting for—for logical brains in the herd to notice and take care of the threat perceived within the difference of opinion.

72   Chopra, D., & Tolle, E. (2017). *Awakening from the illusion of separateness: Spiritual truths to help heal a divided world.* The Chopra Center online seminar, 9/20/17.

You might recognize these do's and don'ts as practices of good listeners you have known:[73]

- Face the speaker in a nonthreatening manner. Keep in mind that staring someone in the eye, directly face-to-face, is what people do when angry or confrontational. If you do likewise, the speaker's gut brain may misinterpret your intentions. However you do want to have eye contact, so the person understands that you truly are listening. Turning your body to face slightly away from the speaker allows him or her to escape your gaze when feelings of vulnerability strike. It also lets you avert your own gaze if you sense the speaker becoming uncomfortable with eye contact.

- Tap into your mindful attentiveness. If stress causes your diaphragm to tighten, take occasional deep breaths. Otherwise, you risk not taking in enough air. Insufficient oxygen messes up ability to focus and think.

- Adopt a calm, relaxed speaking voice, even if that's not how you really feel. A soft, low voice has a relaxing effect for speaker and listener alike.

- Try to be open-minded and flexible, as much as you can be for volatile cogjam topics. Remind yourself that you are not listening in order to be "brainwashed" into some other position, but to gain information. Adopt the objective stance of an investigator or scientist: What is the person really saying? What is the meaning behind the words? What feelings are being expressed?

- Summarize or paraphrase back what you hear. Make sure it represents no more than what the speaker is saying, rather than adding interpretations, conclusions, or other embellishments of what has been said. For example, try something like "so you get really fed up when you hear about the latest federal budget proposals" (validating their angry feelings); or "when they make those comments, it's hard not to feel for those who are unfairly criticized" (indirectly acknowledging their indignant sense of compassion). Or even something as simple as "yes, this really is a mess, isn't it."

- Be mindful of body language, the speaker's and your own. Both provide useful information—such as whether you or the speaker is relaxing or becoming more uptight.

- Do not interrupt. If you need clarification, wait for the speaker to pause before requesting it.

- Ask open-ended questions, rather than ones that require only yes or no. This way the speaker has maximum control over what is shared. For example, try "What are your thoughts about the budget proposal?" rather than "Do you think the budget proposal is too spendy?"

73   Leutenberg, E. A. & Liptak, J. J. (2012). *Coping with difficult people workbook.* Duluth, MN: Whole Person.

- Judge neither the speaker, nor what is said. Avoid any appearance of disapproval. Keep whatever you say or do consistent with principles of compassion and understanding.

Active listening goes far to heal relationships strained by cogjam. Feeling misunderstood by those in your support system is painful and frustrating. Active listening shows the person that you value the relationship and truly seek understanding, over and above importance placed on political beliefs.

Disarm your opponent. Disarming the opponent was the tactic my 13-year-old self used during the sore loser challenge. I took the wind out of the girl's sails by not allowing her words to serve as a weapon.[74] Those who throw out challenging words on at least some level know they are likely to get certain reactions, and that those reactions probably won't be productive. You, however, can break the pattern—or at least begin productive conversation—by not delivering the expected response to the challenge.

Let's revisit that example of a friend or coworker saying something like, "Those [insert party members of choice] have no idea how to put together a sensible federal budget."

- Look for something—anything—you can agree with. Then comment on the point of agreement, rather than let your gut brain lash out at the disagreeable: "It is a mammoth task, isn't it." "They do seem to be struggling with it." "It's hard not to be impatient." The more you agree rather than react, the sooner the rant ends. Eventually the other person's gut brain realizes you aren't a threat to do battle with, and backs down.

- Try an intellectualized approach. Focus on something objective about the provocative comment, and use it to redirect the conversation into a less volatile direction: "What do you think the main priorities for the budget should be right now?" or "I wonder what keeps getting in the way of the two sides agreeing." This not only breaks pattern, but also helps the other person move back into his or her logical brain.

- Ask for additional information. "What is it you don't like about the budget proposal? How would you change it?" If the situation deteriorates into insults or name-calling, try something like "What specifically are you referring to that makes them look like [disparaging label here]?" Or, "What led you to that conclusion?" or "What do you think they could do to fix the problem?" This approach at times leads to productive solution finding.

Of course, we need to be prepared to discover that all we get in return is more snide remarks, rather than a genuine attempt at logical discussion. Not everybody who is angry is interested in discussing the issue, perhaps wanting

---

74 Burns, D. D. (1980). *Feeling good: The new mood therapy.* New York: Avon Books.

only to vent or lash out. When this is the case, the most compassionate course of action is to stop talking and listen, as long as it doesn't turn into abuse.

This technique is also useful when dealing with bullies—who, as you may have noticed, are having a hey-day in this era of cogjammed interactions. The more you say in your defense, the more nasty comments they will come up with. Your defensive reacting is their goal. They are purposely trying to get your goat, rather than just defend themselves. Reacting to their barbs only eggs on more abuse. So—try agreeing with their insults:

"Yeah, I guess I am a little flakey sometimes."

"No argument there."

"I've screwed up a lot worse than that."

"I apologize for being so incompetent."

"You're right. Sometimes I am really stupid."

Bullies can only come up with insults for so long, unless your becoming defensive gives them new material to work with. And, there's really no need to challenge them. Their insistently spouting off nasty remarks doesn't make them true, no matter how many times they say them. Those overhearing the exchange recognize this as well. So choose the high road. The payoff is better in the end.

Careful, caring confrontation. Perhaps there's a specific person in your life who keeps bringing up the same negative theme, knowing—or not yet realizing—that it always makes you uncomfortable. Some people don't take hints easily. Or when upset, they have difficulty noticing how their actions affect others. Occasionally this requires taking out and dusting off the velvet sledgehammer. In other words, we state the problem explicitly, but express it with kindness and compassion. We speak our minds, but in a way that is assertive, rather than aggressive.[75]

Here are the basic steps:

- Pick a time and place where you can expect relative privacy, and are not likely to be interrupted. The worst possible time is when either you or the other person is feeling or expressing strong emotions. That timing would encourage more gut reactions, rather than genuine connecting.

- Prepare by calming yourself, engaging mindfulness if it helps. Consider the bigger picture of your relationship with this individual, the compassion you have for his or her feelings, or how addressing this problem may open at least one tunnel of clarity through the cogjam haze clouding your shared corner of common humanity.

- If possible, begin your statement in a way that includes a positive:

75   Alberti, R., & Emmons, M. (2017). *Your perfect right: Assertiveness and equality in your life and relationships,* 10th ed. Oakland, CA: Impact Publishers.

"I like hanging out with you, so I wanted to talk with you about this."

"We work pretty well together, and I think we can do even better."

"I learn a lot from you, but there's something getting in the way right now."

Such phrases indicate you value the person or the relationship. Conveying empathy first can also lessen the sting of confrontation:

"You're a busy person; I appreciate your taking time to discuss this with me."

"I know this is something that is important to you, too, and I respect that."

- Then get to the point quickly, stating the problem and how you feel when it happens, using a "when . . . I feel . . ." format, such as:

"When people talk about the crazy politics these days, I get uncomfortable."

"When you comment on politicians you don't like, I feel anxious/threatened/like I need to distance myself."

"After those topics come up in the break room, I have trouble concentrating when I go back to my desk."

Be factual if needed, such as reminding the person of a specific comment or incident. Note that you do not use phrases that blame the other person, such as "you make me angry," "what you said upset me," or "you shouldn't do that." Nor do you deny the other person's rights, such as their right to have an opinion. You are only stating the circumstance and how you feel, and taking responsibility for your feelings.

- Give the person a chance to react. Listen attentively, then let the person know you hear and acknowledge his or her feelings.

- Once you both understand each other, find your common ground. Depending on the circumstance, you can either ask for possible options for changing the situation, or offer suggestions of your own:

"Perhaps you could discuss [insert issue here] with other friends, instead of me."

"Maybe you could let me know when you're going to get into that kind of discussion, so I can excuse myself."

"We could just agree to disagree. Then I'll feel excused from responding to further comments on the matter."

- Thank the other person. Tell them you appreciate their willingness to work it through. If you think they may be feeling defensive or hurt after it's over, check it out.

"Are you okay with this?"

"Are we still good?"

"Was there anything you wanted to talk about?"

Keep in mind that not everybody has the ego strength to handle healthy confrontation. If they become disconcerted by the exchange, find a way to reassure them that your opinion of them—or the relationship itself—is not at risk. Immediately back off if you discover zero tolerance for this type of discussion.

There are some who habitually respond to any form of confrontation with inner lizards engaged to the max: "I'll say whatever I #@%& want to say," or "I'm entitled to my opinion." "That's how I feel. Get over it." "I am who I am." If so, apologize for bringing it up and back off. If they aren't ready to deal with it, they aren't ready. So be it. At least you know where you stand, and can think up appropriate avoidance maneuvers to use in the future. After having time to cool off and think it over, some people sheepishly come back and ask to finish the exchange.

Address the real need. This conversation is appropriate for relationships that are intimate enough to discuss sensitive personal topics. Continuing in the spirit of active listening and caring confrontation, we direct conversation toward whatever need appears not to be fulfilled for the person who's unreasonably argumentative, or makes repeated hostile remarks:

"What is it about this that upsets you so much?"

"Is this the only thing bothering you right now, or is there something else?"

"What can I do that might help?"

You already know that there's a fear of some sort lurking beneath it. Otherwise, the person's gut brain wouldn't keep trying to sling rocks. And since this is someone you have a close relationship with, you care that he or she is in a hurting place. Park your compassion there. Then focus on what you might be able to do to help reassure your friend.

Be prepared to discover that many do not yet recognize why cogjam issues feel personally threatening. They may still live in that initial state described in Chapter One: uncertainty, confusion, relationships feeling threatened, troubling self-doubts, guilt and shame, fear of potential violence, and dealing with bizarre realities. They may not yet be able to tell you exactly what they need, or their reasons.

But that's okay. At least you've gotten somebody you care about to give it thought. It may lead to productive conversations at a later date. Let them know that you are available for such discussions, if that is what you desire.

Distraction techniques. When people are only moderately upset, their attention can be diverted onto less testy territory. My father's favorite distraction technique for when we kids got too worked up was to find a joke in the situation, or to pull somebody's leg with some outrageous suggestion.

A little laughter goes a long way. It's hard to stay angry when you're laughing. Humor reminds us that sometimes we get too serious. It is also something you don't see as much of in these times of cogjam, other than hostile humor aiming to ridicule others. I miss hearing the healthy humor that used to make the rounds in political circles.

I also think of those old Bugs Bunny cartoons, where he's being hunted down by ever-hopeful Elmer Fudd. Typically Bugs does something to irk Elmer, then zips off screen. Elmer pulls himself together and dashes after him. He eventually catches up, panting in his fury. Bugs would just be standing there, leaning against a tree and holding his carrot. Then he'd deliver his trademark line: "Eh . . . *munch, munch, munch* . . . what's up, Doc?"

"You . . . wascally . . . wabbit!" the enraged Elmer usually sputtered.

"Say, that's an awfully nice hat you're wearing, Doc . . . *munch, munch, munch.*"

"You think so?" Elmer would blush, take off his hat, and begin talking about its merits.

No, something this obvious isn't the right tool for most lathered-up conversational partners. But there are countless other ways to distract people when they are being unreasonable. As mentioned earlier, diplomatically changing the subject will do this. So will questions that require them to shift gears into their logical brain.

Listed below are a few other tactics for getting through heated situations without making things worse, perhaps even influencing them for the better.

- "I'm having trouble following. Could you repeat that for me, a little more slowly?" When the speaker forces a slower rate of speech, slower and more organized thought processes follow—opening the door for greater influence by the logical brain.

- "You're bringing up something that sounds really important. I need a minute to think this through." While both of you remain silent, the speaker's gut brain has a chance to realize it's been heard, and the logical brain has time and opportunity to move in.

- "It sounds like you've given this a lot of thought." As long as this is conveyed as a compliment rather than sarcasm, the gut brain feels heard. And the individual certainly isn't going to disagree with it. The same goes for the response, "You've given me something to think about."

- "Is there something you wanted from me about this?" or, "How can I help you with this?" People may not even know what they want, other than an opportunity to vent about whatever ails them. The question requires that they stop and think about what they are saying or doing, and why— again, a function of logical thinking.

- "How do you think we might fix this?" is an appropriate question for problems or conflicts that involve the two of you, and must be in some way addressed to get beyond them. As the person turns to higher brain functions, solution finding can follow. If it is a complex or unusual problem, depending on the person, you might be able to get him or her to go along with the problem solving technique described in the previous chapter. The process of doing it together can also contribute to healing emotional consequences of whatever conflict got you there.

An important caveat: Say nothing while the other person is yelling. Interruptions are perceived as counterattacks, and the other person will double down all the more. Likewise, don't nod or say "uh-huh" as the rant continues. The less you react, the sooner it ends. Introduce any needed comments or questions only after your adversary appears to have run out of steam. And while you're waiting, practice tapping into your mindfulness and compassion. That way you better keep your own gut brain under wraps.

WHEN PEOPLE STOP BEING REASONABLE

We all fall victim to an occasional disconnect from our logical brains. For most of us it's a temporary state, popping out when emotions overwhelm or we willingly invite it in for a short visit. Eventually we return to our senses, and bring logic and objectivity back online.

Giving in to emotions and pure experiencing is an asset some of the time, such as when we're immersing ourselves in a play activity or are in the throes of certain passions. Mindfulness itself is exactly this: sensing and noting, without assessing, judging, or otherwise reacting.

But there's a time and place for everything. Sorting through heated socio-political issues is definitely not the time and place to let primitive process take the reins. That's what got us cogjammed in the first place.

Unfortunately for some, distancing themselves from objectivity and logic is a regular pastime. They habitually go by their gut. While traveling the highways of life, their engine lights are always on. Anything that challenges them or contradicts their agenda shifts them into overdrive. It's all they trust to go on.

For such individuals the cogjam mentality is an ongoing way of being, not just a current reaction to socio-political stress. In review, a chronic mental health or other medical condition may play a role in their status. Both neurological and psychodynamic influences can directly interfere with making best use of the logical brain. Or, their differing coping gifts may be because of current life circumstances that are extraordinarily turbulent and stressful.

People tend to be the best people they know how to be. Given varying life experiences, cogjammed reacting may be the best some know how to do.

Imagine what it would be like if this were you: always terrified and feeling at risk, yet defended by little more than gut reactions. Others on the scene seem to draw at least some strength from their wits. Meanwhile you are left feeling as brainless as a stump. Everybody else so clearly has an upper hand. Such perceptions pump up even more feelings of vulnerability, encouraging more irrational behavior.

So what do we do about cogjam-related issues when such individuals are in our midst?

Step One: Awareness. First, we need to identify who they are. If it's someone we spend much time with, we're probably aware of whether he or she has any of the following core characteristics. These are conditions we all have at least some familiarity with, since from time to time our own gut brains get drawn into these stances of excessive self-involvement.

- Major difficulties with emotional regulation: Their anger or anxiety is both extreme and poorly handled. They go way overboard in comparison to how most people live with those feeling states. Others may refer to them as being a "hothead" or "Chicken Little."

- Reactive and impulsive: They often speak or act without thinking. They also may hold the belief that their impulsive acting out is only being "who they are," rather than something they have choices about and control over.

- Do not anticipate potential consequences: Considering what might happen with a certain course of action requires input from the logical brain. Immediate gut reacting does not allow adequate time or opportunity to consult an advisable knowledge base. Thus they often find themselves to be victims of their own poor choices.

- Poor social judgment: Interaction with others requires more than identifying good guys and bad guys, fighting/fleeing the bad guys, or mindlessly glomming onto whichever herd is doing something agreeable. Therefore their morals and moral behavior are often challenged. They may construct and live by their own chosen moral standards, which largely serve gut-brain interests. Or, as in the case of the psychopath, the moral compass is nonexistent. Therefore they frequently do things that hurt or offend others, unintentionally or otherwise.

- Do not learn from mistakes: When their poor choices do not work out, they cannot step back and evaluate what they could have done differently. Instead, they view such misfortune as someone else's fault, which turns them into masters of the blame game. They have extreme difficulty recognizing or examining core beliefs or cognitive distortions that may lie beneath the surface of their ill-advised choices. Change, and learning itself, is extraordinarily difficult for them.

It's not a total wash for these folks. They usually also have traits and abilities that are desirable, or even exceptional. That's why they so often find ways not only to survive in the world, but also to enjoy spectacular successes, in spite of fatal flaws.[76] But their worldview takes them and others on an extremely bumpy ride.

What personal change they make and when they choose to pursue it is their own journey to map out, not ours. But meanwhile, those of us coexisting in the same corner of the world inevitably find ourselves occasionally on the receiving end of their self-absorption. All that acting out in "self defense" and self-interest betrays the trust necessary for any relationship.

Thus whom they consider to be a best buddy frequently changes—not only due to being dumped by friends, but also because as soon as "best buddies" disagree with them or otherwise contradict their agenda, they are enemies: "People are either for me against me." "It can only be my way or the highway." "Whatever I want is really great; anything contrary is a disaster." The gut brain knows no in betweens, and their logical brains contribute little more than rationalizations to support the gut's premature proclamations.

Step Two: Acceptance. A chronically difficult person is a chronically difficult person. We're not talking about those who only occasionally let their gut brains get out of control. This is about individuals whose negative reactions are fairly predictable. From past experience we know we can depend upon them to react in toxic ways. Expecting that our reasoning can get them to see the light is not realistic. Their logic is not in charge, other than when it supports gut conclusions.

Accept this reality. Approach the problems they create assuming you're likely to get more of the usual, because that is what you most likely will get. The bonus to this stance: any headway you do make will be all the more rewarding.

Step Three: Understanding and Empathy. If the person appears to invite engagement or feedback—possibly even demanding it—staying out of trouble means keeping conversation focused on his or her view, as well as displaying understanding and empathy for his or her perceived plight. You need neither agree nor disagree with their assessments. But you do show them that you understand.

Saying "I understand how you feel" may effectively communicate with those who are level headed. However, for those who are overemotional or unreasonable, it often doesn't: "Nobody could know exactly how I feel!" or "If you understood how I feel you wouldn't act this way!" may well be the immediate retort.

Following are a series of steps for exploring a topic or otherwise engaging a difficult person during adverse interactions.[77]

76   Yudofsky, S. C. (2005). *Fatal flaws: Navigating destructive relationships with people with disorders of personality and character.* Washington, DC: American Psychiatric Publishing, Inc.

77   Sesno, F. (2017). *Ask more: The power of questions to open doors, uncover solutions, and spark change.* New York: AMACOM.

- Crank up the empathy: Consider what standing in this person's shoes would be like. If you experienced or interpreted things in the same way, what would you see? What would you think? How would you feel?

- Establish what might be called "intimate distance:" let your empathy, interest, and understanding show; but at the same time, maintain your own emotional distance and objectivity. Don't let it wander off into something about you or your own beliefs. Apply principles of active listening: position your body in a way that is nonthreatening, be attentive, use a calm and soft voice, remember to stay open-minded and flexible, and refrain from judging. There's nothing wrong with loving someone from afar.

- Leave them plenty of maneuvering space. If you must get more information, ask open questions that are fairly broad. Open questions give others room to go whichever direction they want, such as "What are you most concerned about right now?" rather than questions like "Are you afraid you're going to be hurt somehow by this?" Giving them the widest possible breadth of possible directions helps them avoid the uncomfortable or unfamiliar territory that typically scares gut brains. Instead they gain a sense of control, and their gut brains ease up a little.

- Listen beyond the words themselves. For everything we say, there's plenty we don't say. What shows up in their tone, facial expressions, and body language as they share their position or concerns? What is a person not saying, and why? Engage empathy for the position revealed, no matter whether it is logical or something you agree with.

Step Four: Practice Compassion. Chances of changing such individuals' overvalued beliefs are slim to none. Besides, as soon as you offer a view that potentially conflicts, you are the enemy, as far as their gut brains are concerned. So as the person appears about to run dry on material, transition out of the interlude with a show of compassion, rather than reveal what you yourself might believe.

How to bow out of the exchange varies, based on who the person is and the degree of intimacy you have with him or her. It might include parting statements like:

- "I'm sorry this has caused you so much concern."
- "I'm headed for the break room. Is there something I can bring back for you?"
- "That had to be hard for you to share. Would you like a shoulder rub (or something more appropriate for the relationship)?"
- "Don't forget to take care of yourself (if you suspect they're neglecting sleep, nutrition, etc.). These are stressful times."

- "You know, when I've got something like this bothering me I [go for a run, have a hot bath, take part in spiritual activities, etc.]. I hope you have something like that, too, that feels good during hard times."
- "Yes, finding answers to what's going on right now has turned into quite a job for all of us. I hope it gets easier down the road."
- "Maybe there's something you can do to keep from getting so much exposure to these issues. Then you won't have to deal with them so often."

Remember: Safety first. One day I was standing in line at the grocery store. Above the impulse buy display was the usual line-up of tabloids. As always, splashed across the front of every cover was at least one unflattering story about politicians. In fact, I recall one public figure joking that she regularly read the tabloids just to establish what was really going on in her life.

Anyway, as I watched my groceries chug along the woman behind me begin to mutter to herself. Then her voice rose a little, as she made a harsh comment about somebody featured on one of the slicks. It wasn't clear whether she was speaking to the checkout clerk, or me, or somebody else in line. But none of us chose to react.

She threw out another colorful comment, this time even louder. Out the corner of my eye I could see her staring in the direction of myself and the clerk, as if awaiting—or maybe demanding—some kind of response. I busied myself with my purse, credit cards, and the like. It was mostly subterfuge, hoping to give the impression of being distracted or preoccupied. But I could practically feel the woman next to me stiffening up and preparing her next volley.

"Is that really the price of that . . . avocado?" I blurted out to the clerk. "I thought they were going on special."

The clerk, whose forehead was beginning to bead up, handed me a weekly flyer. "Here's the specials. What do you see?"

The clerk and I continued the contrived conversation, the ruse of a mis-keyed avocado successfully filling the void. We finished the checkout transaction in record time, and I was on my grateful way. In the background I could hear the transaction with the distressed customer moving along at an equally speedy pace.

You might wonder: with everything I've had to say about having compassion for those who struggle with cogjam, why did I leave this strung-out customer just hanging there, twisting in the wind? She was obviously rattled. She certainly could have used a little compassion. Why didn't I even attempt to engage or connect?

Because some unreasonable people are dangerous. I had no way to know what this woman really was about. She was a complete stranger. Was she so loosely wrapped that no matter what was said, it would only escalate the situation? Might she have a weapon in her purse, which could enter the picture if our response was interpreted as supporting the "bad guy?" And what if engaging her had a reinforcing effect, and she followed me out to my car as a captive audience, with no end to the rant in sight?

Weakening cogjam and its impact is important. But so is your physical wellbeing, not to mention emotional wellbeing. A personal mission of disempowering cogjam where you find it does not justify forcing yourself to sit through abuse, verbal or physical. Recognize when the better choice is to walk away. Safety always comes first.

Likewise, you probably already know which of those among your personal acquaintances can handle rational discussion, and which ones so rigidly cling to certain propaganda that their beliefs are impregnable. Social media makes it easy to pick up who has not yet realized and abandoned the folly of potshots and inflammatory remarks. Their comments may still be as cogjammed as they were when this all started.

If you have coworkers or other acquaintances that tend to be unreasonable, there's nothing wrong with or cowardly about dodging the bullet. Rather than engaging, use diversion strategies like distractions, disarming their words, or if nothing else simply come up with a believable reason to absent yourself. People gain nothing by forcing themselves to go through rounds of hostility over things unlikely to change. Nor does the person who threw the first verbal punch really benefit. Bringing such exchanges to an end is the true act of compassion, for all concerned.

CHOOSE YOUR COURSE WITH CARE

Sometimes the door opens for discussing difficult topics with others in your life. Other times, it remains tightly locked—or if we find a way to enter in uninvited, it does not end well. There are many choices to consider while interacting on a cogjammed playing field:

Choose your battles carefully. Do not engage every challenge that stumbles onto perspectives you hold dear. Will the battle actually accomplish anything in this particular instance? Or will it only make things worse?

Choose carefully with whom you will or will not freely speak your mind. Not everybody is ready to face the multiplicity of perspectives and opinions out there.

Choose your words carefully. Apply compassion and understanding rather than defensiveness, anger, or judgment.

Choose to keep your mouth shut. This is the best response when recognizing you aren't or won't soon be getting through to a person's overburdened attitude.

Choose to walk away, if that's the only way to protect yourself—and perhaps indirectly protect the unreasonable person from his or her own behavior, as well.

CHAPTER 13

......

Healing the Herd

HEALING A COGJAMMED community takes a village-worth of effort. There's more to it than each of us addressing our own inner lives and interpersonal relations. Cultural fluctuations also contribute to cogjam status, which at times take swipes at both self and other healing.

The path we eventually carve to lead us out of the wilderness will take form as it will. We can't predict much about its final direction at this early stage. But we do know that as individual attitudes change, so does society.

Thus far the incessant warring of conservatives versus liberals, politicians versus pundits, and the like has received the lion's share of attention in describing cogjam's cultural effect. However beneath the surface of more obvious goings on lie other deeply imbedded influences, ones that can fuel polarized worldviews. To escape this ongoing cultural bloodshed, such underlying influences must be outed and factored in.

Cultural change is a long, slow process. As with cogjam, our cultural beliefs and practices didn't turn up overnight. Weeding out cultural concepts that are no longer relevant takes time as well. But limits to immediate gratification shouldn't stop us from doing our part to help slash the eventual path through the jungle. One way we hack away impeding branches is by gaining deeper understanding of cultural norms in which we and fellow community members are currently enmeshed.

THE INTERSECT OF GENDER AND CULTURE

"A whistling woman and an crowing hen are sure to come to no good end."

While working my way through school I was an office assistant at a public service agency. One of the women I worked with, whom I'll call Ethel, was a real livewire. She had reached an age at which most people retire. However she showed no signs of calling it quits. She also had a very active social life. On more than one occasion I heard her finish detailing after-work plans with her mantra that "fun comes first!"

One day she shared a story about an uncle she'd been especially fond of during her growing years. Apparently Ethel was a firecracker back then, too. When her uncle came to visit he'd listen while she told him about her latest exploits. Shaking his head and clicking his tongue, he'd quote the saying about the fate of hens that crow like roosters and women who do unladylike things like whistle. She said that after he left she always sneaked out to the barn, closed the door, and whistled her heart out.

This story presents one major cultural torment in a nutshell. Ethel's uncle believed in a world where people conform to rigid role expectations. Women doing something like whistling was considered every bit as outrageous as a hen learning to crow. Ethel, on the other hand, lived a life of self-exploration. Rather than conforming, she listened with her heart. She climbed to the top of where her gifts and inclinations would take her, to the extent possible for someone coming of age in the day of the flapper. I sometimes wonder where she might have ended up had she been born in my cohort, with its more flexible expectations.

Regardless, conflicting gender role expectations continue to affect us to this day. To understand how we arrived at this cultural crossroad, we need to go back a few hundred years.

Families have not always been so split up regarding how they spent an average day. The more usual scenario was the whole family taking part in whatever efforts were required to meet joint daily needs. Children helped out with basics as soon as they were big enough to manage it. On farms, everybody in some manner worked the fields or tended the animals. Shopkeeper families often assigned tasks so that all family members could pitch in, with shop and home often in the same location. Professions, craft skills, and businesses were passed down through the family, with future vocations predetermined the day a child was born. Though still around, this particular path now tends to be one less taken.

Likewise, child oversight was more shared among family members. Children worked side by side with fathers as well as mothers. Such mentoring activity was a means for learning how to one day support families of their own. Children attending school for a prolonged period was an exception, rather than the norm. Society was comparatively simple. Being homeschooled with basics was often sufficient to become capable of meeting future adult daily challenges.

Gender-based expectations were around back then, too. But they were more socially and behaviorally oriented, and not as deeply fixed in career expectations as they later became. Yes, some things were considered men's work or women's work. But task assignments were often more influenced by pragmatics: only women could have babies, nurse them, and the like. While this was going on, duties that let women be home-oriented were more practical. Men were usually better at tasks requiring brute strength, which often placed them outside the home. As children matured, overseeing children and other work tasks intermingled more.

Then along came the Industrial Revolution, and the beginnings of technology. More and more jobs required that somebody leave home to earn a living. Meanwhile, someone had to stay home and take care of the kids while they were young. Furthermore, to succeed in their more complex society, children began needing longer educations. Thus the splitting of career expectations became more extreme—women working at home and keeping track of children, while men negotiated outside careers and provided financially.

Eventually role expectations became entrenched. Men spent most of their day separated from home and family. Women became less involved in work that was not home related. Children spent increasingly more time in school, with education becoming more critical to making it as adults. Laws emerged that kept children from working as an adult might, expanding the child-tending hours required of mothers. Joint, home-based family effort became an increasingly less common way to make a living or help guide role expectations.

Thus was the stage set for the early to mid-1900s, an era of significant historical trauma. First came the Great Depression, and then World War II. People's lives were turned upside down. Gut brains screamed in terror, for legitimate reasons: basic survival was repeatedly coming under question. Different types of threats and vulnerabilities surrounded them on multiple fronts.

Adrenalin and oxytocin served them well. They energized into the bonded tenacity that later became known as "The Greatest Generation." Joint efforts became tightly focused, with tunnel vision aiming toward getting them through both individual and community battles victorious. Men went off to war, and faced its strife and horrors. The women left behind filled in gaps by playing multiple roles. They went through rationing, or doing without altogether. Victory gardens sprang up where there once had been front lawns, helping to feed a nation in hardship.

Though it was difficult and extremely stressful, they kept their eyes on the prize. They looked forward to that day when it would all be over, when they could go back to life as it had once been. And in the middle of a world war, that vision looked pretty darn good. Families would be together again. Daily living would be easier and less threatening, for men and women alike. Bolstered by trauma chemistry, gender roles previously typical of men and women easily became stereotyped and idolized. The fantasy offered security and comfort for an extremely frightened generation.

Back in high school I saw a documentary about those days. A journalist interviewed a "Rosie the Riveter" type, who was working away on an assembly line. He asked her if she would continue after the war was over. Her answer sticks with me to this day: "This job belongs to some soldier. I'm going to go home and take care of my family."

There's nothing wrong with such a personal life plan, if that is what Rosie and her family would like. But this message was widely trumpeted, both by mouth and media. It was presented as an expectation, rather than as an option. It helped support that vision of a perfect world in a sunny future, where there would be no more threat and uncertainty. Citizens would all know what they were about, and what others were about. They would relax into rigidly carved slots. It was their security blanket, their ace in the hole for better times.

It dared not be challenged. Post-war sitcoms such as *Leave it to Beaver* and *Father Knows Best* reinforced belief in this fantasized world. Mainstream Judeo-Christian beliefs tended to stand behind the ideal as well, even though the cultures of Biblical times—at least as evidenced by scriptural writings—did not portray family roles looking quite like this.

Nevertheless, families of the 1950's did their best to be just like the ones they saw on TV. Men had careers while women typically did not, outside of homemaking. Men took up more dominant roles, while women were expected to be subservient and needing to be taken care of. As parents raised children they passed on to their sons the expectation that if they worked hard and kept their noses clean, there would be a job waiting out there for them. Which was largely true for that era—finishing high school was once all a young man needed to qualify for many family-supporting jobs.

As always, time changed the playing field. Trauma had a chance to heal. Most outgrew the need to cling to rigid gender role ideals as a way to cope. Advancing technology and the information boom lead to the world becoming even more complex for those just entering the workforce. A high school education no longer guaranteed qualification for jobs that could support a family.

Furthermore, the economy changed. The cost of living kept rising, and wages did not keep up. Eventually families with single wage earners struggled to make ends meet. So did single parent families, which had become more common as couples came to terms with the folly of forcing ideals as the answer to guaranteeing a successful marriage. Re-entry of the female workforce was inevitable.

Other changes involved expectations for minorities—first racial and ethnic, then later the LGBTQ and other marginalized populations. Earlier eras' expectation was that citizens of color or minority ethnicities would "stay in their place." The LGBTQ community was hidden or denied to exist, identified as mentally ill, and/or expected to keep their orientation in the closet. Hamstringed by discrimination practices, minorities did not present serious competition to those applying for better-paying jobs.

Civil rights movements addressed much of the institutionalized discrimination, though not all. Nevertheless, as time went on getting a good job became somewhat less challenging for members of minority and marginalized populations. They increased the volume of mainstream competition in the workforce.

Then along came the flood of immigrants. Lower paying jobs, like working in the fields and domestic help, were going unfilled. Child labor laws no longer supported bringing in minors to take care of such work. But for those living in poverty and/or the political upheaval of their homelands, such jobs looked like Nirvana. Immigrants filled the gaps. Many settled and raised families, producing the next wave of American residents. Their second generation took advantage of educational opportunities and moved up in the world, becoming yet another source of competition for those on the hunt for better-paying jobs.

To make matters worse, the ongoing infighting within the DC Beltway had let immigration laws and their implementation stagnate as the constancy of change went its way. The road to citizenship slowly became pitted with major potholes. Thus immigrants ferreted out backdoor ways to be able to work in the United States. Since such workers usually didn't pay taxes, employers were eager to snap them up at lower wage rates than those needed by citizens raising families and paying taxes.

So with all these changes, where did the life of the average white male end up? Michael Kimmel's book, *Angry White Men*, sums up their plight.[78] They were enduring one loss after another. On top of it all, they felt like they'd been "had." Their parents—and society itself—had given them a bum steer.

78   Kimmel, M. (2017). *Angry white men: American masculinity and the end of an era.* New York: Nation Books.

They had grown up believing in certain entitlements. They'd been told all they had to do is follow the right path, and everything would work out. They'd get a good job, buy a house, and step into the time-honored role of supporting the wife and kids. Instead, they found themselves up against stiff competition over fewer good-paying jobs, an economy that required double incomes for most families to get by, needing to rent rather than own their home, and career-oriented wives who expected them to help out with "women's work."

This is not to say that women were not also led down the garden path. The post-war fantasy was encouraged for us girls, as well. We'd been told our expected life path was to get married, have children, and become homemakers. There was supposedly no need to prepare for a career outside the home. As teenagers, required educational curricula for girls included homemaking classes—instruction in skills such as cooking, sewing, and childcare. Boys, on the other hand, were required to take a certain number of shop classes.

We were not allowed to take opposite gendered classes, even if we signed up for them as electives. I, for one, tried to get into the gas engines class. After all, both men and women drive cars. Here was a valuable set of skills and knowledge that would benefit anyone, regardless of gender. It was a no-brainer. But when my class schedule arrived, it always showed me funneled into some other classroom. In the final analysis, the traditional overrode the logical.

Many women of my era were unprepared for the cultural and economic changes to come. Whether we trained for an outside career was only supposed to be a personal choice. We grew up believing in our right as women to stay home and take care of our families, while someone else took responsibility for bringing home the bacon. Instead, both parents working became the rule rather than the exception, with women additionally responsible for most homemaking and childcare responsibilities. Thus there are plenty of angry women to go around these days, too.

However women did get a leg up over men in the process of adjusting to this new world. The ever-present need to juggle both family and career made cultural change impossible for women to ignore. Reality stared back at us daily. Making household ends meet, and feeding and clothing our children—major priorities for the average homemaker—often could not be achieved without simultaneously pitching in with a supplemental income. We may have been as angry as men in regard to having been misled. But we had little choice other than to accept that we were in a different world than the one we'd been raised to expect. So we adjusted path directions any way we needed to in order to succeed.

Most men did not have a similar opportunity. While wives grew into new realities, many husbands continued trying to stay only in provider and family über-leader roles, as outlined by the post-war generation. Belief in the stereo-typical macho male role model also held its own, adding to the conflict and confusion. Many are still left foundering in what it means to be a man in modern society.

How do we define the concept of "a good man," anyway?[79] Typically we envision good men as principled, dependable, responsible, hard workers, adequate providers, protectors, and strong family men. Meanwhile, the popular and idolized male movie characters are cut more from John Wayne or Clint Eastwood bolts of cloth. It's also the model we think of when telling someone to "man up" during a difficult situation: ignore your feelings, and act as if you are invulnerable. That's the first bit of confusion men are faced with sorting out.

The second involves the nurturing and supportive side of men getting shoved under the rug—first by their more restricted role in the childrearing arena, and then the pressure to deny any "femmy" urgings that deviate from the macho-man mold. True, women tend to be more inclined toward nurturing than men, for reasons of biology, psychology, and sociology.[80] But that does not mean men do not have this inner trait as well, or that there aren't also men out there who are better nurturers than the average woman. Squelching that side of themselves in order to fit the mold can be as trying for men as being denied opportunity to climb the rungs of "men's work" is for women. The assumption that women are always the better nurturer also led to wives getting unfair child custody advantages in divorce court, another reason for men to feel burnt.

From these ashes rose a new variety of community trauma. Thanks to diminished provider ability, identity confusion, and feeling deprived of their legacy and social status entitlements, the angry white men experienced dire threat.

The inner lizard awakens: "Survival is at stake! You can't get a good enough job. You can't depend on gender alone to guarantee dominance or power. The herd may look down on you, or even ostracize you for not measuring up to stereotypical expectations. To make matters worse, there's something changing out there. Something's no longer as it ought to be. Sound the alarm!"

In rush the adrenalin and oxytocin. "Which way do we go? How do we direct this narrowed and sharpened focus? Where's the enemy?

"Why, there they are. They're right in front of us. It's those minorities, immigrants, and women who are taking our jobs. It's those politicians and pundits whose efforts support change, rather than protect the safety of the status quo.

---

79   Real, T. (1998). *I don't want to talk about it: Overcoming the secret legacy of male depression.* New York: Scribner.

80   Taylor, S. E. (2003). *The tending instinct: Women, men, and the biology of our relationships.* New York: Henry Holt & Company.

Join up with the herd of other angry white men, and we'll let 'em have it." And a collective inner lizard forges onward, doing battle against the imaginary foe.

In other words right on cue, fundamental attribution error steps in: blaming certain individuals or groups, rather than a situation that has been evolving over many decades. The errant reasoning and resulting behaviors create more infighting and misunderstandings, rather than effective solution finding. Which, of course, is exactly what we're getting.

American culture did not play fair with these men. Nor did it play fair with women whose lives were upended by the changes of the last half-century. Little wonder a number of women joined the angry white men on the far right. Their gut brains insist that things must get back to the way they were, the tried and true: "We need to get back to that post-war fantasy! That's where we'll find reliability, certainty, and safety."

But those who rolled with and adjusted to the emerging new world are coping with equally distressed inner lizards: "You're under attack! Those guys on the right want to take away all the advancements. They'll annihilate everything you've worked so hard to achieve. They want to re-subjugate women, persecute minorities, alienate other nations, and hinder the nurturing and caring that finally infiltrated macho capitalist ideals. Everybody's liberty is challenged."

The right versus left posturing is thus further fueled. More fear and anger, and all the neurochemistry that goes with it. More rigidity. Polarization. Groupthink. And the beat goes on.

We're usually well familiar with the torments that drive our own personal views on hot political topics. However addressing cultural influences and moving forward requires becoming familiar with a different arena, one that embraces the benefits of objectivity and alternative perspective taking.

Culture is largely about attitude, most of which is subconscious. As one of my junior high teachers so often chastised, with his trademark rolling of the "r": "It is strrrrictly a question of your attitude." We view what's going on around us through the attitudinal lens of cultural expectation. Underlying attitude roots have the ability to keep us stuck in place no matter how much contradictory evidence crosses our paths.[81]

Therefore the first step for each of us is to set aside our own biases long enough to stand in the shoes of those who are not like-minded. That's how we get a feel for the whole picture, rather than experience only our own biases, thoughts and fears. What would it be like to live with the alternative set of concerns?

How frightening and uncertain the world can look, no matter which inner lizard's glasses you peer through. At least some bit of compassion stirs as

---

81   Hornsey, M. J., & Fielding, K. S. (2017). Attitude roots and Jiu Jitsu persuasion: Understanding and overcoming the motivated rejection of science. *American Psychologist*, 72, 459–473.

we consider what we see. That compassion can help override the insistence of destructive gut brain urgings, as well as reestablish connection with common humanity.

Debate over gender role expectations will likely go on indefinitely. Meanwhile, the more compassion we introduce into our midst, the less our differing opinions will interfere with daily social functioning:

- We can acknowledge and accept that irreconcilable differences exist between others' worldviews and our own. That is a reality, always has been, and likely always will be.
- We can strive to be accepting and considerate of those individuals who disagree, even while they are being disagreeable.
- We can seek out the common ground, rather than search for and focus on mismatch.
- We can become more knowledgeable about concerns and cultural influences that lead them to see things a certain way.

Successful community healing means actively training ourselves to better get along on the playground, especially when we're among those who display short cogjam fuses. It means getting to know where others are really coming from. Only by arranging meetings of the minds between logical brains can we make this happen. As compassion and common humanity pave the way to this outcome, the path out of cogjam will reveal itself.

LIFE WITH CONSTANT MEDIA

I participate in several writers' groups. Some of them stay in touch using social media. Like everyone else, we've dealt with the occasional interloper sneaking in from elsewhere, sniffing around for ways to stir up trouble.

One day some unknown individual posted a nasty rant in broken English. Its content aimed to stir up one of the day's major cogjam pots. Following similar posts, I usually see a bunch of angry retorts or other defensive comments. But that was not the case for this one. Here's the main gist of how my writer colleagues responded:

"Rework plot. Not very original."

"Is it really worser, or should it be worserest?"

"Um, put down the bottle, mate."

"Great hook. What happens next?"

"I think aragance is how they spell it in Aragon."

"Be fair, you guys. Others in this group make errors in spelling and grammar."

"It's spelled grammer."

"I think [account originator] put this here, just to keep us on our toes."

"Try turning [object of political rant] off, then on again. Works for my computer."

"His editor will need to be paid overtime."

"That poor guy will think twice before hacking into a writers group again."

I have never been more proud of my fellow writers. Why? Let me count the ways:

1. They didn't let their gut brains be baited.
2. They consulted logical brain options for a way to adaptively react to the intrusion.
3. They introduced humor, a healthy coping strategy that also served as a distraction.
4. Compassion dotted their responses, even if at times tongue in cheek.
5. They didn't let a new round of offensive material contribute to cogjam, or poison the atmosphere of the group.
6. They turned a wad of toxicity into an opportunity for creativity, a growth moment.
7. Without anybody directly spelling out what we were trying to do and how we were going about it, we joined together as one and steered clear of ill will.

What would social media feeds look like, if every group behaved this way? More to the point, what would happen with cogjam if we all placed greater priority on herd wellbeing than giving in to gut-brain impulses?

Shining a spotlight on the role media play in cogjam is not out of spite, vindictiveness, or some other gut-brain edict to kill the messenger. News media are simply a reality we live with. Most if not all political material and cog-jammed messaging comes either directly or indirectly from such outlets. They bombard us daily: television, radio, newspapers and slicks, as well as the many internet sources and applications. In the discussion to follow, I cluster them into two broad groups: traditional news media and social media.

TRADITIONAL NEWS MEDIA

For the last couple of years, licensed mental health professionals have been wading through a cogjam-swamped challenge. Many have felt pressured to assign a formal diagnosis to the current president's mental health status, based on what we have seen him say and do.[82] Given all the tweets and other public statements and actions, there's certainly no shortage of data available for forming an opinion. Most everyone else on the planet seems to have already done so. Why are the experts dragging their feet?

---

82   Lee, B. X. (2017). *The dangerous case of Donald Trump: 27 psychiatrists and mental health experts assess a president*. New York: St. Martins Press.

Because we do not diagnose people from afar. As ethical practitioners we follow protocols. They include appropriate psychological testing, and otherwise directly interacting with the individual in question before deciding on a diagnosis. That is how we ensure a fair, valid assessment, rather than one distorted by bias. True, we would probably do better at simply taking an educated guess than the random person on the street. But we can't assign a formal diagnosis without using protocol, no matter how obvious we think the outcome will be.

However, a conflicting consideration also applies to this scenario. Legally, we are charged with duty to warn.[83] In certain circumstances, if we come across evidence that someone is at risk of harming themselves or others, we are to report it to the authorities and/or potential victims. Formal diagnosis is not required. It's recognition of the potential for serious harm taking place that flips the switch.

I am not going to try to second guess whether the confusing and conflicting information filtering down from the top represents a master plan to shake up a polarized Congress, the gaslighting of America, the aimless ranting of unspecified psychopathology, or something lying somewhere in between. Eventually hindsight will give us a few answers. But meanwhile, in the midst of potential threat and uncertainty, how were we mental health professionals supposed to satisfy all that society requires of us?

Most of us elected not to publicly diagnose. But we did find an alternate answer: petitions to Congress. Many thousands of us recommended that the president get a good, thorough, unbiased psychiatric evaluation. Then in a separate petition, we expressed concern about the danger of having someone who regularly calls attention to his seemingly erratic behavior placed in a position of such power. So while we didn't formally diagnose, we did follow through on duty to warn. Having done so, we can at least assure ourselves we have done as much as is ethically possible.

Journalists face a similar challenge. Their reporting needs to jibe with certain professional values, most of them centered on making sure what they report is as accurate and fair as possible. But the public also expects journalists to inform them of potential dangers in the world. People need to know where the hurricane is expected to hit, where the traffic pileup is and how to avoid it, how certain laws have changed, and other potential hazards. News reporting helps all of us look after our own safety and best interests.

Current affairs have pitted journalistic ethics and responsibility to the public against one another, and journalists struggle as they try to do both. They

83   VandeCreek, L., & Knapp, S. (2001). *Tarasoff and beyond: Legal and clinical considerations in the treatment of life-endangering patients.* Practitioner's Resource Series. Sarasota, FL: Professional Resource Press.

appear entrenched in the battle of all cogjam battles, with the rest of us occasionally becoming collateral damage.

Here's how it plays out. The main values that guide the field of journalism are:[84]

- *Honesty.* Journalists do not misrepresent the truth. They report what they find accurately, and do their best to present it in ways that are not misleading.

- *Independence.* Journalists avoid conflict of interest. If they have a personal connection with a news story, they avoid bias by passing it to one of their colleagues or revealing the connection within the story.

- *Fairness.* Journalists endeavor to present both sides of a story, no matter where their personal opinions lie. If they can't be objective, they let someone else cover the story.

- *Productiveness.* Journalists dig up reliable facts—confirming and disconfirming—to support or contradict what they hear an interviewee say. They also report facts they uncover that may be unpopular.

- *Pride.* Journalists take responsibility for what they report. They don't report it if they don't feel like they can stand behind it. When they err, they backtrack and publicly correct their errors.

Journalists are keenly aware of potential dangers brewing in DC Beltway cogjam, not only because of their more constant exposure, but also because they regularly encounter expert opinions that express concerns. No, neither journalists nor experts can say exactly where or when a hurricane will hit, be it natural or political. Nobody does. But they are certainly able to recognize and report on signs of a hurricane on the horizon. And we do want to know about those signs.

To make matters worse, before getting into office a few higher rungs of the DC Beltway contingency openly declared war on the news media. Before the new administration had even begun, an attack against the press was well under way.

"An attack!" Gut brains, to the rescue.

Journalists continue to report things as they see and hear them—still for the purpose of letting the public know. But now what they report is also a form of self-defense, lopsided toward what will back up any risky business that previously had been reported. Since self-defense favors one side, the end result is a hopeless conflict of interest.

Then, thanks to the stories journalists often need to work with, whatever gets reported tends to be uncomplimentary. This stirs up even more gut responding and lashing out among those at the top. In return journalists fur-

---

84   Jennings, M. (1999). The evolution and devolution of journalistic ethics. *Imprimis,* 28. Retrieved at https://imprimis. hillsdale.edu/the-evolutionand-devolutionof-journalistic-ethics/.

ther ramp up efforts to help the public know of facts behind perceived threats they've reported on, including politicians' or pundits' latest rounds of sparring.

It doesn't matter if the hurricane spinning around out there may never hit at all. What matters is the risk it presents should it hit. People need to know it's there, so they can prepare and do what they can to potentially save themselves.

And on goes the battle, with the truth buried somewhere out in the trenches. The primary focus in both camps has ceased to be getting the truth to the public. Instead, it more often deteriorates into doing whatever can be done to discredit the other side.[85]

On the other hand, we know there's no such thing as an unbiased opinion. We deal with personal subjectivity on a daily basis. Everybody's opinions are at least somewhat biased. It's why personal positions are called opinions, rather than facts.

The issue here is more about how *much* bias affects a particular source or story. As reasonable adults we weed out (or at least, should be attempting to weed out) bias in any new information we get from anywhere by looking at verifiable facts and internal logic, as well as applying other forms of ordered thinking.

These days, longstanding conservative complaints about biased media have gone into warp drive, perhaps rightly so. New populations of believers have joined them. Many liberals now agree that "truth" is harder to make out, given the biased reporting practices and murky or questionable direct word from the top. The distinction between the play-by-play announcer and the game commentator has lessened or disappeared altogether, the objective and the subjective seeming to intermingle freely. Pulling facts from what comes out of either camp of the journalism/DC Beltway battle has become a formidable task.

I see no silver bullet to end their battle any time soon. It's likely something those directly involved will need to sort out for themselves.

But meanwhile, what do we do to keep our gut brains from overreacting to all this negative energy, confusion, and uncertainty? How do we contribute toward community change regarding the impact of traditional news media, rather than unwittingly reinforce a regrettable status quo?

I suggest the following:

Adjust expectations. Based on what we've seen so far, we can safely predict there will be more of this back and forth going on. A certain amount of unpleasantness will be there as well. When it does, do not let yourself be thrown off. Instead, plan ahead for how you will manage such incoming assaults to sensitivities.

Soothe the gut brain. When outrage manages to filter in, let your inner lizard know he's been heard. Provide reassurances. Point out how the situation only

---

85   Kurtz, H. (2018). *Media madness: Donald Trump, the press, and the war over the truth.* Washington, DC: Regenry Publishing.

feels excessively trying because steering clear of the news is so much more difficult than it used to be. Such ridiculousness has always been out there, in some form. Still, we got by. It's time to habituate to it as background noise, and refuse to be baited. Save the alarm for the real battles, not the ones you hear are going on elsewhere.

Engage compassion. We're all hurting over this. We all deserve compassion. Remember the extra kindness people shared with one another during the first days following the events of September 11th? Even while among complete strangers, people reached out and connected. We can do that now, too. Think of something nice you might do for someone—perhaps even for the benefit of a philosophical adversary.

Get selective. Use a discriminating eye when selecting which news sources to follow. Most of us have always done so. For example, most people readily recognize that tabloid stories are largely fiction. We can apply that same scrutiny to other news sources and their biases. When you can't avoid them, think of these extreme, questionable, and/or otherwise biased stories and quotes as a form of entertainment, rather than representing reality. The old saying of "don't believe everything you hear" was never truer than it is in this era of cogjam.

Separate the subjective from the objective. We cannot necessarily count on political reporting to do this for us, at least not the way it did in the past. So while watching or reading the news, note what is objective, rather than subjective. Is it a direct quote? Actual footage of a speech or behavior? Direct data from a trusted source of expert information? Or, is it possibly taken out of context? Is it a conclusion being drawn from what is reported—in other words, only a reporter's opinion or conjecture? There's nothing wrong with listening to an opinion, whether you agree or disagree. But keep in mind that such reporting is at greater risk for bias. Do you keep an eye out for inferential leaps, those reasoning errors that so easily promote cogjam? Is there disconfirming data that is not being taken into account? Remind yourself of what you know about scientific reasoning. You can be the judge.

Limit exposure. The more you are exposed to stressful events, the greater your chances of experiencing stress or trauma symptoms—even when you're only watching a recording of it.[86] Television news broadcasting has become better about not excessively replaying traumatizing footage, like the Twin Towers coming down or gruesome athlete injuries. The field of journalism heeded the advice of experts: watching tragedy over and over creates trauma. However, these days it's easy to create that same result for yourself, regardless of media broadcast practices. So in addition to being selective about which sources to trust, limit how often you check in with them. Likewise, avoid initiating ex-

86   Schuster, M.A., Stein, B.D., Jaycox, L.H., Collins, R.L., Marshall, G.N., Elliott, M.N., et al. (2001). A National Survey of stress reactions after the September 11, 2001 terrorist attacks. *New England Journal of Medicine, 345*, 1507-1512.

posure by bringing up the latest with others, and getting your herd started into directions that are regrettable for all concerned. When possible, save those conversations for a select and close few, preferably in private.

Don't forget to breathe. In, then out. In, then out.

SOCIAL MEDIA

Currently social media appear to succeed as the most effective, as well as most destructive circulators of cogjammed information. Internet postings are often no holds barred; anything goes. The truth doesn't matter. Neither do social sensibilities. Nor has most postings' potential impact on others gotten much vetting. Even terrorist recruitment propaganda finds ways to get through. Why should we expect any different for cogjam-promoting hype?

In recent days social media platform providers have begun addressing this problem. Even so, information coming from social media requires a lot more of our individual scrutiny than stories put out by traditional news outlets, where a more standardized degree of journalistic ethics and oversight has been applied. And sadly, false news tends to be more widely spread on social media than reports that are true.[87] Likewise, thanks to the negativity bias, stories about various problems at the top are both circulated and remembered better than those about what actually is getting accomplished by the DC Beltway contingency. We always need to filter what we hear or read, adjusting for these natural biases.

Furthermore, knowing where a particular story originates is difficult if a trusted outlet is not referenced or cannot be otherwise checked out, though some outlets are taking steps to try to remedy this. Nonetheless, plenty of evidence has surfaced that certain foreign powers serve their own nefarious agenda by stirring up discord through social media. Nobody likes being played. But it happens.

Some social media output, like tweets, are inherently limited in how accurate they can be. They are set up to let people use no more than a certain number of characters. Whatever makes it into print can easily be under-explained, misunderstood, blown out of proportion, or taken out of context. Follow-up comments can help clear any confusion. But how many people go to the trouble of looking for follow-up? We never get a second chance at making that first impression.

Then there's the omnipresence of social media. Now that we carry around devices like smart phones and spend significant periods of time in front of computer screens, we rarely escape it completely. We receive constant reminders of ongoing discord. The gut brain ends up perpetually on alert.

---

87   Vosoughi, S., Roy, D., & Aral, S. (2018). The spread of true and false news online. *Science,* 359,1146-1151.

The emotional intelligence so necessary to social reasoning also pays a price. Reliance on communication devices over face-to-face socializing lets familiarity with empathy cues get rusty. Truly knowing where people are coming from takes more than decoding a set of words. There's also tone, emphasis, volume, facial expression, body language, and other factors that aren't communicated by simple written words. There's also wordless interconnecting, such as what takes place during something so simple as two people looking one another in the eye. Human interaction has much more to it than whatever verbally oriented data makes it out of our minds and mouths.

It would be nice if there were some kind of vaccination out there that would keep people from succumbing to social media overexposure. Who knows, maybe someday someone will come up with something. Meanwhile, the best way to protect ourselves is by bucking common herd practices that increase the likelihood or impact of overexposure.

Don't get baited. No matter how ridiculous, offensive, shortsighted, insensitive, or illogical a posting, do not respond. Angry objections, no matter how legitimate their content might be, only add fuel to the fire. So will benign objections, as far as that goes. Whatever you post or tweet is highly unlikely to change anybody's mind at this stage of the game, anyway. If you must unload, do so in private, with someone you know you can trust to simply listen, rather than react.

Note post origins. Where did it come from? Is there any way to check out the validity of what is said? All posts, tweets, and the like need to be taken with a grain of salt—they all represent opinion, one way or another. But if you can't even tell where the information originated, the entire saltshaker may be required.

Steer clear of unrecognizable original sources. Could a divisive post actually be a form of outside interference, seeking only to stir up trouble? Or is it only someone stating an opinion as a fact, trying to further an opposing position? Don't let yourself be played. If your gut brain takes over and cooperates with divisiveness, the bad guy wins.

Limit social media input. Pick certain times to check social media postings, and stick to the schedule. Then keep your phone in your pocket, rather than sitting where it serves as a constant reminder. Consider whether you really need to follow as many types of social media as you do.

Be selective about reading newsfeeds. The fact that someone is your BFF does not mean you must read and/or respond to all of his or her newsfeeds. If a post is toxic or unfairly biased, ignore it. If you can't resist reading such material when it pops up, unsubscribe to that particular individual's newsfeed. If your friend asks you why, be honest.

Adjust your apps. Protect your sanity by not setting apps to ding every time your device detects an incoming media post. You can check it out later, during the time you've allotted for it.

Repost selectively. If one side or the other is likely to experience a particular post as inflammatory, let it die a natural death. Do not pass it on, and force others to deal with it as well.

Remember to press your own reset button. After running up against cogjammed social media, find a way to shake it off before returning to the real world. Use mindfulness techniques or other strategies to set it aside and refocus, so you don't risk contaminating your living environment.

Be a role model. There's a whole generation of teenagers and millenials out there whose internet devices seem to have become natural appendages. Anybody that wrapped up in living through their devices is especially vulnerable to overexposure to cogjammed attitudes.

Positive and negative impact of heavy device use is currently a hot topic of study. In terms of effects on young people's wellbeing, social connectedness, empathy, and narcissism, it gets mixed results in multiple directions.[88] Of particular concern, however, is that the accuracy of our empathy is best when a message is heard, rather than read or taken in by multiple senses—another reason why so much miscommunication happens with social media.[89] Young people are proceeding through their developmental window of building sensitivity to social, behavioral, and emotional cues. So much preoccupation on communicating by device rather than direct interaction interferes with important developmental learning.

Someday experts, policy makers, and educators will have more to go on. As research findings pile up they will likely develop strategy for how to best guide the next generation. Meanwhile, we can avoid becoming poor role models for the rest of the herd by biting the bullet and pocketing our devices when we can.

I wish I had more certainty to share about what I expect to happen with cultural attitudes in future generations. Paradigm shifts are always a mystery—until they happen. But that's okay. In spite of having lived forever with this type of uncertainty, we've survived quite well. Nonetheless, tending to our own needed adjustments plays an important role in helping set the cultural compass for a healthier direction.

88   James, C., Davis, K., Charmarman, L., Konrath, S., Slovak,P., Weinstein, E., & Yarosh, L. (2017). Digital life and youth well-being, social connectedness, empathy, and narcissism. *Pediatrics*, 140 (Suppl. 2), S71-S75.
89   Kraus, M. W. (2017). Voice-only communication enhances empathic accuracy. *American Psychologist*, 72, 644-654.

CHAPTER 14

......

What Now?

BY NOW IT'S no secret that the cogjam story is about process, not content. It's not a treatise on gun control, minority rights, foreign war involvement, immigration laws, the environment, or the budget deficit. Those are merely a few of the more active battlegrounds upon which our cogjammed attitudes duke it out these days.

Process, on the other hand, is strategy for *how* we go about resolving an issue or dispute. Is now the time to address the problem, or do we wait until a certain line is crossed? Do we go for diplomatic measures, or send out a warship? Do we use major artillery, or peashooters? Process decisions similar to these apply to any situation, no matter what the setting or specifics of the problem may be.

Furthermore, process issues must be settled before content details can even be set out on the game board. How do you move chess pieces around, without any mutually accepted rules? This concept has always been a counseling basic, especially when issues involve relationships. If two people cannot communicate effectively, or are unable to draw up and exchange logical, common sense ideas, resolution of any conflict is dead in the water.

This appears to be a major reason why DC Beltway leaders ended up so adrift. They've been overly caught up in testing the potency of their peashooter collections, rather than seeking tools and strategy that could actually get us out of limbo. Furthermore, the questionable role modeling provided by some of their behaviors leaves many constituents feeling disgruntled toward them, which interferes with how much social support leaders receive.

Truth be known, we constituents haven't done a whole lot better than the peashooter contingency. We cry out mightily about hot issues—including the polarizing itself—in more ways than we can count. But how we're going about it hasn't been getting us very far. Mainly we seem to get more cogjam.

We all need to step back, take a deep breath, and consider which tools are right for the job. We also need to make better use of the tools that have been readily at hand all along, like anger. That's right, anger—that focus-limiting haze I've thus far treated as if it's a bomb dropped by some evil empire. It can actually be a useful tool, when used appropriately.

Anger is more than an aggressive force unleashed by a threatened gut brain. As an energizer, it serves a vital purpose: it motivates us to look after best interests when things turn south, for ourselves or for those we care about. Presence of anger following trauma is actually a good predictor of future post-traumatic growth.[90] Anger only becomes a destructive force when misused or misdirected.

Addressing the impulsive lashing out that creates a cogjammed society is an absolute necessity. However, curbing angry behavior alone does not necessarily take care of all the adrenalin released. During an overload, mindfulness and compassion may not be enough to reset body chemistry. In this case, going for a brisk walk and other forms of exercise help work it off.

But how about if we also figure out how to turn that anger and adrenalin loose on the matters that so often deliver us into cogjam's clutches? Not the content of the specific problem arising, but the process—in other words, focusing on *how* we strategize and interrelate when trying to get results, and applying that to the issue we address.

Such maneuvers require thoughtful and purposeful change. Remember the words attributed to Einstein—that we cannot solve problems with the same level of thinking that created them. Likewise, repeating the same thing and expecting a different result is irrational. And those who are not aware of history are destined to repeat it. Not just the history of humanity, but also our own. Poor awareness or understanding of our past guarantees repeating the same mistakes.

The other day I sat through hours of grueling testimony, supposedly part of a Supreme Court confirmation hearing. Instead, along with millions of other

90   Strasshofer, D. R., Peterson, Z. D., Beagley, M. C., & Galovski, T. E. (2018). Investigating the relationship between posttraumatic stress symptoms and posttraumatic growth following community violence: The role of anger. *Psychological Trauma: Theory, Research, Practice, and Policy*, 10, 515-522.

viewers, I was subjected to some of the most outrageous cogjam abuse to date. Not just how an accuser and the accused were treated, but how the overall process ensured that as many people as possible would be exposed to this florid level of divisive community and fractured science. I can only imagine where it might lead newly oversensitized inner lizards in weeks and months to come.

It also struck me as ironic. Two sworn enemies, politics and media, actually getting together long enough to create something big and impactful. Unfortunately they couldn't have produced a more destructive outcome if they'd intentionally coordinated effort toward this aim.

This represents a new crossroad for each of our cogjam journeys. Do we let anger over a new piece of outrageousness cause us to act out, taking sides and lashing out at whoever we choose to blame? Or do we let this anger fuel something that will actually make a difference, no matter how small the change may be?

Back when I was dragging around heavy luggage, practically keeping my eyelids open with toothpicks in order to board wee-hour flights to disaster assignments, I couldn't help but question why I did this to myself. The same answer reliably bubbled to the surface: if I made a significant difference in just one person's disaster survival, it would all be worthwhile. And it always was.

The world can only be saved in increments. When we each do our share, both community and common humanity blossom. Thus this newest cogjam-fueled anger only strengthened my resolve to publish this book. If the material within it makes a significant difference in the lives of only a few, it is still worth the time and effort taken to produce it. My aim will have been achieved.

And, my own inner lizard can go stretch out again on that sun-warmed rock.

WHICH PATH IS MINE?

Finding your path requires steps other than the ones that brought you here. In addition to working on inner selves and how to interrelate with the herd, there's concrete civic involvement galore. There are so many simple things that can make a difference in our individual villages.

We all have causes that matter to us. If your chosen cause intersects with the domain of bizarro world, plans to pursue it will likely need to be novel, focused, and well thought out—some perhaps seemingly bizarre in themselves. We take off the white gloves and start looking *way* outside the box for our answers, as did our founding fathers. Possibly lessons carried around by our inner children will once again come out to play.

This actually could be fun.

All the same, stepping outside comfort zones and taking risks, even when carefully thought out, is not for everybody. Besides, do one person's efforts really change an entire culture? Not very often. But joint insistence and surgically inserted efforts toward specific changes do add up. We contribute by focusing on what we can do, rather than moaning and groaning over what we cannot.

We miss the sense of unity we once shared, back before so much gasoline was dumped on divisive trends. Little wonder many passionately yearn for "the good old days." But the sands of time can't be crammed back into the upper half of an advancing hourglass. Our past social structures, economy, and world situation are long gone.

But we can rebuild that same sense of unity and common humanity we once had, within the new constraints of what is now. We can join together, pool excess adrenalin, and use it to fuel creation of "the good new days."

So. Where are our niches in the quest to advance the herd? What cogjam-fueling factors can we personally take action on, all on our own? Whatever you do, don't let this powerful energy go to waste. Or worse, let it lure you back into a pattern of pointless acting out, despair, or empty resignation. Funnel your energy into something that matters to you, no matter how small a deed. Even if it doesn't immediately get results, you at least will use the energy for something positive.

WHERE LIE YOUR PASSIONS?

If you could invest time and energy into absolutely anything, what interests would you delve into? Not vague goals like fame, fun, and fortune, but specific activities you might take part in, ones that help you achieve or contribute toward something you value. Passion joined with excess adrenalin can be a great thing indeed.

The path you choose need not directly address cogjam to help relieve it. Pursuing passions helps in general by redirecting efforts into healthier common humanity. It could even involve something you think of as play. There are always ways to make a play setting, the player experience, or access to a pastime more attainable or enjoyable by others. Think about it as ways you might pay it forward. In other words, figure out how you can leave that particular corner of your world in better shape than you found it.

COMMUNITY INVOLVEMENT

Many major shifts in community thinking begin with individual grass roots efforts. Dr. Allen Frances, a prominent psychiatrist, outlined several.[91] For example, the hoax about bottle-feeding being healthier for infants than breastfeeding and the claim that smoking tobacco is not harmful were both derailed in recent decades. These changes began with individual efforts, then with many coming together to apply scientific method and common sense. Redirected outrage has also been successful in changing practices such as littering, lax drinking and driving laws, buckling seat belts, and releasing certain damaging chemicals into the ozone. They all started somewhere.

CIVIL PROTEST METHODOLOGY

This is a tricky one. We do want to let our leaders and others know of our objections to an undesired status quo. But we don't want our actions to become weapons of mass destruction, should they end up frequently reposted, rebroadcast, expounded upon, or blown out of proportion. Constant exposure only keeps gut brains on high alert, messing with our reasoning and potentially creating trauma. When extreme, constant exposure can even lead to tuning it out all together, and spending our lives hiding out in the relative safety of the underbrush.

Yes, we organize and express concerns. But perhaps we need to reexamine the purpose or role of such gatherings. Maybe the focus should not be on how big, loud, or insistent a protest our joint chemistry achieves, or how severe the disruption to others' daily lives. Maybe protest efforts should be thought of more as a beginning point for doing something productive.

Such gatherings offer opportunity for like-minded people to organize, implement, or otherwise support the surgically precise actions that directly result in institutional or social change: communicating with representatives, supporting campaigns, voting, giving direct aid to disadvantaged groups, or helping with petitions. There's also the option of giving presentations or otherwise spreading the evidence-based facts and common sense behind a cause, rather than using such opportunities to get a gut-brain audience to catastrophize over imagined extremes.

In other words, protest gatherings may better serve us as calls to educate, plan, and implement goals, rather than considering them an end in themselves. This does already happen here and there. But we need more of it.

Yes, throwing a tantrum so that Mommy comes running and fixes everything was once great strategy. But today, it's the wrong tool for the job. We need the logical brain to take the wheel. We need to unearth and experiment with the other treasures buried in the contents of our cognitive toolboxes. How else might we do no harm when we protest, and achieve desired goals?

---

91   Frances, A. (2017). *Twilight of American sanity: A psychiatrist analyzes the age of Trump.* New York: HarperCollins.

POLITICAL PARTY EVOLUTION

While the two major parties have functioned lately as extremes, not all of their members hold extreme views. Those with more moderate, common sense views are getting frustrated. Some have left to join minority parties. Others have left politics altogether.

Restructuring the entire political party system would be a massive undertaking. But who knows, that may be the direction we're headed. The Independent party certainly continues to grow. Other minority parties are at least well established, if not yet as successful at getting candidates into office. However some minority parties take up extreme left- or right-leaning views similar to the two mainstream parties.

Maybe what we really need is something completely new, based on an entirely different paradigm. Rather than liberal, moderate, or conservative slants, how about creating a party that's organized around common sense itself? The Independent party is already somewhat like this, focusing more on what pans out in the final analysis than pushing candidates or extremes.

What we may need to build, however, is a novel platform. Like, effective process serving as the party platform. Specific problems of the day arise as they do; so also does the need for solutions that are sometimes more liberal and at other times more conservative. Membership in such a party would be based on dedication to effective process and decision-making, regardless of personal liberal or conservative biases. All solutions would be embraced as possibilities to sort out. Candidates would be supported as they demonstrate ability to use common sense and effective problem solving. In other words, the first thing they would need to show us is that they have the right tools for the job.

What might we call this new party? (Like I said, this thinking outside the box business can be fun.) I suggest we go back to our founding fathers, where it all started. Who among them sums up such a stance? I'm thinking Benjamin Franklin. You know, the author of Poor Richard's Almanac (in earlier days, "Almanack"), that tome of wisdom whose contents are at times confused as originating in the Bible. How about if we call ourselves the Almanack Party?

It's hard to say whether such a paradigm shift would actually work. Making it happen would require considerable discussion and reorganization. But that's what spawned democracy in the first place: dedicated founding fathers starting from scratch, and hashing out details for what might work for their new world. There were some who wanted to set up a kingship, and stick to familiar political structures and practices of old. But had they done so, would democracy have evolved as it did? Taking the risk of thinking outside the box, as did our founding fathers, could well provide solutions for today.

However, the most important lesson our founding fathers taught us is how to be winners. The American Revolution did not succeed by highlighting everybody's differences and stockpiling them as objects for receiving fear-driven ridicule. Success rode in on the back of shared common humanity.

The war would have been lost if not for the sympathies of the multiple European allies coming to our aid. The colonial army itself was made up of widely varying cultures that instinctively mistrusted one other: fisherman, farmers, backwoodsmen, and others. African Americans and Native Americans fought side by side with them as well, at times pitted against others of their own ancestries, depending on which side of the conflict they supported. All had differing irons in the fire.

Yet General Washington pulled them together by reminding them not only of their shared goal, but of their common humanity: they were all citizens of the great nation yet to be, and as such were one. It worked, as he even underscored his position by living in a tent alongside his troops rather than accepting the more comfortable lodgings to which he was considered entitled. He emphasized that he, too, was one with the rest of us. And he could only have done so by keeping his inner lizard in its proper place.

His example and teachings apply today as we struggle with cogjam. And they will likely continue to serve for generations to come, as our nation evolves with the ever-changing times.

THE NEXT GENERATION

My generation has been miserably failing the next, every bit as much as the Greatest Generation failed the cohort that followed them. It's happening in different ways, and for different reasons. Perhaps it's inevitable. How do you help a generation prepare for a world that has not yet appeared on the radar? But the end result has been the same, regardless of generation: leaving behind an entry world more shaped by trauma symptoms than bolstered by common sense.

To some degree we've failed the next generation as role models, as well. One way its members learn to think straight, problem solve, express themselves, and interact with others is by watching older and established herd members. Unfortunately cogjam has us acting in ways that violate basic principles of all of these. What in the world do they come away thinking? How will they map their own life trajectories, given the questionable material they have to work with?

Having come of age in the sixties, I well remember how we reacted to the Greatest Generation fantasy: letting hair grow long, the advent of flower power, "don't trust anyone over thirty," Beatlemania, the popularizing of sit-ins, "make love, not war," a growing drug culture, and a nonconformist style of dress that to this day is tied to the hippie generation. Norms were put on trial, and at times soundly rejected.

I don't think any of us really knew where this path would lead us. But on some level, we'd figured out that the status quo wasn't going to cut it in the world we had before us. Something new was needed. So we explored mightily, in multiple directions. We adjusted.

What will those of this next new generation create, as they correct for our shortcomings? For eons, older generations have been critical of younger generations, my cohort no exception. Among peers I sometimes hear judgmental complaints about kids shooting up schools, or becoming gang-bangers, drug dealers, hackers, internet zombies, or the like.

However our generation also had its collective of heavy metal ne'er-do-wells. Of course, not everyone of our generation was like that. Those standout types were just more visible than those of us productively working behind the scenes. As a group we applied a variety of ways of thinking outside the box, some of us more adaptive with it than others. Our generation's members eventually found courses that helped us make do in the world we had entered.

I actually have high hopes for up and coming generations. I already see a promising shift. As I write this, our nation is recovering from yet another school shooting. As usual, the topics of mental illness and gun control have resurfaced. The black or white reasoning of "it's all because of guns" pitted against "it's all because of mental illness" is back, once again spotlighting the DC Beltway's cogjam-fogged stalemate. The truly objective observation is that both factors, as well as others, play into these tragic incidents. All need to be explored and taken into account for ferreting out viable solutions to be possible. But as long as policymakers are trapped in trauma-guided tunnel vision, serious discussion of comprehensive solutions is unlikely to take place.

Near as I can tell, the next generation is as fed up with it as we are. After all, it's their schools that keep getting shot up. It's their friends they see bleeding out before their eyes. They're the ones who will be stuck with the mess we're leaving behind for them.

I've watched them push their way toward microphones and into government settings to express their outrage. I've heard them meet with leadership and demand that they do something about it. And, they appear to be organizing for an ongoing battle toward change. They are already taking responsibility for the adult world they will become part of—and it's a great start. These days I'm more interested in what they have to say than the latest pundit commentaries.

What is our role? How do we assist them in their generational quest? Open conversation is needed, rather than condemnation of faults, perceived or real.

We need a dialogue that helps both older and younger generations work together to redirect this hurting world. We need to admit to our own mistakes, rather than cling to defensiveness or insist it's our generation's way or the highway.

The answers they find may be very different from ours. But our job is not to determine answers for them. Our job is to help them find answers of their own, for the world they recreate.

Consult your past adolescent self. What would have helped you at that tender age, when you were just beginning to sort out a future niche? Perhaps you recall a mentor, leader, or other role model whose efforts were especially helpful. Consider standing on the shoulders of these others who went before you, and shine a new beacon for those who have yet to carve out their paths.

And, for those of you readers who represent the next generation: you're absolutely right. In some ways we botched it royally. We blew our big chance. If we baby boomers had more effectively planted the platform we'd stumbled upon, perhaps we wouldn't have ended up here. For our era-defining "make love, not war" chant was merely an adolescent expression of the abstractions for which we were then and are still now striving: ending the fighting, sexism, racism, violence against the environment, and abuse of authority.

We did leave our footprint in moving the herd forward. But how much further might we have gotten if we had focused more on firmly establishing that base of caring and compassion for common humanity that originally spurred us on? So many social issues would be less pervasive if only this base had become an expected norm. How do we reestablish these values, ones that keep getting lost as lessons of history are seemingly ignored?

Little doubt your cohort has work to do to clean up the spilt milk, just as my generation needed to come up with something to replace Greatest Generation fantasies. So far it's obvious we aren't very successful at dealing with cogjam stalemate. Maybe the problem is that we're too enmeshed in our cohort, as were some of those of the Greatest Generation.

But the platform of caring and compassion endures, regardless. Perhaps as the next generation you can better scaffold onto it, and help move us forward. Are there things those of us who've been around for a while might do to help you in your own mission to think outside the box? What tools do you need, that we might share and pass on? Seek, and ye shall find.

THE THING WITH MEDIA REPORTS

Not long ago there was a mall shooting in my area. Media coverage was quick to arrive on the scene. I followed the incident as it played out on television, hoping for the best possible outcome for those in harm's way. As usual reporters stopped those who were leaving the mall area, seeking whatever details they might have to offer.

However there was this one reporter who kept insisting on asking people—barely out of the throes of escaping mass casualty, mind you—"how do you feel?"

My blood pressure hit the roof. The last thing those poor people needed in the thick of crisis was to be directed toward the status of their feelings. Resilience purposely shoves them in the background so that in the heat of the moment, they can focus and think clearly. Resilience lets feelings resurface and be worked through soon enough, when the particular survivor is ready to face the task.

But that reporter's zealous pursuit of a story was interfering with this priceless and irreplaceable survival strategy. She was screwing around with people's chances for healthy recovery, perhaps retraumatizing them in the process.

I got hold of the television station, threw around a few fancy credentials, and succinctly stated my concern. I suspect a few others from my collegial herd did likewise. Shortly afterwards the "how do you feel?" queries stopped—at least regarding interviews that particular station put onscreen that sad afternoon.

This is an example of re-funneling anger into productivity. The journalists involved with the incident responded appropriately. They're people, after all, the same as the rest of us. They want to get things right.

But sometimes the public needs to let them know what they consider to be right. We, the public, live outside the world of journalism. We are in position to have more objectivity about their actions than what they are able to see through the ever-present haze of personal subjectivity and sub-herd influence.

So what else do we tell them? What do we want them to do differently?

- We do want them to let us know what's going on in the world.
- We also want their reporting to be up front about which parts of a story are factual, and which are commentary.
- We want reports centered on the entire truth, regardless of whether content fits their defensive agenda.
- We want journalism to stop overlooking its own ethical standards.
- And as members of our tribe, we hold them accountable for their behaviors within these roles we have entrusted to them.

Just as we should also hold accountable those whose internet platforms spread cogjammed newsfeeds. Social media conglomerates should establish airtight methods for tracking who posts what, rather than having to establish origins and evidence by way of painstaking searches after the fact. The general public does not have the skills necessary to perform such maneuvers on their own. Social media providers need to know we hold them responsible for what they create and so widely distribute. And, perhaps once again be reminded that we don't appreciate being set up to be played by foreign ne'er-do-wells.

AND NOW FOR THE POLITICIANS

First, *breathe.*

There. That feels better.

Politicians also live in a world of hurt. They too deserve our compassion. They are trying to do the right thing and forge onward, all the while buried under mounds of conflict of interest and criticisms. Their daily lives surely must seem like, or may even be, one long string of no-win situations. Can it get any more frustrating and demoralizing than that?

That does not excuse them from following through on the jobs they agreed to do. The founding fathers never intended the party system to function as antagonistic broken-down opposites. The system was supposed to establish a way to be sure all points of view sat at the table when decisions were made. The decision-making process itself was not supposed to be kept from happening.

But over the last several decades, DC Beltway herd behavior has evolved into exactly that. It has restructured congressional practices and procedures until parties no longer work well together—literally, as their collective herd seems more and more determined to scamper off that infamous cliff. No wonder so many politicians have thrown in the towel and veered off onto more productive career paths.

Part of the problem is that in some ways, our representatives behave as if they confuse Congress with a court of law. In spite of certain similarities, it's not the same paradigm. In court, attorneys are supposed to take sides and defend whichever side they're hired to represent. Which side wins then determines whether their client will experience consequences of one sort or another. Agreeing with anything that supports the opposing side's position is therefore taboo.

In Congress, establishing that kind of black or white answer is not the goal. They're not supposed to be establishing blame or legal consequences for specific individuals, which is what it at times turns into. The goal is to problem-solve in the real world.

The issues that come before Congress are about finding answers for realities we all must live with. All perspectives need to meet up, mesh, and draw joint conclusions. Simply aligning with a specific set of pros or cons about an issue does not solve problems. Both sides need to be examined by all, and evaluated in a spirit of goodwill. The entire problem solving strategy must be applied in order to work effectively.

Elected office is one of the few highly placed positions in our society that are not based on whether we have the appropriate training, knowledge base, and practical skills to do it. Instead we hire for these jobs by voting, usually based on the quality of the candidate's sell job about supporting what we want. In the final analysis, whether they have the right tools for the job appears to be placed much lower among voting priorities.

So what's the answer here? What do we do about cogjammed representatives?

- We let them know what we think—less about the content of the day's arguments, more about the cogjam haze blotting out the priorities of problem solving and promoting civilized community, and that we want them to refrain from needlessly traumatizing those they represent.

- We want them to recognize and acknowledge how their behavior affects everybody—not just the consequences of a particular decision, but also the community destructiveness of some of their decision-making tactics. We are tired of our communities becoming collateral damage.

- We are also tired of having our anger and fears so often toyed with—pumped up and manipulated to serve political purposes. Please leave our inner lizards alone.

- We let them know that we want *them* to think, too, rather than defensively react or blindly follow the herd. If we can rein in gut brains and herd instinct, so can they. If they continue to pursue the groupthink that cocoons them from natural consequences for dubious behaviors, we don't stand a chance. It's time for politicians to rejoin the mainstream, rather than stage elite, overprotected sideshows.

- We watch for evidence of fractured science in their thinking and behavior: the over-simplifications, cherry-picking the data, ridiculing and dismissing, straight-up fabrications, and other forms of willful or unintended mangling of valid information.[92]

- We tell them we want to hear valid logic during stump talks, rather than proclamations and emotional extremes. Those serve only to prod gut brains into running with herd instinct. In case they're still missing this point, we really don't like being played. It's no longer enough to appear to support our position. We want to hear them using the right tools for the jobs of decision-making, and serving as healthy role models.

- We tell them to listen to those with opposing positions. We want them to actually discuss relevant factors behind positions, rather than talk about how supposedly evil and misguided they and whoever supports opposing positions may be.

92   Levitan, D. (2017). *Not a scientist: How politicians mistake, misrepresent, and utterly mangle science.* New York: W. W. Norton & Company.

- We demand that politicians no longer comply with the stereotype of not answering uncomfortable questions. Talking around issues won't cut it any more. We want to hear real evidence behind their stance, even if they're still deciding what their stance will be. And we want to hear better evidence than "because so-and-so said so."

- We want to see evidence that they are listening to and supporting voters, rather than party extremes or whichever lobbyists support their campaigns. We are going to pay closer attention to which lobbyists finance their presence in office.

- We encourage them to show compassion toward their own inner lizards. Reassure them that they are heard, and that you will use their feedback to help understand what is going on around them. But, your logical brain will take care of the decision-making.

- And highest on the list: We are watching. We are listening. If they stick to the status quo no matter what we say, it will affect our votes. And we do keep our word. Or perhaps we give them a second chance, if it's needed for them to realize we noticed what they are doing, and that we really do mean what we say. But after two strikes, they're out. Even if they tightly agree with our personal positions, they're of little use to us if they can't effectively work with the other players.

We confront them without insults, ridicule, or giving in to other suspects pushing their way to the forefront during outrage. We take a deep breath, engage compassion, and explain our positions assertively rather than destructively. Besides, they cannot successfully represent us if we don't let them know where we stand. Communicating with them, rather than condemning them, is a greater act of compassion than standing back and humoring them. Compassionate confrontation also provides a role model for those politicians who still appear to need one.

Thankfully, not all politicians are worst-case scenarios. We've seen many of them experiment with reintroduced logic and reaching across the aisle. There are also those who appear well aware of what is messing up process. But whether due to neglect, not knowing what else to do, or doing it on purpose, they let their herd continue to lead anyway.

So exactly what do we say or write to politicians that will get our points across? Let's try out this new approach with examples. Two current polarizing issues are: 1) gun rights, and 2) Affirmative Action. Below are typical cogjammed statements and behaviors that relate to them, and how confrontations might be crafted to guide representatives down a more rational path.

Right: *They think government should meet the entire population's every need.*

Left: *They think Wild West shoot-'em-up is the answer to everything.*

First of all, you don't know what every person of a similar perspective thinks. You can't see inside people's heads. We only know what individual people think when they tell us—and then, we must actually listen. Individuals with similar perspectives have opinions that vary widely, as do their reasons and motivations for believing what they choose to believe. Such "they think" statements are gross overgeneralizations, as well as thinly disguised dismissiveness.

Taking their position to the extreme and treating that as reality brings negotiation to a grinding halt, as well as stirs up more cogjam. Telling people what they think instead of listening to them also alienates those supporting opposing positions, further tearing down bridges. Plus, implying that Joe and Jane Public will blindly buy into this type of illogic indefinitely is insulting. We are offended. Consider the Emperor's New Clothes routine outed. Please stop it.

Right: *They won't be satisfied until they've taken all our gun rights away.*

Left: *They won't be satisfied until all Affirmative Action is done away with.*

Yes, there are those who would prefer having such rights scoured from the face of the Earth. But basing interpretation of opponents' beliefs on the most extreme possible meaning is absurd, no matter which direction you take it. Insisting that anybody who has opposing solutions wants to take ridiculous measures is a cop-out. Where's your data? From where the rest of us stand, it looks more like an excuse to not negotiate. No, we don't want you to go along with the most extreme possible view. But we do expect you to fully examine both sides. Take a deep breath, and do your job.

Right: *The real problem is about mental health issues, not gun control.*

Left: *The real problem is that the white male majority wants to reestablish their legacy.*

Factors like these may well play into problems. But that doesn't mean they're the only factors that contribute to the final outcomes. Addressing only the factor that is most convenient to deal with, supports a political party extreme, or satisfies certain lobbyists does not necessarily solve the problem, even if it were possible to follow through on a single-factor "solution." Other causes for the problem would still be alive and well.

Besides, the proposal that one specific cause is the "real" problem is only a hypothesis. Where's the outcome study that proves your point? You cannot justify what you are saying with such certainty. You're only rationalizing and guessing, and hoping your hypothesis turns out to be true. So stop proclaiming what causes what, and objectively look at all relevant causes—including the disconfirming data.

Right: *They're only saying/doing that because they're obstructionists. It's their fault.*

Left: *They're only saying/doing that because they're obstructionists. It's their fault.*

The name-calling and snide remarks must end. There may well be some people with opposing views whose behavior suggests an extremist or challenged mentality. Nonetheless, their taking a particular position on any issue does not make it the entirety of who they are. Saying they want to block one thing does not necessarily mean they want to block everything, regardless of how congressional herd behaviors may make them look these days. And when unfair remarks are made about those who are championing our own positions, it is not only offensive to them. It is also offensive to us. You don't win people over by insulting them.

Name-calling doesn't change the validity of whatever facts or logic a person presents. The information and logic either have reasonable merit, or they don't. Start using facts and common sense to back your positions. Stop calling names, pointing fingers, and making snide remarks about those who disagree with you. We want your logical brains leading, not your gut brains.

The blame game in general must end. Blaming solves nothing. It's only cheap, transparent trashing behavior—focusing on your opponent's role, and ignoring your own contribution. In other words, it's another cop-out. Its inflammatory tone also leaves the impression that you're purposely egging on gut brains, so that our logical brains will miss what's really going on here.

Even if it were completely the other side's fault, you can't change "them." But you can change what you yourselves do. Is what you're doing now really getting you any closer to what you're aiming for? What kind of unfortunate social side effects do you get, or do we the public end up being forced to deal with, largely as a result of how you are handling things? Please stop beating your heads—and ours—against the wall, and change course.

And then, of course, we should waste no time in pointing out when we hear politicians talk around an issue rather than answer the question. Reminding them "that's not a direct answer" may be all you need to say to get the point across. Or, let them know that "I don't know," "I still haven't decided" or "I'm still going over the data" is an okay answer, so long as they also fill you in on the competing pros and cons they're sorting through. But if they repeatedly dodge revealing where they stand, continuing to trust them is ill advised. Would you trust a spouse, friend, or supervisor who treats your questions this evasively? Possibly those politicians who do this regularly have become too caught up in the "Game of Lies" to continue to be useful.

Did you notice in these examples that the same response options apply to statements heard coming from either side of the aisle? That is exactly what we want them to understand. Both sides are guilty of dysfunctional process:

- We want our representatives, not cogjam, running the show.
- We want the terms "our side" and "their side" to be wiped from their vocabulary.
- We want to stop being traumatized by toxic rhetoric—commentary more

reminiscent of gaslighting than common sense—and marginally functioning government.

- We want them to run our country as one—the systematized legislative, judicial, and executive branches of our United States of America, not as a split of two warring tribes.

Otherwise, future decades will hold only more of this ridiculously swinging pendulum, with what little that is accomplished determined by whichever extreme holds the most power at the moment, later to be undone by another. Ignoring voters will get a lot dicier for them if we consistently point out all that smells of cogjammed polarizing and disrespect for sensibilities.

Our representatives are already aware that their process is broken. In fact, a couple of years ago they stepped back to revisit the topic of congressional ethics, which essentially serve as guidelines for process. This worthy effort got nipped in the bud when the new administration came on board.

We can let our representatives know we support their setting aside the issues of the day long enough to establish socialized and effective problem-solving process. Without them, their ability to problem solve will continue to suffer. It's not like they accomplish that much on major issues with how they currently spend their time. Why not take a break and sort it out? We can also ask them if there's anything we, Jane and Joe Public, can do to assist them with fixing process.

You know, we could turn this whole thing into a grand experiment. Would repeatedly confronting politicians this way actually result in less cogjammed behavior on their part?

Yeah, that'll do for a working hypothesis.

How many of them, and which ones, do you think will respond to our intervention experiment? And who will not, and simply hang in there with business as usual?

It would at least let us know where we stand with the particular representatives we communicate with. All we'd have to do is sit back and watch what they do with our feedback. How much does our opinion matter to them? What are they personally doing to fix cogjam? Sometimes feedback or lack thereof lets us know that finding a different candidate for the position is in order.

CAUTION: ROADBLOCK AHEAD

Uh-oh.

There's a fly in the ointment with this business of introducing political parties or novel political process. Actually a grotesquely large one, also relating to process rather than content. Getting out of this bugaboo requires thinking outside the box on steroids. Perhaps as you seek out your own personal mission, a strategy for resolving it will cross your path.

Current political system process mirrors the workings and preferences of the gut brain. Two options are judged as all good or all bad, safe or dangerous, etc., with groupthink stomping out gray areas and striving to perpetuate the norm. In spite of the mutual oppositionalism, the two sides do collude to maintain election practices that make sure their "duopoly" survives.[93] The deck has been stacked to support the existence of only two political parties with major influence. As a result, any new parties or practices that might more accurately represent the needs and wants of citizens have little opportunity to get a foot in the door.

Here's what's happening. Remember that in terms of political careers, how election rules and regulations are arranged is in fact a matter of life or death. Politician gut brains are sensitized to jump in and cling to whatever ensures political survival, despite the needs of the citizens. And it's a darn shame. Politicians typically run for office because of their drive to serve the public and make a real difference in the world. Thanks to cogjam, they can end up doing the opposite of what they originally set out to accomplish. Clearly, they have yet to find the way out of this no-win situation. Otherwise, they'd be headed there already.

They're stuck. They need our help.

So what do we do? We chip away at entrenched groupthink, even if it is only one citizen or politician at a time. But we can also search for ways to adjust process within the system—one state, one county, one city, one agency, one community, one neighborhood at a time—so that legislative inner lizards can go back to their sun-warmed rocks and save their energy for issues that matter.

Individual states and other democracies already experiment with election process, helping wean major parties away from gut-brain politics. Groups such as *Unite America* and others champion some of these new ideas. Following is a sampling of innovative bandwagons, which may help jog your logical brain in the direction of potential solutions.[94]

Eliminate closed primaries. Most states require that in order to vote in the primaries, citizens must belong to a major political party. As a result the field is narrowed to represent what the two parties want, not necessarily what the majority of the citizenry wants. Everyone should be allowed a vote in primaries. We should be allowed to vote for a candidate in any party, so that we can support various ideas and approaches no matter which party presents them.

---

93   Gehl, K. M., & Porter, M. E. (2017). *Why competition in the politics industry is failing America: A strategy for reinvigorating our democracy.* Paper presented at Harvard Business School.
94   Ibid.

Abolish gerrymandering. "Gerrymandering" means legislatively doctoring election requirements to favor the interests of whichever party is in control. Most well known is moving around electoral district boundaries to increase the likelihood that winning candidates and issues support the interests of the party currently holding power. Gerrymandering has always been around, despite how obviously squirrelly it is. But many states have yet to reel it in.

Adopt ranked-choice voting. Currently voting rules let us show preference for one candidate over the others in the field. A ranking system of all candidates would come closer to representing our true opinions. So if there were four candidates, we could designate second, third and last choices for the position. After the math, the candidate with the lowest score wins. Another version of this idea would be to give every voter a certain number of "points" to spread out over the various candidates. This would allow for even greater depth of expressing opinions.

Increase the power of small-donation supporters. The government could provide matching funds for small campaign donations. This would even out some of the imbalance of finances between citizens and big money interests, as well as help smaller parties get more traction.

Take day-to-day legislative rules away from the legislators. We should be the ones who decide their parliamentary procedures, salaries and benefits, how many days they work, and other rules that have been monkeyed with to benefit groupthink and cogjam. We are a government of the people, for the people, and by the people, not warring tribes of liberals and conservatives who routinely change rules to suit their agenda.

So in addition to content of potential solutions, we need to address formal political system process itself. What steps might we take to accomplish solutions such as these? Where are the entry points? Ideas, anybody? Revamping the formal system itself may become your mission.

CONTINUING YOUR COGJAM RECOVERY

The impact of a traumatic event never goes away completely. Like any other life experience, it gets absorbed into our personal history. Learning takes place because of those experiences. As our lives go on we apply and build upon that learning, which hopefully is represented more by posttraumatic growth and wisdom than ongoing angst.

Here's an example that illustrates this type of learning. It evolved out of my frequent exposure to disaster trauma.

Caregivers of toddlers often develop what has been called a third ear. It means picking up on cues or sounds—or perhaps even absence of sound—that suggest Junior is getting into something. I developed a similar skill while on the disaster trail. My disaster third ear emerged from the need to quickly pick up on who most needed help.

Everybody on a disaster scene is affected somehow. Emotionally the atmosphere can easily drain or overwhelm staff as well as survivors, if allowed to do so. I could not let that happen—not only to them, but also for myself. Effectively doing my job meant identifying those who most struggled, rather than being distracted and swallowed up by a vast sea of stress and misery. I had no choice other than to get selective about how to focus my compassion and empathy.

So I learned a lot about how people behave when gut brains get stuck on overdrive. And as it turns out, that disaster third ear contains transferable skills.

After leaving disaster fieldwork I began a stint of fiction writing. The learning curve was massive. I'm pretty sure I learned more from my mistakes than my successes. Much learning came by way of reviewer feedback.

However there are reviewers, and then there are...reviewers. Those who are skilled at giving feedback are worth their weight in gold. But if they don't have their feedback ducks in a row, it doesn't matter how knowledgeable they are. Their nuggets can only be unearthed with deep mining. And, unfortunately, I found that those with communication limitations also tend to have trouble handling questions about their recommendations.

A couple of them were especially memorable. One reviewer's feedback took form as a pompous speech. She brushed off requests for clarification with "I'm not done yet," "you just do it that way," and other evasive responses. As I looked up from the pages we were reviewing, I saw she was sweating bullets. So I backed off. Her unleashed gut brain was not of much use to my writing skills. Better luck next reviewer.

On another occasion a reviewer actually went into attack mode when I dared question a point. The rest of his feedback consisted of angry rhetoric about everything he could possibly find to trash. At one point he even said of my psychotherapist characters, "I don't think that's how therapists really talk to each other." *Uh . . . hello.*

If I hadn't been attuned to recognizing stressed-out defensiveness, I might have been crushed. I even might have given up on a pastime I'd been looking forward to my entire life. Instead I noted that something having nothing to do with me, or my writing, was keeping their engine lights blazing away. I had no idea exactly what it might be. But it was not likely something I could to do much about in that particular setting.

Except, it did further along this one ongoing lesson: compassionately adjust interaction with such folks, put the experience on a shelf, and move on. It works out best that way for everyone involved.

The disaster field is also where I encountered the concept of psychological first aid.[95] Much of my approach to cogjam was inspired by practices learned by disaster immersion. I developed confidence in how simple listening and showing compassion could do so much for those working through trauma. It did require taming my inner lizard, but also had gifts for my logical brain.

Which brings us to the present. I am in a different place now than when I first began tapping out this book, just as my inner status moves on following any stage of my disaster career. It required that I be open—to novel experience, incorporating learning that followed, and taking a chance on applying similar methods for a cogjam disaster. Rather than fearfully withdrawing and rigidly clinging to same-old same-old, I progressed. My reward is a worldview that has moved ever closer toward placing greatest emphasis on joy, intimacy, and play, rather than the overwhelming dread and negativity spread by the cogjam effect.

Where does the experience of reading this book leave you? For that matter, where does cogjam in general leave you now, at this moment? The previous pages are obviously not a cure for cogjam. The material they hold only begins the journey of recognizing where you stand, and options for moving forward. You alone need to examine how you are affected by cogjam, and which path is likely to help you find your way out of the weeds.

Be thankful for this opportunity for new discoveries. Whatever skills you learn and apply to cogjam are likely as transferable as my disaster third ear. You may not yet know exactly how or where they will once again come to your aid. All the same, the suggested methods within this book jacket are useful for any form of stress, at any time in your life.

One thing we can be sure of about life: there will be stress. But it need not destroy our wellbeing. And it need not turn into cogjam.

THE FINAL FRONTIER

If only I were younger, that I might live to see what history books say about this era another fifty years from now. Where will we go from here? Will we learn from this experience? Will we avoid having it happen again?

Back in the sixties, an innovative platform for hashing out social issues hit the screen: *Star Trek*. It tackled the day's controversies with themes like racial prejudice, flower power, and limits to authority. It also introduced a fantasy world of technology, one that became factual in modern times: cell phones as communicators, electronic writing tablets, talking computers, human travel away from Earth, and sending unmanned ships even further into the final

95   World Health Organization (2011). *Psychological first aid: Guide for field workers.* Published by World Health Organization.

frontier. The era's blossoming fascination with sci-fi entertainment did help its high ratings. However the popularity of the series and its underlying messages continue to this day.

This year a farcical version of the old classic entered the scene: *The Orville*. At first I dismissed it as not having much more to it than an hour-long *Saturday Night Live skit*. Later episodes proved me mistaken.

One episode struck an especially relevant chord. It told the story of a planet where reality, justice, and the like were determined by the entire population. However, citizens did so by way of voting in the moment on social media. As the Orville's brainiac character aptly pointed out, they confused opinion with knowledge. As the crew posted frenzied fictions aimed to spare a captured colleague from a fate worse than death, a benevolent native assured them not to worry about anyone checking the truth of their postings. Nobody ever did.

Sounds familiar, doesn't it? Maybe someday *The Orville* will achieve the same status as *Star Trek*. A half-century from now, perhaps we'll look back on its reruns with fond nostalgia: recalling the pain of the cogjam era, yet rejoicing in the progress we've made beyond it.

My, oh my. And what will that progress look like? What will the answers be, and where will they turn up? Maybe it's like Dorothy's ruby slippers in the *Wizard of Oz*. The power to see everything there is to be seen has been here in front of us, all along.

Exploring beyond planet Earth isn't the famed final frontier. That honor belongs right here at home—within the unexplored territory of our own minds and hearts.

ABOUT THE AUTHOR

......

Laurel E. Hughes, Psy.D. participated in over 50 disaster operations, ranging from major catastrophes such as the events of September 11th to minor local flooding. Between deployments, she wrote books, and developed numerous program and training materials for agencies and organizations that provide mental health services following disaster. Now semiretired, she is still watching and listening— and stepping back into the ring for this opportunity to out "the cogjam effect." Dr. Hughes may be reached by email or through her website.

laurel@keeperconnections.com | www.thecogjameffect.com

ABOUT KHARIS PUBLISHING

......

Kharis Publishing is an independent, traditional publishing house with a core mission to publish impactful books, and channel proceeds into establishing mini-libraries or resource centers for orphanages in developing countries, so these kids will learn to read, dream, and grow. Every time you purchase a book from Kharis Publishing or partner as an author, you are helping give these kids an amazing opportunity to read, dream, and grow. Kharis Publishing is an imprint of Kharis Media LLC. Learn more at

www.kharispublishing.com

CPSIA information can be obtained
at www.ICGtesting.com
Printed in the USA
FFHW011851100719
53565091-59218FF